Freedom, Faith, and Dogma

Freedom, Faith, and Dogma

Essays by V. S. Soloviev on
Christianity and Judaism

Solovyov, Vladimir Sergeyevich

Edited, Translated,
and with an Introduction by

Vladimir Wozniuk

STATE UNIVERSITY OF NEW YORK PRESS

Published by
State University of New York Press, Albany

For information, contact State University of New York Press, Albany, NY
www.sunypress.edu

Production by Kelli W. LeRoux
Marketing by Michael Campochiaro

Library of Congress Cataloging-in-Publication Data

Solovyov, Vladimir Sergeyevich, 1853–1900.
  [Essays. English. Selections]
  Freedom, faith, and dogma : essays by V. S. Soloviev on Christianity and
Judaism / V. S. Soloviev ; translated, introduced and edited by Vladimir
Wozniuk.
      p. cm.
  Includes bibliographical references and index.
  ISBN 978-0-7914-7535-5 (hardcover : alk. paper)
  1. Christianity and other religions—Relations—Judaism. 2. Judaism—
Relations—Christianity. 3. Christianity. 4. Judaism. 5. Russia—
Religion—19th century. I. Wozniuk, Vladimir. II. Title.

BM535.S668213 2008
261.2'6—dc22   2007048683

10 9 8 7 6 5 4 3 2 1

Contents

Acknowledgments

Successful completion of this project would have been more difficult without the course release time granted to me by Western New England College, and the library resources made available to me through my affiliations with Harvard's Davis Center for Russian and Eurasian Studies and Yale Divinity School. My sincere thanks go to these institutions, as well as to various reviewers, whose comments proved helpful in many ways.

Introduction:
Freedom, Faith, and Dogma

In prefatory comments appearing in a revised edition of one of his better known books, *Justification of the Good*, the idealist Russian religious philosopher Vladimir S. Soloviev (1853–1900) stressed the intrinsically close connection that existed between "true religion and sensible politics."[1] Soloviev's understanding of the relationship between religion and politics emerged organically from his reading of the New Testament, which he believed required that continuous progress be made toward perfection in all human affairs. The key to the eventual achievement of this goal of perfection could be found in the core Christian mission of moral reconciliation, which, as Soloviev himself observed, could be translated into philosophical language as *synthesis*—the Hegelian resolution of two opposing claims, or a contradiction, into a third, higher truth.[2] According to Soloviev, this Christian mission of reconciliation applied to all of reality, both past and present, and included the rationality of Greek philosophy as well as the elements of ancient pagan religion that seemed to him to be a necessary preparation for the future appearance of Christianity and subsequent human progress.[3] He also proclaimed this mission of moral reconciliation to be a major part of Russia's role in universal history, situated as it was both geographically and culturally between East and West.

Soloviev relentlessly critiqued all of European culture for its seemingly unremitting abandonment of Christian principles in favor of secularization, while he at the same time indicted all three major branches of Christianity for the failure to preserve and promote unity among believers in light of this circumstance. Yet Soloviev's main focus remained his native Russia and Eastern Orthodoxy, not because there was less to find fault with in Western Europe but because he understood his own mission as directed first and foremost to his homeland. And yet, since the collapse of the Soviet Union in 1991, Soloviev's writings have not only been reissued in Russia, but also have attracted a growing audience in a West that has become even more secularized and more riven by sectarianism than in Soloviev's day.

Ten of the eleven articles that I have selected for this, my fourth, volume of Soloviev's writings have not previously appeared in English translation, while one (the lengthy "The Jews and the Christian Question") was only rendered into English incompletely in the middle of the last century. All the essays included in this volume illuminate Soloviev's concerns about the obstacles that religious and political dogma present to the free pursuit of faith; they assist in deepening our understanding of Soloviev's complex views on the relationship of church and state in both East and West. Many of these pieces resonate with answers as to how and why Eastern Orthodoxy deviated from its mission to work toward the establishment of a truly Christian society—the Kingdom of God—first in Byzantium and then in Moscow. But at the same time they also remind the reader that Orthodoxy was by no means unique in this regard: Soloviev offers insights on how and why the Mosaic Law—the heart of ancient Judaism—eventually became subverted and trampled over by the kings of ancient Israel and Judah, and how and why Catholicism in Western Europe became co-opted and corrupted by the political milieu in which it grew during the Middle Ages. For Soloviev, the difficult but necessary path to Russia's fulfillment of its historical calling to "spiritual nationhood" required not just recalling, but also learning the hard lessons that history had taught since antiquity about the tendency of dogmatism to first shackle and then abuse faith.[4]

The seemingly intractable dispute and deep chasm that existed between Christianity and Judaism, out of which the former had organically arisen, constitutes a secondary issue that links a number of these endeavors as well. Soloviev championed full religious and civic rights for all minorities in the Russian Empire over the course of his career: several of the essays in this volume evidence Soloviev's steadfast and outspoken defense of Judaism and the Jews throughout the rest of Europe as well as in Russia.[5] Unlike some of his contemporaries, Soloviev never lost sight of the fact that Jesus had lived his earthly life as an observant Jew, and that it was this *Jewish* teacher and prophet who subsequently became the Christ of Christianity. This significant, yet often neglected, consideration helps to explain Soloviev's special concern for the plight of the Jews, a concern that takes shape in different ways throughout his work, but appeared most adamantly in an 1890 denunciation of pogroms, a collective protest written by him and signed by many Russian artistic and literary personalities (including Lev Tolstoy) and subsequently published in the *Times* of London.[6]

A problem that insinuates itself ubiquitously throughout this book is how to reconcile the commandment that Jesus gave to render to Caesar what is Caesar's and to God what is God's (Mt 22:21; Mk 12:17; Lk 20:25) with the gist of Romans 13, in which St. Paul counsels Christians to obey their rulers—that is, the State. Reconciling these two norms without doing damage to the intent of either can be seen as one of Soloviev's special purposes throughout his *oeuvre*. Soloviev never discussed church history for its own sake, nor did he engage in biblical exegesis simply to understand the moral values of ancient Israel and the Greco-Roman world, nor did he analyze political history in order just to clarify power relationships in the ancient and medieval worlds. Rather, he directed his efforts at explicating how and why such issues should matter to his contemporaries, and the lessons that these issues could teach about the relationship of church and state throughout Europe and the Russia of his day.[7]

The vast majority of the dozens of references to power that Soloviev makes in the essays that comprise this book appear in a context that is other than a purely spiritual one: he often highlights either political or ecclesiastical power, or at times discusses them both together, but rarely does he discuss spiritual power without referring to a social context. Reminiscent of a variety of Christian writers from Augustine to Thomas More, Soloviev's major concern here seems to be with the distorted power relationships that have developed in human society and the damage they have inflicted on the idea of community. Not unlike these Christian saints, he insisted that extant reality and normative ideals not only could be related in society, but that they in fact must be.[8] In fundamental agreement with the church fathers of both East and West, Soloviev, the religious philosopher, believed that individual freedom, religious faith, and the common good could only be reconciled in community through a serious application of a noncoercive Christian ethic. Early in his career, Soloviev saw More's Utopianism as resembling a norm sooner than a fantasy, and he postulated that "utopias and utopians have always ruled humanity and so-called practical people have always been only their unconscious instruments."[9] And later, he indirectly suggested that Augustine's *City of God* had provided some inspiration for his *Justification of the Good*.[10]

At the risk of oversimplification, I would suggest that three overarching and interrelated questions form the backdrop against which

Soloviev framed the discourses on freedom, faith, and dogma that are found in this book. And since these writings span much of his adult life, it can be suggested that these are the questions that persistently occupied Soloviev, sometimes even appearing in places where one might expect to find a more "spiritual" treatment of issues: What does "reconciliation and reunification" of the church actually mean and how might this be achieved? What is the proper relationship between clerical and secular authorities? How can the tendency of the powerful to exploit the powerless be curbed more effectively? These are questions that have continued to resonate in the corridors of power, in both East and West, since Soloviev's day—it is left to the reader to decide what relevance his answers to them have for us today.

The first selection in this volume, "On Spiritual Authority in Russia" (1881), represents one of Soloviev's earliest and harshest critiques of the Russian Orthodox church hierarchy, which in his view had lost its way and did not offer the Russian people very good role models. Soloviev implied that the church hierarchy was hypocritical in separating itself from the people on the one hand, while issuing grave warnings about the state of the nation's spiritual health on the other. Whose fault was this lamentable situation? Soloviev traces the roots of the situation back to the seventeenth century and in so doing presents the officials of the institutional church with some unflattering assessments, including a strong suggestion that it had abandoned its basic mission to embody Christ's love on earth.

He reasoned that a "calamitous illness" had befallen Russia because of this failure, and that the seventeenth-century schism had contributed heavily to the weakening of the hierarchy's spiritual authority. Harsh treatment of schismatics and sectarians of all sorts, as well as people of other faiths, had undermined the spiritual and moral authority of the church hierarchy. Soloviev blamed the seventeenth-century Patriarch Nikon and his attempt to establish himself as a "great sovereign" side by side with the tsar for a significant portion of the church-state situation in Russia in his day. Interestingly, Nikon reappears in subsequent essays in this book almost as a kind of leitmotif or symbol of Russia's deep-seated spiritual and political problems. Soloviev equated Nikon's tendency to follow what he termed the medieval "Latin principle of religious coercion" with papal excesses, which represented the "fundamental error" that "spiritual authority is acknowledged in and of itself as a principle and goal," while the only truly Christian goal must be the kingdom of God.

Soloviev boldly called for a Russian church council to convene for the immediate "abolition of all restrictive laws and measures against schismatics, sectarians, and those of other faiths," as well as the renunciation of ecclesiastical censorship. In effect, this would constitute an abandonment of an illegitimate "police authority" by the hierarchy and would have the effect of restoring true moral authority to the church, which would then be more capable of influencing society in a positive way. Soloviev encapsulated the task of both such a re-energized church and state in a pithy, yet compelling, formula: to work together freely toward "one common goal—the building of true community on earth."

Although the second essay, "On the Ecclesiastical Question Concerning the Old Catholics" (1883), seems less universal in scope than the others in this volume, it conforms to one of the key general attributes shared by all the writings in the book: it focuses on the tendencies of both politics in general and the State in particular to intrude into clerical affairs and matters of faith across Europe. In this short piece, Soloviev took issue with those in Russia who were eager to identify and take political advantage of potential schisms appearing in the West. Looking back at the results of the Vatican Council of 1870, Soloviev suggested that the initial dissent surrounding the papal claims established at this council hardly qualified as justifiable schisms, based as they were on dubious premises. The pretext for Soloviev's essay was the action of the self-proclaimed "Old Catholics" who split with the Roman Catholic Church in Germany after the council. Soloviev pointed out that Otto von Bismarck's support of this split was crudely motivated by raw political considerations. But there is a subtext in this essay as well: the Russian state was just as used to interfering with the Church in Russia—after all, they were essentially fused—which Soloviev repeatedly referred to as an unhealthy circumstance. In this essay, Soloviev displayed his writing talent with sparkling pun and double entendre, exploiting the image of the ecclesiastical "laying on of hands," a tradition for installment of bishops going back to the foundations of the church, in order to point out what he understood to be the absurdities encountered when the interests of the State were interjected into disputes over faith issues and dogma.

The third selection presents a thumbnail sketch of a good deal of Soloviev's future writing agenda about the relationship of religion to society and faith to dogma. "The Jews and the Christian Question" (1884) is one of Soloviev's longer essays, and it covers much more ground than the title suggests. The inversion of the standard understanding of ethnic relations in this early and vigorous defense of Judaism brilliantly turns the table on those who put any blame on Jews for their situation in Russia or elsewhere in Europe. This is one of Soloviev's earliest attempts to explain the principle of "spiritual corporeality" in Judaism and link it to the Divine plan to create a Kingdom of God on earth. In this piece, Soloviev began to develop the idea that Judaism will not only play an integral role in Christian eschatology—an idea harking back to St. Paul—but that somehow this will have a particularly powerful effect upon Russia itself as history draws to its perfected conclusion. Perhaps most significantly, this article represents Soloviev's opposition to any involuntary subordination of one element to the other in church-state relations, to any structural dependency of one on the other. Here we find as well an early exposition of the argument for "free theocracy," drawing on the distinction made in the Hebrew Bible (and reinterpreted in the New Testament) among the three offices of prophet, priest, and king. The idea of "free theocracy" became a central project for Soloviev in the 1880s, but it fell on deaf ears. One commentator even referred to it as "a fantastic utopia." Soloviev abandoned this project, which he called his "theocratic Leviathan" and which he later suggested that he had wasted his "best years" on; but this later resignation to the project's failure came in part because of his audience's inattention to refined points in his argument.[11]

He worked to reform the sad state of affairs in Russia peacefully, taking the admonition of Romans 13 to heart, but neither sugar coating the ugly reality nor accepting or justifying the monarchic idea without careful qualification. "The Jews and the Christian Question" evidences these concerns, condensing various elements of medieval and early modern debates about whether the source and justification of secular power is other worldly (a question that harks back indirectly to the disquisitions of such thinkers as St. Augustine, St. Thomas Aquinas, John of Salisbury, Dante, and Marsilio of Padua). Soloviev understood that church and state needed to remain separate and distinct, in part because each had different functions to perform independently toward the eventual goal of achieving a perfect society. Thus, while the "anointment" of the monarch by a priesthood "does not give the ecclesiastical hierarchy any rights in the realm of state power" in Soloviev's theocratic idea, the monarch is nevertheless obligated to faithfully serve the "Divine enterprise." Moreover, there is a clear statement in Soloviev's argument that divine sanction depends on the monarch being a "faithful servant," for "only under this condition does he have the significance of Christian emperor, one of the formative organs of true theocracy." His chief example of the devastation caused by the theocratic idea when dogmatized is, of course, Byzantium, which he only comments on briefly in this 1884 piece, returning to it later in greater detail in two 1891 articles (see below). Russia had to act resolutely in order to avoid the fate of Byzantium, a point that Soloviev would continue to make throughout his writing in various ways. In order to escape this cataclysmic fate, the most important task was the emancipation of religion from the political authority to which it had been yoked for centuries. Harmful for both church and state, this situation in Russia required sweeping changes according to Soloviev. In order to give the state truly moral guidance, it was "necessary that the spiritual authority, personifying the religion element in society, *have full independence*" (italics added).

Soloviev went on in "The Jews and the Christian Question" to explain how Western Christianity had also failed to inaugurate a Kingdom of God on earth, adding some insightful comments on the subsequent schism within the western church itself. For Soloviev, all the problems of Christian societies stemmed from an unwillingness and inability to balance correctly the requirements of human freedom, spiritual faith, and religious dogma, that is, to apply the full meaning of the tripartite (priestly, prophetic, and monarchic) definition of a godly society that he posited early on. Soloviev's principal criticism of Protestantism, one which he held throughout his career, is lucidly presented here in capsule form. The fundamental problem with Protestantism, according to Soloviev, is that it gives so much preponderance to the prophetic role that it virtually eliminates the other two as effective counterbalances. This has the effect of:

> reduc[ing] all religion to the single status of faith and thus cedes to every believer the absolute right to act as a self-appointed and peremptory arbitrator of religious matters.

Returning to the point of reconciliation as a prelude to any hope for beginning to realize a Kingdom of God on earth, Soloviev suggested that both the Jews and the Poles were key to any future reunification of the people of God. An early version of Soloviev's well-known triad of reconciliation emerges: Russia holds out hope as the potential staging ground for a reunification of God's people, East and West, because the Russian Empire contained a large number of Jews and (at that time) the Catholic nation of Poland. Soloviev's reasoning about the Jewish role in any future reconciliation and reunification drew directly upon the Apostle Paul's proclamation of a special place the Jews would have in an eschatological theocracy, or the Kingdom of God. Moreover, Soloviev also posited the issue in terms of a triad upon which the future of Russia would depend: if Russians, Poles, and Jews did not work out their mutual relations, Russia's economic future and material well-being would be cast in doubt.

Soloviev's fascination with a particular community of Jews on the fringes of the Russian Empire in Kishinev, Moldova appears in the article "New Testament Israel" (1885). In this piece, he discussed the thought of Josef Rabinovich, who is generally recognized to have represented an early version of what has since become known as "Messianic Judaism." Through correspondence with Rabinovich, Soloviev became impressed with the way in which this community had apparently acquired faith in the Gospel message, pointing out that the minimal dogmatic content of the new community's free profession of faith resembled that of the New Testament community of the early (Jewish) Christian church in first century Jerusalem. Soloviev went back and forth from the New Testament to Rabinovich's own preaching in order to demonstrate what he understood to be the extensive and prominent resemblance. Soloviev characterized Rabinovich as remaining a Jew who rejected, however, the Talmudic tradition as diverging from the simple faith of the Gospel message, seeing at the same time the fulfillment of Torah in the person of Jesus as Messiah. It should be pointed out that Soloviev did not really subscribe to any of this Jewish Christian's own bleak characterizations of the centuries old problems of Talmudic Judaism in diaspora, as can be seen in a subsequent, more extensive, discussion of Talmudic literature (see below).

"The Teaching of the Twelve Apostles" (1886) originally appeared as a foreword to the Russian edition of what was at that time the recently discovered Greek manuscript Διδαχη των δωδεκα αποστολων (*Didache ton dodeka apostolon*), about which there was a considerable amount of debate, particularly regarding its precise time of composition. Soloviev critiqued the predominant German scholarship of the time, which argued for a relatively late date of authorship for the "Didache," as it quickly became known. Stressing the importance of the principle of Apostolic succession throughout, Soloviev pointed out distinctive features of the text that he insisted indicated a first century, rather than a second century origin of the text. In this foreword to the Russian translation of the Didache, Soloviev displayed his wide-ranging knowledge of New Testament scholarship and ancient history, highlighting this text as a testimony to the universal unity of the early church regarding matters of basic doctrine. Soloviev postulated that the Didache could be reduced to seven basic points about the nature of the early (first century) church, and that all have to do with the principles of a basic hierarchical structure and a minimum amount of fundamental dogmatic content regarding the nature of Christ. Soloviev pointed out that the Didache undermined two polar opposite views regarding the character of early Christianity: (*a*) "the view that wants to reduce Christian religion to a single teaching of morality without any dogmatic foundations and sacraments," and (*b*) "the contrary view which maintains that all the forms and hierarchical and dogmatic definitions that exist today in the church, as well as the sacraments, also existed unchangingly from the very beginning *in the very same form* and with the very same significance as now" (italics in the original). According to Soloviev, both these views reject the idea of progressive development in the Universal Church, which is fundamental to the basic nature of the universe as one of "spiritual corporeality." This principle encapsulates his teleology about the material and spiritual growth of humanity toward final union with God—what he termed *bogochelovechestvo*, usually rendered into English as God-manhood or Divine humanity.

"The Talmud and Recent Polemical Literature Concerning It in Austria and Germany" (1886) returns to a vigorous defense of Judaism as an integral part of Russia's path to salvation and the special role it would play in an eschatological future. The lengthy article appeared in the Russian journal *Russkoe obozrenie* (Russian Survey), and should be considered not just as a searing indictment of anti-Semitism, but a painstaking analysis of its *psychology*. Soloviev first laid out the theological and historical situation of Judaism in the context of first the pagan and then the Christian world amidst which it developed. He carefully analyzed the differences among the three parties in New Testament times—the Pharisees, Sadducees, and Essenes—in order to explain more clearly to those in his Russian audience unfamiliar with biblical history the several sources from which Christianity drew. After setting this background, Soloviev gave a largely standard explanation of the growth of Talmudic tradition as a function of first the Babylonian exile and later the Diaspora after the destruction of the Temple in 70 AD, proceeding then to his main purpose: to address the fabrications and distortions of European anti-Semites regarding what the Talmud teaches.

The result is a dazzling subversion of all German, Austrian and—by direct implication—Russian attempts to portray the Talmud's teachings about the necessity of segregation and a different treatment of non-Jews as somehow evil:

It would be very surprising if the Jewish codex of the 16th century acknowledged an obligatory equality among Jews and Christians, when in the most enlightened Christian countries such equality was acknowledged only several dozen years ago, and in the country with the greatest amount of Jews, they do not have full citizen rights to this day.

In 1891, Soloviev twice publicly defended his orthodox Christian views by critiquing what he called "pseudo" and "false" Christians who failed to take their faith seriously, and even distorted it beyond recognition. The attacks on Soloviev's Christianity never ceased over the course of his public evangelization of his faith; these attacks were not unlike those that Dostoevsky, Soloviev's friend, had suffered earlier at the hands of his detractors in Russia. If the best defense is a good offense, as the saying goes, Soloviev's piece "On Counterfeits" stands as perhaps his most finely honed offensive against such opponents. He based his argument on the overwhelming amount of data in the Gospels themselves about what Christ, as the "founder" of the religion, taught. Soloviev adduced over ninety direct references to "the *Gospel of the kingdom*—the good news about the Kingdom of God" in support of his claim that this is the fundamental Gospel message, which is not meant to be a passive, or quietist message, but one of action toward a positive fulfillment of love and justice within the framework of the Kingdom of God, a kingdom progressively being realized in bits and pieces imperfectly in the fallen world of humanity, only to arrive in fullness with the Second Coming of Christ.

"On the Decline of the Medieval Worldview," the second of his public defenses of the meaning of Christian orthodoxy in 1891, was presented as a public lecture at the Moscow Psychological Society. The tone of the piece is somber, and it follows up the analysis of "pseudo" and "false" Christianity that appeared in "Counterfeits." Here Soloviev reviewed the myriad reasons why Christianity failed to live up to its obligation to transform human relations and usher in the Kingdom of God. His criticism of the universal church does not only extend back to the Christianization of the Roman Empire by the Emperor Constantine in 310 AD, a more common Christian critique, but also to its failures almost immediately after Christ's earthly life ended. Soloviev not only indicted Byzantium for preferring paganism to Christianity in its political and social culture, but also established an unbroken line of continuity of pagan values permeating the early church from the time of the Apostles up through modernity. According to him, the socially transformative power of the Christian faith was lost in "the pagan midst" as the Christian society of the post-Constantinian era "assumed [paganism's] character," putting a de facto end to the possibility of the redemption of politics as the Gospel exhorts. Thus, "all public life" was now left to conservative secular and religious authorities who would not initiate "radical transformations," inevitably eventuating in redemption being limited to the personal sphere. Pointing out that the situation was somewhat better in the West, Soloviev observed that "contrast between *the paganism of the city* and *the Christianity of the desert* was manifested especially acutely in the East." Soloviev did not, for the most part, view asceticism very positively because it tended to relinquish the key Christian role to be played in a proactive establishment of the Kingdom of God.

At the very center of this "historical process" of establishing the Kingdom of God, which cannot make do without a human commitment to the divine purpose, there is the uniquely Christian (according to Soloviev) idea of progress. And yet Christians have been instrumental in stalling progress: does this mean that the Kingdom of God has been doomed to *not* being realized, or as Soloviev put it, has been "forsaken"? The answer to this question is no, because the social, moral, and intellectual progress of modernity contributes mightily to the realization of the Divine purpose. He observed that:

> The majority of people who create and have created this progress do not acknowledge themselves as Christians. But if Christians in name have betrayed the purpose of Christ and nearly ruined it—if they only could have done so—then why can't those who are *not Christians* in name, and who renounce Christ in word, serve the purpose of Christ?

Moreover, in abandoning nature and treating it as a mere "machine," pseudo-Christians contributed as well to serious ecological problems, which appear as a direct response to abuse and cast further doubt on the Christian stewardship of nature; such treatment is tantamount to rejecting Christ "in the flesh."

In 1896, Soloviev published a rather extensive review of a rather small book issued several years earlier in France and titled "When did the Hebrew Prophets Live?" (Ernest Havet, *La modernité des prophêtes* [Paris, 1891]). Here we see two aspects of Soloviev as a professional writer that rarely appear anywhere else in his work: finely detailed historical analysis of Old Testament texts (primarily Isaiah and Kings) in the context of attested historical and archaeological records, and harsh castigation of a scholar who misused and abused texts not only with the goal of validating his spurious theory, but also in order to deceive "readers unfamiliar with the Bible." Soloviev drove the point home in different ways, concluding that "bias, and not logic, governs these pseudo-critical exercises." The result is a tour de force, however, this ostensible book review served another, more veiled, purpose: Soloviev had long criticized the inadequate attention to increasingly sophisticated methods of biblical scholarship in Russia. The review offered him an opportunity to demonstrate to his Russian audience, which included clergy as well as the secular "intelligentsia," how the reliability and authenticity of the biblical witness could pass any test that modern methods had devised. And so, it is not the treatment of biblical texts that recommends the piece, but rather the partially veiled critique in the last section: two "extremes" of traditional and modern "scholarly abstraction" have beset those who study the Bible, the former extreme constituting a "blind literalism" that appeared only in countries "wittingly alienated from knowledge"—an indirect broadside at Russian religious scholarship in general and the church hierarchs in particular, both of which Soloviev sharply criticized else-where as well.[12] According to Soloviev, both these extremes suffered from the "same *indifference* to the essence, to the intrinsic meaning of the Bible and prophetic writings in particular." Soloviev's purpose was to emphasize the key element in biblical history—the Hebrew nation and its special place in universal history. For scholars to ignore this aspect of the Bible was to approach it "falsely [and therefore] *unscientifically*," and for clerics and laymen of the church to view it as "a fossilized and inviolable relic, means to demonstrate dead faith and to sin against the Holy Spirit, who has spoken through the prophets." Harsh condemnations indeed for both "schools" of thought.

In 1896, Soloviev undertook as well an extensive examination of Russia's relationship to Byzantium—how Byzantium influenced Russia for good and ill. He embarked on this project as he was at the same time also writing about the religious teachings of Muhammad, the founder of Islam. It seems clear that both topics were linked in his thinking. The article "Byzantinism and Russia"—one of the most powerful and somber that Soloviev ever wrote—begins by exploring the reasons why the "second Rome," the eastern Christian capital of the Roman Empire established by Constantine in the fourth century, fell to the Ottomans, leaving Moscow as its apparent heir—a "third Rome." He averred that empires "perish only from collective sins." Following up on his indictment of Byzantium in the earlier essay, "On the Decline of the Medieval Worldview," Soloviev now deepened his critique of Byzantine political-religious culture for utilizing dogma to shackle true believers, helping to sustain an eastern despotic vision of societal relations at the expense of human freedom and dignity.

According to Soloviev, it was not Muslim military superiority, but rather an "intrinsic, spiritual reason" that ultimately explains the fall of Byzantium—and by extension, augured ill for Russia as well: a false application of the Christian idea, a collective sin of indifference to universal truth and progress, and a forgetfulness about its calling as a Christian kingdom, constituting

> total and general indifference to the *historical advancement of the good*, to the providential Divine will in the collective life of the people . . .

Russia strove to be a Christian kingdom under Vladimir the Great, who was unlike his Greek "pseudo-Christian mentors" in that he valued this principle, as did certain of his successors. But the Mongol threat created a political environment in which "the idea of autocracy appeared for the entire nation as a banner of salvation." Soloviev applied himself to explaining how the monarchic idea solidified and the Western idea of the State as a "balance of independent and equivalent elements" never got a chance to develop in Russia. A good portion of the blame goes to Ivan IV, the tsar who, just as the Byzantines before him, rejected faith in favor of dogma, truth in favor of power, and freedom in favor of despotism, nearly leading his nation to destruction. His reign represented

> a vivid and distinctive repetition of the contradiction that ruined Byzantium—the contradiction between a verbal confession of truth and its denial in fact.

The irreconcilable duality of the dictates of Christian conscience on the one hand and the attractiveness of the pagan ideas of power on the other, according to Soloviev, led rulers to choose the latter and dispense completely with the former, and in Russia this meant "a reversion [. . .] to the ancient pagan deification of a limitless power engulfing everything." At this point Soloviev, displaying a penchant for storytelling, related a legend about how the Byzantines received the tokens of imperial power that they themselves traced back to Nebuchadnezzar's Babylon, and then bequeathed to Russia.

One of Soloviev's principal purposes in this article was to explain how ostensibly secular reforms instituted by Peter the Great, who understood the need for human progress, qualified as part of the

Divine plan to bridge the distance between East and West, a chasm that Soloviev blames upon Greek Byzantines and their loyal Muscovite successors. To those who claimed that it was the Imperator Peter who destroyed church independence in Russia, Soloviev responded by explaining how the ecclesiastical hierarchy's spiritual and moral failures made it quite logical for Peter to subsume the administration of the Russian Orthodox Church under the rubric of a government "department." This merely reflected the de facto reality that had developed over the course of several generations. Soloviev, while recognizing the many deficiencies of Peter, gave him high marks:

> Through European enlightenment the Russian mind was opened to such concepts such as human merit, the right of the individual, freedom of conscience, etc., without which a worthy existence, true improvement, is impossible . . .

"Byzantinism," as Soloviev defined it, is an insistence on "particularism" over against universalism in both values and traditions. In this regard, as well as many others, Soloviev stood much closer to the West than to the East, seemingly supporting the position of Rome—although it too was not without sin—over against Byzantium regarding the East-West schism, whose origins can be traced back at least as far as the ninth century. Soloviev summarized the gist of the matter, combining all the petty dogmatic issues (except for the filioque), into one fundamental problem related to the despotic impulse on the part of the Greeks: the transformation of *"ecumenical* tradition into a tradition of *local antiquity."* Soloviev illustrated how all schisms flowed from this original Byzantine "movement toward particularism," including, most significantly, the Russian schism that occurred under Nikon.

The last, and briefest, composition included in this volume bears the intriguing title "The Secret of Progress," which has been added to the present collection as a kind of *coda* at the request of one of the project's initial reviewers. In it, Soloviev relates a fairy tale that he claims everybody—at least in Russia—knows in one variant or another: a lonely young hunter lost in a forest performs a good deed, albeit somewhat reluctantly, for a haggardly old woman, who then miraculously becomes transformed into a beautiful damsel and leads him to a paradise—a "happy-ever-aftering" ending of sorts. Soloviev analogizes the main characters in this tale to the attitude of a humanity that is lost in modernity, but that retains an ambiguous—if not outright hostile—predisposition toward antiquity. What is the lesson here? The only way forward is to take full account of the past and to cherish it, by carrying the best legacies of humanity into an uncertain future for the purpose of building a more perfect society, not unlike the classical image Soloviev offers at the end: Aeneas embarking on his journey to Italy from the ruins of Troy.

Some general comments about translation matters are in order. First, the many biblical citations in these texts, which in some ways reflect their evangelical nature more than most other essays that Soloviev penned, come in different forms—often in contemporary Russian, but also regularly in older Slavonic forms when the subject of his thinking seems to require it. I have attempted to vary the translations of these biblical citations accordingly, moving from something akin to the King James to a closer approximation of the New Revised Standard Version when called for. Elsewhere, issues of precision and clarity dominated my choice of words, phrases, mood, and so forth, with stylistic considerations entering only secondarily into the calculus of the translation. I have attempted to convey some of the flavor of Soloviev the master stylist, striving (just as I have before) for justice in rendering the complexity, brilliance, and humanity of Soloviev, the Christian scholar. However, whenever and wherever conflict arose between style and substance, the latter prevailed.

In matters of transliteration, I have stayed close to the Library of Congress system, except where commonly used spelling of names (such as Dostoevsky) is preferred, and I have also omitted diacritical marks in the Greek and Hebrew passages Soloviev himself transliterated into Latin script.

All emphases are as they appear in the original, except for those places where Soloviev himself used an alphabet other than the Cyrillic; I have italicized these places to set them apart from the text that I have translated from the Russian. Ellipses are likewise as they appear in the original unless noted otherwise. Notations by the author appear for the most part as they do in the original, at the bottom of each page in footnote form or parenthetically in the text while my comments and clarifications for the most part appear at the end of the book in notes consecutively and separately numbered for each essay, except for the numerous biblical citations and casual references that Soloviev himself made without direct indication, or sometimes misidentified. In these places, I have added precise scriptural references, and in other places where I have had to add a word or two to the text for clarity's sake I have utilized square brackets to indicate my editorial interventions into Soloviev's text.

1

On Spiritual Authority in Russia

The terrible moral condition of Russia is bewailed in the Holy Synod's recent pastoral appeal, and all the sins and lawlessness to which we have descended are here enumerated in detail: unbelief, indolence, selfishness, unbridled free thinking, pride, cupidity, the craving of pleasure, intemperance, and envy. The reproaches are just, and no one has a right to deflect them from oneself. But the Holy Synod elicits a bewilderment that is truly lamentable: in bewailing the calamitous situation of Russia and speaking in a long-winded manner about the moral disorders attending all natural humanity since the time of its Fall, not a single word is concerned with the particularly great affliction that today dispirits the Russian nation in its entirety and constitutes the true reason for its distressing situation. Such silence is strange and lamentable not only owing to the importance of the matter, but also because this great national affliction relates intimately to the hierarchy of the Russian church—it is situated in the sphere of the hierarchy's direct jurisdiction and it can and must await healing first and foremost from the hierarchy.

Quite apart from all the sins and lawlessness of individual persons and classes, the Russian nation is spiritually paralyzed in its totality; its moral unity has been violated, the *actions* of a single *spiritual* principle that would intrinsically govern all life, as the soul does in the body, are not visible within it. This kind of supreme life principle is given to Russia, as a Christian nation, in the truth of Christ. The spirit that engenders our societal organism must be the spirit of Christ, the spirit of love and free consent to unity; a higher ideal for the entire societal structure of Russia must also be determined by it. If Russia is a Christian country in truth, and not only in name, then a voluntary moral unity of people in Christ—which forms a spiritual community, or the church—must lie at the foundation of its societal organization and life.

The church is an "assembly of believers." Believers in what? First of all in the Christian God, Who is love. But is it truly possible

17

to believe in love, not having love in oneself? Thus, the church is not only an assembly of believers, but also an assembly of lovers. Love can not exist without action, and a union of love in humanity or in an individual people, that is, the church, can not isolate itself within the circle of a religious cult, can not remain indifferent to life outside it, to all human matters and relations. Love is a force of limitless expansiveness, and the church, founded upon love, must permeate the entire life of human society, all its relations and activity, descending into everything and elevating everything to itself. Existing outwardly in the milieu of civil society and the State, the church can not segregate itself and separate itself from this milieu, but must influence it by its spiritual strength, must attract state and society to itself and gradually make them like itself, convey its principle of love and harmony in all spheres of human life. And the institution of spiritual authority, or the church hierarchy, exists as a special instrument or organ of such church influence on secular society. This hierarchy is especially designed in authority and influence to be devoted to the spiritual unification of human society, bringing the principle of love present in the church into civic life and state affairs, not just praying in word, but being concerned in deed that the *name of God be hallowed* within people, that the *Kingdom of God come* in the world, and that the *will of God be done* not only in heaven, but *on earth as well.*

So it should truly be, but in practice we see something else. I am not speaking about the Western world, where in papism the Church substituted Christ with the pope, while in Protestantism it disavowed itself; neither am I speaking about a Christian East, where the church, having long been oppressed by a qualified slavery, could not manifest its strengths. But if the West is not Orthodox, and the East is not free, then what is to be said about an Orthodox and free Russia?

Instead of the Russian church serving as the foundation of true unification for all Russia, it itself now has served as a subject of division and enmity for more than two centuries. Having been divided into a multitude of sects, a significant part of the Russian nation quarrels amongst itself belligerently about faith and concurs only in a common denial of a "reigning" church. And the hierarchy of the Russian church, instead of acting outside the church likewise by the great power of love, has disavowed it within itself: in striving by coercion to bring back into unity those who had fallen away, it has produced even greater division; in attempting to maintain its supreme authority by force, it subjects itself to the danger of being deprived of it completely.

As a Christian country, Russia searches for life in the church of Christ, but the Russian church has lost its strength in church schism, and before it can vivify, it has need of revival itself. This is what all of Russia suffers from profoundly, this is its great affliction— which the Holy Synod forgot to mention in its enumeration of our moral disorders.

In truth the Holy Synod contends justly and in a Christian manner, ascribing all our calamities to our sins and lawlessness. A sown sin will reap misfortune.

This eternal moral law has force not only for individual persons, but also for entire human societies and institutions, inasmuch as they live and act as collective beings and, consequently, can also sin, that is, evade their purpose. But neither individual nor collective beings are responsible for their actions and sufferings uniformly in their entire makeup. So, if someone lifts his hand in offense against his neighbor, then the responsibility for this falls not on his hand, but on his head. In precisely the same way there are central and ruling organs in human societies as well, and the galvanizing principle belongs to them, and it is therefore they who carry responsibility for their fate. Thus, if the Russian church, and within it all Russia, suffers from the great and calamitous affliction of church schism and a weakness of spiritual authority, then isn't some sin of the very authority representing the galvanizing principle in church life the reason for this calamity? The Church of Christ is holy and chaste, but the Russian hierarchy can, without doubt, sin; it can evade its duty and its calling, and by doing so lead the church governed by it on a path of great calamities. And it is not necessary for us to dwell on presuppositions about the possibility of such evasion, when history manifestly attests to its reality.

There was a time, however, when the spiritual authority in Russia, though sparse in dynamic energies as well, represented the Christian principle in society and, faithful to its calling, possessed a generally recognized moral authority. It really occupied the exalted position befitting it both in the eyes of the State and in the eyes of the people, not competing with the authority of the State, but also not abasing itself before it, not pandering to the bad instincts of the nation, but also not alienated from it. Thanks to this, ancient Russia possessed the rudiments of proper social relations and a healthy national life, notwithstanding bizarre customs and the absence of education. Whatever the woeful and dim reality of old Russia might have been, the nation could not get bogged down in it as long as its faith was firm in the moral principle of another life and as long as there were in its midst people of authority devoted to this moral principle and representing in the eyes of the nation a faithful, even if not complete, image of this true life. The secular state authority itself, voluntarily acknowledging a higher purely moral spiritual authority and relying on it, also received moral significance and internal strength.

Today, when they speak of the strong unity of state and land in ancient Russia, and the mutual trust and rapport between sovereign and people as expressed in assemblies, then it must not be forgotten *what* this unity was based *on*, whence emanated the moral authority of the sovereign that allowed him both to convene assemblies of the land fearlessly and to listen to their opinions willingly.[1] This rapport of state and land, ruler and people, was based on the fact that they both alike bowed before the common spiritual authority of Christian principle; this principle had firm and faithful spokesmen in society in the person of church hierarchs. Thus, the force of the people and the power of the State were brought into rapport by a third force that was above the other two, the moral force of the church. The societal life of Russia split in two, but did not disintegrate into State versus local councils thanks to this third higher principle, which was devoted both to the people's will and to governmental activity, setting a single eternal goal for them both—the establishment of Divine truth on earth. And if the State protected the Russian land, then the prelates of the Russian church protected it. It was for the good of the Russian land that Metropolitan Alexis went to the [Golden] Horde as an intercessor and by virtue of his holiness, apparent even to unbelievers, rescued the prince of Muscovy—here is a true historical symbol of the foundations of Russian society.[2]

Muscovite sovereigns served the Russian land with the blessing of prelates. They derived their moral authority from this blessing, their resolve in the business of ruling; and their trust in the people, incidentally, was expressed in the assemblies. Here is why the same sovereign who first rebelled against the moral requirements of the spiritual authority and did not want to subordinate his arbitrary will to its veracity, was the first to lose trust in the people, detached himself from the country [*zemlia*]. Ivan IV, who tortured Metropolitan Philip, feared the country and out of a fear of it set up the *oprichina* [secret police]. And yet Ivan IV's evil acts did not have fateful significance in Russian history, did not muddy the source of the nation's life; on the contrary, they gave the nation occasion to display its strength. There were neither disputes over power nor any personal scores between Ivan IV and St. Philip. The prelate performed his duty as the representative of moral principle, denouncing the tsar who had betrayed this principle, and, as the bearer of spiritual authority, Philip did not fear physical force and death. The tsar's lawlessness was the prelate's triumph. In the person of Ivan IV the State came off its moral foundations, but the people did not lose anything essential, for what was essential to them was—spiritual power and sanctity; and the blood of the prelate who died for a holy cause only made this higher ideal sparkle in the eyes of the people.

Metropolitan Philip justified the people's faith and did not besmirch the Christian standard, and afterwards the people remained calm, notwithstanding an outright pogrom by Ivan IV. Going by Russian sensibilities, it was still possible to "live" during the reign of Ivan the Terrible. Why then in a hundred years did a significant part of the Russian people suddenly feel that it was not possible to live during the "quiet" reign of Aleksii Mikhailovich, when they plunged in despair into forests and wilderness, and scaled mountains to live in log cabins? What was it that happened? It appeared to these people that the greatest of disasters had occurred on earth, that the hierarchy had deviated to Latinism, had ceased to be the true spiritual authority in the Orthodox world, and that an anti-Christian kingdom had arrived; a patriarch-torturer sat on the throne of the metropolitan-martyr, and in adopting Latinism forced others to do so as well.

So say the schismatics. In actual fact, although no one went over to Latinism, it is absolutely beyond doubt that from the time of Patriarch Nikon and after his death the hierarchy of the Russian church, remaining Orthodox in faith and teaching, adopted in its outward activity tendencies and methods revealing neither an Orthodox nor an evangelical spirit, but an alien one.*

Patriarch Nikon did not go over to Latinism, but the fundamental error of Latinism was instinctively adopted by him. The fundamental error consists in the fact that spiritual authority is acknowledged as the principle and goal in and of itself. Meanwhile it is truly not the principle and goal in the Christian world. The principle is Christ, and the goal—the Kingdom of God and his truth. Spiritual authority is only a necessary instrument in the earthly makeup of the church for the possible achievement of this goal, that is, for the establishment of Divine truth on earth; and the true [istinnyi] authority and rights of spiritual authority directly depend on its faithful service to Divine truth, and they are the natural consequence and appurtenance of such service. Church hierarchs must chiefly be concerned before all Christians only with what the whole needs, knowing that everything else will

---

*If, in earlier times, it was possible to indicate an example of spiritual coercion in the Russian church—in the persecution of "Judaizers"—then the influence of Latinism in this case is absolutely beyond doubt as well.

be given to them. The ancient hierarchs of the Russian church knew this as well, and that is why they did not present their authority as a special principle and were not concerned about their rights when they acted authoritatively for the good of the land. In actually representing the spiritual Christian principle, in which all Russia believed and before which it bowed, church administration found itself by the same token indissolubly and intrinsically united with the people and the State, as the inspirational force of their life; and consequently it could in no way oppose itself to them and contend with them, could not compete with the State or oppress the people. Patriarch Nikon was the first to decidedly isolate spiritual authority in Russia, ordaining it as something detached, apart from the people and the State, and in so doing inevitably elicited hostile relations between them and estranged them. Since then the moral unity of Russia has disintegrated, and there has arisen that spiritual absence of authority in which we now find ourselves, for with the detachment of a spiritual authority that betrayed its calling, the people and the State are bereft of a guiding principle for their life in common, and they lose sight of the intrinsic meaning and goal of this life.

Patriarch Nikon is usually indicted for an excessive exaltation of spiritual authority; in truth he should be reproached for the opposite; it is not possible to excessively elevate spiritual authority, for it is in essence the highest authority in the world. "All things have been committed to me by my Father" [Mt 11:27], says the Founder and the Eternal High Priest of the church, who committed to his *faithful* Apostles the authority to interpret and discern in Heaven and on earth. It is not possible to exalt spiritual authority, but it is possible to abase and to pervert it, separating it from that which its serves, for the sake of which it exists and by which it is sanctified—from love and Divine truth. Separated from its divine content, spiritual authority becomes a chance historical force on a level with other such forces, with which it inevitably also has to contend. Understood as higher authority in a juridical sense, it first of all collides with the existing higher authority of the State. Rivalry and litigation with the tsar constituted life's chief mission for Patriarch Nikon. The patriarch took to signing as the "great sovereign" on a level with the tsar,* interfering in military and diplomatic affairs and in all the details of governance. But did such rivalry and troublesome interference in the trivialities

---

*Patriarch Philaret Nikitich also signed as "great sovereign" together with the tsar, but exclusively through his personal relationship to the tsar as his father; Nikon elevated the personal right conceded to him to an integral appurtenance of his authority.

of state affairs really serve the exaltation of the spiritual authority, and not its abasement? Could the supreme high priest of the Russian church, who represented the Heavenly King and High Priest in it, really receive further sanctification for his great name from a title of earthly authority? And if Nikon himself, following medieval catholic writers, compared the relationship of spiritual to secular authority to the relationship of the sun and moon in his note of justification, then isn't the contradiction with his own activity obvious? Indeed, does the sun compete with the moon or seek its light, and not itself give light to it? Spiritual authority is not homogeneous and not commensurate with secular authority; it must sanctify and direct the latter, but can not dispute with it over preeminence. Christ did not compete with Caesar and did not struggle with him, and true representatives of Christ's kingdom never competed with earthly authorities. Metropolitan Alexis did not compete with the prince of Muscovy, but protected him; Metropolitan Philip did not compete with Ivan the Terrible, but denounced him with authoritative words and through his martyrdom showed the true superiority of spiritual authority. Orthodox prelates did not contend and did not struggle with secular authority, but the Roman popes of old did contend and struggle with it; and even if we did not have direct evidence of Patriarch Nikon's sympathy for the papacy, his attitudes to the tsar alone would sufficiently show whose spirit was introduced into the Russian hierarchy by him.

Having reached for the enticement of earthly authority, the hierarchy manifested the first digression from its true calling; after this followed a second, even more decisive digression. Having retreated from the Christian ideal, the hierarchy by the same token discredited its moral authority in the eyes of the Christian people, lost its intrinsic spiritual connection with them—only an extrinsic coercive authority remained for it. This kind of authority elicited discord and protest because it was something alien. But the hierarchy, once having taken the position of an *extrinsic* authority, viewed discord with it as criminal rebellion and responded to it with persecution and punishment. Chopping blocks and stakes were erected in defense of authority and church unity; the spiritual authority had need not just of a crown, but also of the sword of the State.

When Apostle Peter took up a sword in defense of Christ in the Garden of Gethsemane, Christ stopped and condemned him.[3] Did the Russian hierarchy take up its sword in defense of Christ? Had the schismatics attacked Christ? Or was Patriarch Nikon, with his corrected books, dearer than Christ? Or were Archpriest [protopop] Avvakum with his friends worse than the servants of the high priest?[4] Let the Russian bishops themselves say who and what they were protecting with their torture chambers and bonfires—let us hear their own admission:

In 1682, at the time of the *streltsy* sedition, one of the old-rite followers, Pavel Danilovets, said, turning to Patriarch Joachim: "You say truthfully, most holy prelate, that you yourself bear the image of Christ; but Christ said: learn from me to be meek and humble of heart, and he did not threaten either with beheading or with fire or sword.[5] It is commanded to obey masters, but it is commanded as well to listen to the Angel if he proclaims otherwise. What is the heresy and abuse in crossing oneself with two fingers, what reason is there here to burn and torture?" And how does the patriarch respond? "We do not burn and torture for crossing and prayer, we burn for the reason that *they called us heretics,* and for not obeying the holy church—but cross yourselves as you wish."

Here is the reason the bearers of the image of Christ spilled Christian blood, here is the reason they tortured and burned thousands of Christians as in the most evil periods of pagan persecutions. "*They called us heretics*—but cross yourselves as you wish." Jesuits say: live as you like and believe as you like, only acknowledge the pope.

The great prelates of the Orthodox Church were not generally renowned for the persecution of heretics. The papacy was renowned for such persecutions from old, and here again it is beyond doubt whose traditions were adopted by the Russian hierarchy from the time of Nikon.

It would be well to forget all this as business long since past. But unfortunately the Russian hierarchy has still not repudiated the Latin principle of religious coercion brought into it by Nikon. A Moscow council condemned the person of Nikon and affirmed the correction of books as substantially good; it also as if consecrated the ruinous spirit of coercion and despotism with which Nikon conducted this business by their ill-fated curses. After this, the successors of the patriarch that was removed from power followed his footsteps decisively, increasing bloody persecutions against schismatics. The forms of these persecutions soon relented, though this took place not at the initiative of the church but of the secular authority. When Peter the Great, out of considerations of state interest, replaced the execution of schismatics with fiscal measures against them, and later Peter III, Catherine II, Alexander I, and Alexander II, out of personal motives of tolerance and love of fellow man, gradually weakened religious repression more and more, the hierarchy not only did not lead them in this, but also retarded their good undertakings, zealously protecting the Latin principle of coercion in matters of faith and conscience. By this the spiritual authority decisively acknowledged that it rests not on intrinsic moral strength, but on extrinsic, material strength. But the hierarchy, having separated itself from the corpus of the whole people, in and of itself does not have even material strength. It must seek it in the same secular government that controls through material power, but for this it is necessary to repudiate its independence, *to go into the service* of the secular authority. And the Russian hierarchy did not delay in committing this third sin against its great calling. Instead of teaching and leading the secular government in true service to God and country, it essentially went into the service of this government. At first, during the time of Nikon, it reached for the *crown of the State*, then it grappled persistently for the *sword of the State*, and finally it was forced to don the *uniform of the State*.

The alien seed that was transplanted by Nikon into the soil of the Russian church grew over the course of two centuries, and now we can judge it by its shoots.

The contemporary situation of the Russian church is known to all: a manifest weakness of the spiritual authority; the absence in it of generally acknowledged moral authority and societal significance; its silent subordination to secular authorities; the alienation of the priestly hierarchy from the rest of the people; the bifurcation in the hierarchy itself between the commanding black and the subordinate white priesthood, a despotism of the higher over the lower that elicits from the latter covert, ill-disposed and forlorn protest; the religious ignorance and helplessness of the Orthodox people, giving free range to countless sects; an indifference or enmity toward Christianity in educated society.

Over the course of these two centuries, notwithstanding the personal merits and holiness of many hierarchs, the hidden poison of the alien principle that permeated the church administration prevented it from manifesting Christian activity in the life of society. The same bonds of an alien spirit rooted out fruitful activity in the sphere of spiritual study and education in our teaching churches.[6]

What were our Orthodox theologians doing when human intellect in the West, revolting against the coercion and falsehood of Catholicism, relinquished the religious principle and, evolving its own initiative, created outside of Christianity an abstract rational philosophy and natural science, against which all the efforts of Catholic theology turned out to be unsuccessful? They reiterated the positions and arguments of the very same Catholic theology that had already turned out to be manifestly groundless, or they timidly juxtaposed the less acute forms of rationalism in Protestant theology. And meanwhile our church preserves the uncorrupted dogmatic truth of Christianity, and a direct obligation rested upon our theologians, in view of the great intellectual development of the West that permeated Russian society as well, to show that Christian truth does not fear human thought and knowledge, and that it can make use of all the products of the intellect while not disavowing itself; it can combine religious faith with free philosophical thought and the disclosures of divine life with the discoveries of human knowledge. It is a great mission, but the authoritative theologians of the Orthodox church do not even put forth this mission. And here, notwithstanding the personal talents and learning of many hierarchs, and notwithstanding the many useful learned labors of our church hierarchy, *independent* spiritual study does not exist in Russia, Russian theology has not added anything essential to the treasures of spiritual knowledge bequeathed to it by the East, and to this day holds exclusively to the definitions and formulas of the seventh and eighth centuries—as if nothing has occurred since then, as if the human intellect has not raised new questions and doubts since the time of the last great teachers of the East, St. Maximus the Confessor and John of Damascus, and as if, finally, modern European philosophy and science do not represent for contemporary Orthodox theologians the same kind of intellectual food that the great theologians of former centuries found in ancient Greek philosophy.

The Russian hierarchy can not be placed at fault directly for this intellectual sterility; it serves only as a sign of its decline. It is directly at fault in the fact that it digressed from its *social* calling, from conducting and realizing in human society the new spiritual life that is revealed in Christianity. For the church can not reject this great social mission as a united community unifying people through the most profound and most powerful bond in the world—through religion.[7]

To maintain that Christian spiritual principle should not enter into the life of society as a guiding force, and through it also into the activity of the State, is to maintain that it has no place there—this means to deny the church as a social institution. But Orthodox hierarchs can not deny that the church must act upon human society in the spirit of Christ, permeating and regenerating all societal forms and relations with this life-creating spirit. Neither can they deny the fact that the visible conductor of this spiritual influence on land and state must first of all be the ecclesiastical administration, centering in itself the *dynamic* forces of the church. And so what has the Russian church administration done for the performance of this mission? In the last two centuries, where and in what has it manifested its salutary influence on the Russian State and society? More than a few social successes have been attained in Russia in these two centuries: serfdom gradually abated and was finally abolished completely, criminal laws were tempered, torture was eliminated and capital punishment almost eliminated, and a degree of confessional freedom allowed. All these improvements were without doubt undertaken in a Christian spirit, and meanwhile the spiritual authority, representing the Christian principle in society, did not take part in any of this. Is it possible to point to the visible active participation of the hierarchy in a single good social undertaking in Russia over the last two centuries? Who is then at fault if all the good undertakings of the secular authority, bereft of a spiritual authority's superior leadership, did not lead to positive results and, in frustrating evil, did not create good? Who is at fault that people freed by the State, but not finding sufficient leadership on the part of the church, are left to their own dark instincts? And is there any wonder, finally, if among the people those in whom the spiritual need is stronger go into schism and those in whom it is weaker—into taverns?

True, the situation of Russia is miserable. And is the spiritual administration of Russia indeed faulting all of us for its miseries while exonerating itself alone? Christ saved the human soul and promised His church to save the people and all of humanity. But here a Christian nation finds itself on the path to ruin. And who will resolve to indict it—to indict a people who, in the darkness of ignorance and in a continuous struggle with material necessity, preserves the faith of Christ more than all of us, and strive to live in a godly way as well? Will we indict the wretched, without knowledge and without power, while we *acquit* those who are free from need, know the truth and have in their hands the power to act in its name. May God save us from such hypocrisy.

Without doubt, the existing ecclesiastical authority is not responsible for the historical sins of its predecessors. This is a ruinous legacy that it must renounce. The Orthodox church is maintained on tradition, but on a *tradition of truth*, and not on a tradition of falsehood. Love for ancestors and a true connection with them consists not in the imitation of their sins, but in striving to atone for them by our good deeds. If every tradition is holy, then it is not necessary for us to preach the Gospel to pagans, who stand on their patriarchal tradition. If every tradition is holy, then let us bow to the Roman pope, who firmly holds to his anti-Christian tradition.

Truly, ill tradition weighs over even the Russian church, but it is easier for the Russian church to renounce it than it is for the hierarchy of a West that has elevated its error to dogma. Although the eastern hierarchy has also deviated from the Spirit of Christ in its activity, it has not risen against him consciously and has not placed itself in place of Christ. And if the spiritual authority in Russia adopted alien, un-Orthodox endeavors in a certain historical period, then why can it not renounce them and return to its calling in another period? In truth it can and must.

And no extrinsic extraordinary measures are necessary for this, neither the restoration of the patriarchy, nor the convening of an ecumenical council. If pluralism is not good, then neither is autocracy salvation in and of itself. The autocracy of the popes did not save the Roman church from error, but on the contrary led to it, and patriarchal autocracy did not preserve the Russian church from sin in Nikon's time, but sooner promoted it. The Spirit of Christ can act both through one and through the many alike. Restoration of this spirit is required in the hierarchy of the Russian church, as the essence and basis of its authority. The spirit will show as well the best forms for the church.

Neither is a special ecumenical council necessary for the regeneration of the Russian church: the sin lies not on the universal church, but on the Russian, and first of all it must be cleansed of it on its own.

The church council of 1667 in Moscow ratified the division of the Russian church and undermined the true meaning of spiritual authority with its anathemas. Such a council must remove these anathemas and open a path for schismatics to reunite with the church.

A council of the Russian church must solemnly confess that the truth of Christ and His church have no need of coercive unity and defense by force, and that the Gospel commandment of love and mercy is first of all obligatory for the ecclesiastical authority. Having acknowledged this commandment as the supreme rule of engagement, a council of the Russian church must also petition the secular government for the abolition of all restrictive laws and measures against schismatics, sectarians, and those of other faiths.

Finally, having acknowledged that true faith does not delimit reason of conviction and does not fear free inquiry, a council of the Russian church must renounce spiritual censorship as a coercive institution, reserving for the church its inalienable right—or better, obligation—to pronounce its censure and condemnation of all publicly expressed opinions that contradict Orthodox Christian truth.

Thus, with the church having renounced outward police authority, it will reacquire inward moral authority, true authority over minds and souls. No longer needing the secular government's material protection, it will be liberated from its trusteeship and will stand in a relationship to the government properly befitting it.

We know that in the non-Orthodox part of the Christian world the church and state either strive to absorb one another or strive to so delimit their spheres that they do not concern themselves with one another at all, conforming to the theory of a free church in a free state in complete and mutual indifference. The theory looks good but in essence is bankrupt, and is in any event not applicable to the government of a Christian nation. For a Christian government can not be free from Christian truth and, consequently, can not be indifferent to the church, which represents this truth on earth.

If civil government really acknowledges the higher authority of Christian principle, then it inevitably desires to be guided by it in its activity and thus becomes intrinsically morally dependent on the church, insofar as it embodies in itself this Christian principle. And if *this kind* of government does not want to coercively support religious unity and ecclesiastical authority, then it is not out of indifference to faith and the church but, on the contrary, out of faith in the Christian and ecclesiastical principle of grace and love, which does not require or permit coercion.

The correct relationship of church and state, without doubt, is one of mutual freedom, yet not a negative freedom of indifference, but a positive freedom of harmonious cooperation in the collegial service of one common goal—the building of true community on earth.

A correct attitude toward church and state existed among us at one time in rudimentary form. And if this attitude was disrupted, then the blame for this does not fall on the State. For before Peter the Great subjected ecclesiastical authority to external state subordination, this ecclesiastical authority itself had already allowed within itself an anti-Christian spirit of pride, despotism, and coercion, and through this subjected to doubt its right to exist independently. And as long as the hierarchy of the Russian church does not renounce this alien spirit and does not return to the strength and reason of true Orthodox Christianity, it will neither recover its freedom nor its significance.

Ecclesiastical authority exists for the social good. Can it remain inactive when, according to its own acknowledgment, society is so near to ruin? And who must act, if not the ecclesiastical authority? The light of truth is entrusted to it, the keys of understanding are given to it. Both the reverence of a nation for all that is divine and its parched quest for higher truth call it to task. It has taken up arms against schism and sects, seeing in them only darkness and evil. Must it always remain in this one-sided view? Hasn't an extreme reverence for the Divine evoked the old-rite schism, doesn't a true quest for Divine truth, a striving to adopt and realize it, give rise to numerous sects in the Russian nation? Shouldn't the spiritual authority respond to this quest, removing its ignorant and bizarre forms in humility. But it turned its gaze only to the bad aspect of the popular movement in the schism, to fanaticism and ignorance, and began to act against this bad aspect in an even worse manner, beginning with chopping blocks and stakes, and it still enacts prohibitions and restrictions to this day.

The church was not glorified by this, and the schism was not destroyed. Isn't it obvious that this path is a false and ruinous path? Isn't it time to leave it? Why wouldn't the spiritual administration interpret the religious movement among the people from its good aspect? It should strengthen its enlightened earnestness against the backward zealousness of the old believers for all that is Divine. It should show that Divine truth [pravda] and a Christian life in spirit and truth [istina] are just as dear, and even more so, to it than to all these questing sectarians—then they would come to it and would receive from it that which they seek—a living Orthodox ecumenical faith. This faith, unconsciously languishing in the soul of the Russian people (both orthodox as well as sectarians), would then become acquainted with itself in its ecumenical unity and would resurrect to new life.

Then the best people of cultured society as well—estranged from Christian truth by the semblance of morbidity and decomposition that this truth has taken on in today's teaching churches—would recognize the higher truth they have searched for in a new illuminated image of Christianity, and would devote themselves to it out of free conviction.

In its all-national appeal, the Holy Synod points to the decisive significance of these fateful times and to the necessity to act against the ruin threatening us. For Christians who know that nothing can be done by human effort alone, the foundation and source of all action is prayer. But in order that prayer not be merely empty pagan words, total faith is necessary in the power of the Spirit of God, perfect devotion to a most beneficent Divine faith, decisive renunciation of all extrinsic, material means and instruments unworthy of the Divine undertaking. Only this kind of prayer attracts divine forces to us and allows us to act to the glory of God and for the good of the Earth.

For us, those who are imperfect in faith—semi-Christian and semi-pagan—such self-renunciation is scarcely accessible, and real prayer is also scarcely accessible to us. But representatives of the spiritual kingdom on earth, according to their very mission, are called to true prayer and truly spiritual action. They can not waver between the Spirit of God and the forces of the material world, they must show that in them resides and acts He Who is greater than the world, Who conquered the world with divine love, Who came not in order to judge the world, but in order to save it [Jn 12:47]. And true spiritual authority, which for the most part carries the image of Christ, must rely on Him alone, abandoning all considerations of human wisdom, which is an affront before God, and fearlessly rejecting all the decayed props of human traditions that are dust, for to dust they will return.[8] Christian Russia rests its hopes on this kind of spiritual authority, and it awaits its salvation from this kind of spiritual authority; and Russia did not and does not now believe in human contrivance and in material power.

2

On the Ecclesiastical Question Concerning the Old Catholics

About ten–twelve years ago, a movement began among a group of Catholic theologians of Germany, one which all Europe followed attentively and which found an echo among us as well. The participants of this movement, dissatisfied with the decisions of the Vatican council of 1870 on the infallibility of papal authority in questions of doctrine, separated themselves from the Roman Catholic Church and adopted the name "Old Catholics" for themselves. Western adversaries of papism placed great hopes on them, and on the other side, some among us awaited anxiously their conversion to Orthodoxy. However, the artificial, affected character of this movement, which had emerged from professors' offices, was soon exhibited. All those who had hoped to make use of the Old Catholics for their own purposes were deceived in their estimations, and these Old Catholics, who had made their appearance with such a clamor, departed from the stage very quietly and unnoticeably.

Nevertheless religious questions that are connected with this unsuccessful movement still retain all their significance, and it is necessary sometimes as well for their sake to recall the Old Catholics. Thus a brief apologia was recently published in a letter to the editor of *New Times* [*Novoe vremya*], no. 2666 [August 1], both with respect to its factual origin and with respect to its general principle, which amounted to freedom of ecclesiastical life according to the opinion of the writer. This apologia was elicited by my note on the concurrence of Russia with Rome; in it the amicable sympathy with which certain of our fellow countrymen at the time related to the Old Catholics is noted in passing, how they had revolted against the pope under the patronage of Prince [Otto von] Bismarck, and so forth.

Although the remarks of the writer were evoked by such an insignificant cause, they touch upon very important and interesting

33

matters. The question of the character of Old Catholicism* can even help us in the illumination of other more important questions.[1]

The venerable author of the letter to the editor desires more than anything to defend Old Catholicism from any suspicion of Bismarck's patronage. But what is it that is particularly bad in this patronage, and who would fault them for this alone? As if Prince Bismarck can not patronize a good enterprise, or as if any good enterprise will become bad from his patronage alone! But the so-called Old Catholics, apart from any of their attitudes toward the German chancellor, merit indictment first for the fact that they placed their own personal views, or more precisely, the views of a professorial group, above a matter concerning the universal church, and preferred it to a resolution concordant with the entire catholic world: this world accepted the Vatican decisions and did not change its ecclesiastic relations with the pope.[2] And second, they merit an even greater reproach for the fact that in rising against ecclesiastical authority in the name of freedom of private opinion and thus taking a position on the Protestant point of view, they did not resolve directly to proclaim themselves Protestants, but used the spurious name of "Old Catholic Church" as cover. If we apply the unvarying rules of the universal church, which are compulsory both for Western Catholics and for us alike, to Professor Dollinger along with his comrades and followers, then it will doubtlessly turn out that the individuals who broke every hierarchic connection with the rest of the church and who are excommunicated by their own legitimate spiritual authority, can not constitute any church and any Catholicism, neither old nor new, but represented in themselves that which in the languages of the ancient canons is called an "unauthorized congregation."[3] But this unauthorized congregation declares itself to be the Old Catholic church. The patronage of Prince Bismarck obtains a reprehensible significance only in light of such pretension. In recalling this patronage, I understood first of all the fact the writer of the letter himself indicates, and, namely, that Prince Bismarck hurried to acknowledge the Old Catholics as a church, and to legalize the organization they granted themselves. This hasty legalization consisted mainly in the fact that in the several parishes where a certain number of Old Catholics appeared, Catholic churches taken from actual Catholics were given over by the German government for their disposition. This organization of Old Catholic parishes at someone else's cost was connected with the selection of an official representative by them for their community, to whom they wanted to confer the significance of a bishop.[4] When they separated from the Roman see, there was not a single bishop among them—a fateful circumstance for a movement that had named itself *Old Catholicism*. For when, in which *old* times did the Catholic Church make do without an episcopate? In searching for an exit from this spurious situation, they landed in one that was even worse. Since none of the hierarchs of the Catholic Church wanted anything to do with them, they turned to a Jansenist* bishop in Utrecht who had been excommunicated from the church, and he single handedly installed for them as bishop a Doctor Reinkens.[5]

I do not think that our author or anyone else from among the Orthodox could consider the ecclesiastical position of the Jansenist bishop as proper, nor consequently Dr. Reinkens, who was installed by him with a laying on of hands. For ten years prior to the beginning of the Old Catholic movement the late Khomiakov in a letter to the excommunicated bishop of the Jansenists, Loos (if I am not mistaken the very same one to whom the Old Catholics subsequently turned), proves very convincingly that the Jansenists, judged and excommunicated by the legitimate authority of the Catholic Church, can in no way remain Catholics, but should either declare themselves directly Protestants, or join with eastern Orthodoxy. "You don't have an argument," writes Khomiakov "with the Roman court alone, with that which it would only be possible to call a secret counsel. True, the verdict which condemned you was pronounced by the Roman court, but it is accepted by the entire Roman church. . . . No, you really are in schism, and not with Rome alone, but with the entire Catholic Church; and up until now there has not been a more manifest schism. . . . But will there be enough courage among you to acknowledge Rome and all those faithful to Rome as schismatics? Can you do it? If there isn't enough and you can't, then you condemn yourselves. . . . Rome has no need of us, and simply calls us schismatics; but you can not repay it the same way, because you can not do without Rome, not having changed the basis itself of your teachings. . . . Let me say that you yourselves do not believe in your righteousness and in the justice of your enterprise."†

---

*It is well known that the Jansenist sect was formed in the seventeenth century on account of theological disputes concerning free will and grace.

†*Works of Khomiakov*, Vol. II (Prague, 1867), pp. 265–267.

"It is possible to leave Rome and not return to the (eastern) church, through only one door, and this door is Protestantism. Only two roads are open in the West for a person's spiritual life: the road of Romanum (without any basis of differentiation from ultra-Montanism) and the road of Protestantism."*

"But you do not dare to be followers; you do not dare to acknowledge yourselves as in contradiction to your teachings and you remain vacillating, indecisive, negating in fact that which you acknowledge in words, alone in the universe and condemned by yourselves in the depth of your own consciences."†

Everything said here about the Jansenists applied in full measure as well to the ecclesiastical situation of the Old Catholics. Having separated themselves from the legitimate authority of Catholicism, having repudiated the very principle of the supreme authority of the pope, they had to choose between eastern Orthodoxy and Protestantism.‡ The question arises: *in the name of what* did they reject the authority of the Roman altar and the decisions of the Vatican Council? If they rejected them as *new* dogma in the name of old tradition (as, apparently their name demonstrates), then this is precisely the point of view of Eastern Orthodoxy as well: it is now a thousand years since the Eastern church began to reject papal authority in the name of antiquity and tradition, and in this respect there was no need for the Old Catholics to raise their own particular banner. If they were Old Catholics in name only, and in essence did not care about *antiquity*, but rather about the *freedom* of personal opinion, and rejected Catholic authority in the name of this personal freedom (as the beginning of their movement demonstrates), in such case what is their distinction in *principle* from Protestantism, the essence of which is precisely in the affirmation of freedom of personal faith? But they resolved neither to join with Orthodoxy, nor to announce themselves as Protestants, and meanwhile they did not contribute any new religious idea of theirs to the world, and even feared to do so, valuing the spurious banner of Old Catholicism. Not having any religious or ecclesiastical grounds for their existence as something separate and special in the Christian world, they could only rest upon *political* foundations.

When the unification of the German people took place in 1870 through the establishment of a new German Empire, there turned out to be 15 million Catholics in this single empire—members of

---

Works of Khomiakov, Vol. II (Prague, 1867), p. 271.

†Ibid., p. 268.

‡I. S. Aksakov eloquently developed this thought in his open letter to Professor Dollinger.

another and greater union, of the Catholic church with its religious center outside the boundaries of Germany. It is for this reason that this religious center, that is, the papal throne, in that same year of 1870 solemnly affirmed its supreme significance for the entire Catholic world at a Vatican Council. Fifteen million German Catholics could seem to be a great danger for German unity under such conditions. One of the chief concerns of the German government, that is, Prince Bismarck, became the elimination, or at least the weakening, of this danger. The Old Catholic movement appeared to be the most feasible means for this. By arming themselves against the pope and separating themselves from the center of a church outside Germany, the Old Catholics were also serving the new empire; by preserving the name and all the appearance of Catholicism, they could all the more easily act on the multitude of German Catholics—if not diverting them from papism, then in any case weakening the latter with a new schism. Each success of the Old Catholics would be a success of German unity and a defeat of its enemies. No one supposes, of course, that Professor Dollinger and his comrades began their opposition to the papal throne at the direct suggestion of Prince Bismarck; but it is doubtless that the latter seriously thought to make use of the new movement and that Old Catholicism was organized as a church only thanks to the powerful cooperation of the German chancellor, as by the way our author acknowledges.* Why the Old Catholics neither joined with Orthodoxy nor with Protestantism is explained by this as well: for then they would have stopped being a convenient instrument of German politics, which had need, of course, not of the religious consistency of these professors, but only in their possible influence on German Catholics.

But all calculations based on this influence turned out to be mistaken. Old Catholicism did not produce any effect on the multitude of German Catholics, it did not turn into a national movement anywhere, but remained only within a close-knit group of professors, students, and a few liberal burghers. A new schism of such insignificant dimensions appeared completely harmless for the papacy and useless for the

---

*An occasion at a meeting of Old Catholics in Koln serves as the only argument for our author against the existence of a political connection between the Old Catholics and the German chancellor. One of them, in the presence of a great number of people, proposed a toast in honor of Prince Bismarck, to which another Old Catholic, Dr. Michelis, answered that, notwithstanding the service of Bismarck, such a toast was out of place in view of the religious subject of the meeting. It seems to us that this occasion demonstrates only that there were more naive people and less naive people among the Old Catholics.

German Empire. Applying to this affair the rule of the wise Gamaliel, we must acknowledge that the Old Catholic movement turned out to proceed "not from God, but from man": its failure made it useless for man too.[6] The German government and the social opinion of Europe as well then stopped indulging it and it disappeared into obscurity, leaving the world only the lesson that human personality is powerless and its action fruitless any time that it comes forward only in the name of its own opinions, sentiments and reasons, and not in the name of a common universal-historical idea.

There was such an idea in Protestantism, for it raised and affirmed the great principle of the freedom of spiritual life in the Christian world—the independence and inviolability of personal conscience. But captivated by the intrinsic power of this truth, Protestantism profoundly erred with respect to the place in religious life that belongs to this principle. *Freedom* of the individual spirit is the *summit* and crown of the church, but Protestantism took it not only as a summit that is the necessary end, but also as a *foundation* as well, repudiating the real foundation—orthodox *tradition* and a real *fence* or wall of the church—an independent spiritual *authority*. But both this error and the one-sidedness of Protestants have some justification in the fact that they already found the forces of Christian humanity divided in a one-sided way: instead of agreeing both to preserve the foundation of the church and to collectively endeavor in raising its fence, it will soon be a thousand years that people of the church have been divided in hostility and have stood in isolation; some (in the East) preserve exclusively the foundation of the church, others (in the West) just as exclusively fortify its fence. Both the one and the other have forgotten that the purpose of the Divine undertaking is not in a foundation and not in a fence, but in the entire edifice of the church, or God-manhood, which apart from these two things is still in heed of a third, higher thing—freedom of spiritual life.

The fault of the present troubled condition of the Christian world does not fall on any one individual—it is the general consequence of the *division of the church*. This is the sad event through which the progress of the Christian undertaking in history was violated.

It is doubtless that the practical deficiencies of ecclesiastical life we have in the East—apathy and inactivity, absence of ecclesiastical independence and of influence on social life, and so forth—developed after the division of the church as a result of our religious solitude and isolation from Europe. On the other hand, everybody knows the historical sins of the papacy, which provoked as a consequence the error of Protestantism, and were bound through their origins to the division of the church, thanks to which the Catholic Church, bereft of the mitigating influences of the East, adopted an exclusively juridical character and with unilateral effort began to introduce its principle into practical life.

The spiritual ailments of our Western brothers are clearly apparent to us Russians, but we can not acknowledge our own ecclesiastical condition as healthy either. Knowing the general reason for our own evil as well as that of others, we will not begin to turn for assistance and support to artificial and spurious phenomena, such as the movement of the Old Catholics, who broke from the papacy, did not join with Protestantism, and have no business with us. It is necessary for us to leave aside the absurd and pitiful dream of the conversion of Western Catholics and Protestants to Eastern Orthodoxy, and strive instead for mutual and multilateral agreement among our church—the church of tradition—and Roman Catholicism, as the church of authority, for then the church of freedom as well—Protestantism—will take its appropriate place, and the fullness and wholeness of Christian life will be restored.

Whether this is good or bad, the fortunes of the Catholic Church today are found in the hands of the Roman high priest. Every attempt to create a catholicism without a pope turns out to be resolutely unsupportable. On the other hand, it is without doubt that the Russian imperial government appears as the representative and leader of the Eastern church in every historical matter (for an independent *ecclesiastical* administration does not exist either in Russia or in other places of the Orthodox East). It would therefore be unforgivable to deny in a doctrinaire manner the important influence that the mutual relations of the Russian government and the papal throne can have in the resolution of the great ecclesiastical question. But there appears here in various respects the objection that no matter how one looks from a religious point of view at rapprochement with Rome, it is in any case undesirable and impossible from a political point of view, for the papacy has always come forward as the greatest political enemy of Russia. This is an indisputable fact, but the conclusion that they draw from it falls of its own accord, because the age-old enmity between Russia and the papacy was inarguably caused by ecclesiastical discord, and consequently it is not possible to cite this, when the point is about the removal of this discord. But even allowing that the enmity between Russia and Rome is an ineradicable fact, at least for now, in any case this fact does not impede the Russian government, but sooner calls it to rapprochement with the papacy *not in the sense of union*, but in the sense of a better familiarity with the posture, resources, and prospects of the adversary—a purely diplomatic rapprochement. It is not friends alone who draw closer, but enemies—for businesslike efforts. The more the papacy is for us hostile and dangerous, the more such a rapprochement is necessary for us. Sensible politics will hardly counsel shunning and avoiding the adversary.

Therefore our recent agreement with Rome—apart from its local ecclesiastical significance, as satisfying the religious requirements of our Catholics—deserves full approval also from a political point of view, inasmuch as it was conducted with a renewal of diplomatic relations and was the first step on the path of political rapprochement with Rome. Having entered into a diplomatic agreement with the papal throne, our government demonstrated that it recognizes the papacy as an independent political force, and in that case a further step—the establishment of regular and permanent diplomatic relations between the two governments appears as the direct logical result of such a recognition. The pope is only nominally the ruler of the Vatican and consequently according to the measure of his rule can compete with the Prince of Monaco (who, however, sends his ambassador to Petersburg). But it would be too strange not to see that the real political significance of the Roman high priest extends far beyond the boundaries of the Vatican. True, the pope is no longer "a king of kings," as in the Middle Ages, but he truly remains the supreme leader of the many millions of Catholics of the whole world who acknowledge in him the undisputed authority in all the most important matters of human life.*

The most authoritative representatives of our political press themselves love to cite—and they are quite well-founded in this—the example of Prince Bismarck in various political questions, indicating as instructive the keenness with which Germans relate to their political adversaries. But is it possible to be perceptive of one's adversary when you do not even want to know him? And if one indicates the example of Prince Bismarck, then it is necessary to remember that this statesman, after several years of stubborn and fruitless internal struggle with Catholicism, had to ultimately risk a direct diplomatic rapprochement and appointed a German ambassador to Rome.

But we have a special additional reason for the establishment of regular relations with the papal throne, namely, the need to separate the interest of Catholicism from Polonism. Separating them is a

---

*It should be noted that of all the Christian confessions Catholicism has recently gained the greatest number of followers. In Great Britain and North America the number of those crossing over from Protestantism to Catholicism in the present century is in the millions.

difficult and complicated matter, but the first condition for it in any event is a direct mutual representation between Russia and Rome. Without this the sole representatives of the Roman Church among us, the sole intermediaries between us and the papacy turn out to be the Polish bishops, and thus the identification of Catholic and Polish affairs becomes unavoidable. Natural sympathies between Rome and the Poles will of course remain, and let them; nevertheless an Italian or Spanish nuncio in direct relations with the Russian government will be able to differentiate the interest of the Catholic Church from Polish nationalism.

There was a time when Russia did not have any political significance in Europe. This was precisely the time when Russia shunned Europe and was apprehensive of every rapprochement with it. As soon as Peter the Great brought us close to Europe, he created a politically powerful Russia and a significance for it in the world. We believe that Russia is called not to political power alone, but that it has a religious task in history as well. Here as well Russia can in no way fulfill this task, achieve religious significance for itself in the Christian world, through alienation from the Western church, but through a conscious and reasonable rapprochement with it. In gazing at the surrounding confusion of intellects and affairs, it is frightful to even ponder such a great task. But an ancient historian had a comforting saying: *hominum confusione ac Dei providentia Ruthenia ducitur.*

3

The Jews and the Christian Question

> In that day shall Israel be the third with Mizraim [Egypt] and with Assyria, even a blessing in the midst of the land, whom the Lord of hosts shall bless, saying: Blessed be Mizraim, my people, and Assyria, the work of my hands, and Israel, my inheritance.
>
> —Isaiah 19:24–25

The relations of Judaism and Christianity in their life together over the course of many centuries present one remarkable circumstance.[1] Jews have always and everywhere viewed and acted with regards to Christianity in harmony with the prescriptions of their *religion*, according to their *faith* and according to their *law*. Jews have always related to us in a Jewish manner; however, we Christians, to the contrary, have yet to learn to relate to Judaism in a Christian manner. They have never broken their religious law with respect to us, but we have constantly broken and continue to break the commandments of the Christian religion with respect to them. If Judaic law is deficient, then their stubborn faithfulness to this deficient law is certainly a sorry phenomenon. But if it is wrong to be faithful to deficient law, then it is even worse to be unfaithful to salutary law, to an absolutely perfect precept. We have such a precept in the Gospel. It is perfect, and for that very reason it is quite difficult. But special means have also been revealed to us—the assistance of grace, which does not annul law, gives us strength for its fulfillment. Thus, if we first reject this assistance and then renounce the fulfillment of the gospel precept under the pretext of its difficulty, then we have no excuse. The point is not in whether or not the gospel precept is difficult or not difficult, but in whether it is able to be fulfilled or not. If it is not able to be fulfilled, then why has it been given? In that case those Jews who reproach Christianity for introducing into the world fantastic principles and ideas that cannot have any actual implementation will be correct. If, however, the gospel precept is able to be fulfilled, if we can relate in a Christian manner to everyone, not excluding even Jews, then we are wholly guilty when we do not do this.

Instead of directly repenting of this, we search for someone to heap our guilt upon. We are not guilty—the Middle Ages with all their fanaticism are guilty—the Catholic church is guilty. But now persecutions against the Jews have begun in our time, and in countries that are not Catholic. Here it turns out that those that have suffered are now guilty instead of us. If Jews living among us relate to us in a Jewish manner, then clearly, we should relate to them *in a pagan manner*. If they do not want to love us, clearly, we ought to hate them. If they stand for their segregation, if they do not want to intermingle with us, if they do not want to acknowledge solidarity with us, but on the contrary, they attempt to utilize our weaknesses in every way, then clearly, we should eradicate them.

True, the persecution of Jews and the more or less open justifications of these persecutions do not at present constitute a *general* phenomenon in Europe; on the contrary, generally speaking, Judaism not only makes use of tolerance, but also has succeeded in occupying an ascendant position in the most progressive nations. England has been governed by a Jew, Disraeli, more than once, and in other countries as well finances and a great portion of the periodical press are in the hands of Jews (directly or indirectly). But this preponderance of Jews not only does not refute my point that the Christian world has never related to Judaism in a Christian manner, but rather directly supports it. For does contemporary tolerance, pliancy, and even subjection with respect to Jews really originate from Christian conviction and sentiment? It is completely to the contrary: all this flows not from the breadth of our religious views, but from the *absence* of any religious views, from a total indifference to matters of faith. It is not a Christian Europe that tolerates Jews, but an unbelieving Europe, a Europe bereft of its vital principles, a Europe in decay. Jews live not by our moral strength, but by our moral, or better immoral, weakness.

They speak of a Jewish question; but in essence the entire matter is reduced to a single fact that elicits a question not about the Jewish people, but about the Christian world itself. This fact can be expressed and explained in a few words. Money is the major interest in today's Europe; Jews are masters of monetary business, so naturally, they dominate in today's Europe. After many centuries of antagonism, the Christian world and Judaism have converged finally in a common interest, in a common passion for money. But here as well an important difference between them has turned out to be in favor of Judaism and to the shame of a falsely Christian Europe—a difference by virtue of which money liberates and exalts Jews, but binds and degrades us. The point is that Jews are tethered to money not at all for the sake of material benefit alone, but because they find in it today the major instrument for the triumph and glory of Israel, that is, in their perspective, for the triumph of the Divine enterprise on earth. Indeed, there is yet another peculiarity among Jews besides passion for money: a strong unity among all of them in the name of their common faith and common law. Only thanks to this does money work to their benefit: when any Jew grows wealthy and is elevated—all of Judaism, the entire house of Israel, grows wealthy and is elevated. Meanwhile, cultured Europe has fallen in love with money, not as a means for any kind of higher goal *in common*, but solely for the sake of the material goods that every possessor of which obtains for money *individually*. And here we see that cultured Europe *serves* money, while Judaism *compels* both money and a Europe devoted to money *to serve it*. Contemporary attitudes of advanced Europe toward Judaism are as if to parody one of the prophetic images: ten Gentiles grab hold of the hem of a Jew's garment so that he can bring them, not into the temple of Yahweh, but into the temple of Mammon; and they have as little to do with Yahweh as with Christ.[2]

Thus, there is nothing for cultured Europe to blame on the darkness of the Middle Ages with its religious fanaticism, no reason for it to praise its religious tolerance. Religious tolerance is fine on the part of believers when it originates from a fullness of faith, from consciousness of a higher moral power; but on the part of unbelievers religious tolerance is only an expression of unbelief. If it is all the same to me what Christianity is, what Judaism is, what idol worship is, then what is the virtue of my tolerance, and how can I contrive to be intolerant in faith? No matter how far religious fanaticism is from Christian perfection, it is in any case a moral force, only in an undeveloped, crude form, an unregulated force, and that is why it is inclined to abuses. This is in any case a positive quantity, whereas religious indifference shows the absence of heartfelt warmth and inspiration; it is a moral freezing point, the chill of spiritual death. But when lower interests and material goods become extremely attractive in the face of a societal indifference toward higher ideas, then it is clear that social *decay* has set in.

Thus, the Christian world *in its totality* has displayed up to now in relation to Judaism either irrational zeal or decrepit and powerless indifference. Both of these attitudes are alien to a truly Christian spirit, and are not found at the height of the Christian idea. But beginning with the thirteenth century, we meet up with isolated attempts on the part of distinguished representatives and thinkers of the Christian world, attempts at another, truly Christian, attitude toward Judaism.* While such attempts did not lead to any explicit results either, they nevertheless constitute the beginning of a true resolution of the Jewish question, which is already prophesied by the Apostle Paul in his letter to the Romans (ch. 11).

Acknowledging only this kind of religious resolution of "the Jewish question," and believing in the coming unification of the house of Israel with Orthodox and Catholic Christianity on *theocratic* soil common to them, I had the occasion to express this, my conviction, in brief outline from the lectern.† Now I resolve to give a more detailed elaboration and more publicity to this view on Judaism. Incidentally, I am reinforced in such a resolution by the imposing voice of one of our arch-prelates, whom I may follow without danger of somehow being led astray.

In April of this year, His Holiness Nicanor, Bishop of Kherson and Odessa (the author of a remarkable and still insufficiently appreciated work on religious philosophy), gave an inspired and truly Christian speech in Odessa on the most immediate kinship between Old Testament and New Testament religion.[3] The main idea of this excellent speech was the unity of Judaism with Christianity, but not on the basis of indifference or any abstract principles, rather on grounds of real spiritual and natural kinship and of positive religious interests. We should be united with Judaism, not rejecting Christianity, not contrary to Christianity, but in the name and in the power of Christianity, and Jews should be united with us not contrary to Judaism, but in the name and in the power of true Judaism. We are separated from Jews because we are *not yet fully Christian*, and they separate themselves from us because they are *not yet fully Jews*. For the fullness of Christianity also embraces Judaism and the fullness of Judaism is Christianity.

My thoughts about Judaism, which follow below, constitute a direct supplement to that which was expressed by His Holiness Nicanor, and therefore his words appeared to me as the best reassurance and occasion for the exposition of these thoughts in print.

---

*Justice requires us to note that in general in the Middle Ages the supreme representatives of the church, in particular the Roman popes, related to the Jews relatively philanthropically, and several of the popes even defended them directly, for which they were even exposed to severe indictments by their contemporaries.

†In 1882, in a lecture about the universal historical significance of Judaism given at [St.] Petersburg University and in the higher women's courses.

The fortunes of the Hebrew nation, in our view, are connected chiefly with three facts of their history. The first fact is that Christ was a Jew on his Mother's side and Christianity came out of Judaism; the second fact is that the greater part of the Jewish people rejected Christ and took a decidedly hostile position with respect to Christianity; the third fact is that the chief part of the Hebrew nation and the religious center of recent Judaism is not in Western Europe, but in two Slavic countries—Russia and Poland. The first of these facts—the Incarnation of Christ in Judea—defined the *past* of Israel—its original designation as God's chosen people; the second fact—the nonacknowledgment of Christ by the Jews and their alienation from Christianity—defines the *present* situation of Judaism in the world, its temporary rejection; finally, the third fact—the population of Israel on Slavic soil among nations that have not yet spoken their piece to the world—forecasts the *future* fortunes of Judaism, the ultimate restoration of its religious significance. Former Judaism lived by faith and hope for a *promised* God-manhood; present Judaism lives in protest and enmity to the unacknowledged Messiah God-man, the *seed* of God-manhood on earth; future Judaism will live a full life when it finds and acknowledges in a renewed Christianity the image of a *perfected* God-manhood.

This hope has the firmest foundation in the word of God. Yahweh preselected Israel, concluded a covenant with it, made it a promise. Yahweh is not a man to be deceived, and not a Son of Man to repent of His promises. A part of the Israelite nation rejected the first appearance of the Messiah and for this suffers a difficult requital, but only for a time, for the word of God can not be violated; and this word of the Old Testament, which is resolutely confirmed in the New Testament through the lips of the Apostle to the Gentiles, clearly and incontestably says: *all Israel will be saved*.[4]

The Jews who demanded the death of Christ cried: "His blood be on us and on our children" [Mt. 27:25]. But this blood is the *blood of redemption*. And the cry of human evil is surely insufficiently powerful to silence the Divine word of remission: "Father, forgive them, for they know not what they do" [Lk 23:34]. The bloodthirsty mob that gathered at Golgotha consisted of Jews; but Jews were also those three thousand and then five thousand people who, according to the preaching of the Apostle Peter, were baptized and comprised the original Christian church. Anna and Caiaphas were Jews, as were Joseph and Nicodemus. To one and the same people belonged both Judas, who betrayed Christ to Crucifixion, and Peter and Andrew, who themselves were crucified for Christ. Thomas, who disbelieved the Resurrection, was a Jew; he did not cease being a Jew when he believed in the Resurrected One and said to Him: "My Lord and My God!" [Jn 20:28]. Saul, the most terrible persecutor of Christians, was a Jew, and as Paul, who, persecuted for Christianity and "having labored more abundantly than all" [1 Cor 15:10] for it, remained a Jew among Jews. And what is greater and more important than everything else, He Himself, the God-man Christ, who was betrayed and killed by Jews, in human body and soul was the most faultless Jew.

In view of this striking fact is it not strange for us to condemn all Jewish people, to which Christ himself inalienably belongs as well—*in the name of Christ*? And is this not especially strange on the part of those among us, who, if not directly renouncing Christ, in any case do not manifest in any way their connection to Him?

If Christ is not God, then the Jews are no more guilty than the Hellenes who killed Socrates. If we acknowledge Christ as God, then it is necessary to acknowledge in the Jews a *God-generating* nation.[5] Romans are together with Jews to blame for the death of Jesus; but His birth belongs only to God and to Israel. Jews, they say, are the constant enemies of Christianity; however, not Jews, not Semites, but those who were born Christians of the Aryan tribe stand at the head of the anti-Christian movement of the last few centuries. The denial of Christianity and the struggle against it on the part of several thinkers of Jewish descent has a more honest and more religious character than on the part of writers who came out of the midst of Christianity. Better Spinoza than Voltaire, better Joseph Salvador than Mr. Ernst Renan.

To despise Judaism is insane; to quarrel with Jews is useless; it is better to comprehend Judaism, although this is more difficult. It is difficult to comprehend Judaism because those three great facts with which its fortunes are connected do not appear as something simple, natural, and comprehensible in and of themselves. They have need of specific and complex elucidation. These three facts are at the same time three questions, three problems for resolution:

1. Why was Christ a Jew? Why take the cornerstone of the universal church from the house of Israel?

2. Why did the greater part of Israel not acknowledge its Messiah? Why did the Old Testament church not dissolve in the New Testament church? Why do the majority of Jews prefer to be entirely without a temple rather than to enter into the Christian temple?

3. Finally, why and for the sake of what have the sturdiest (in a religious sense) parts of the Jewish people been thrust into

Russia and Poland, set on the border of the Greco-Slavic and Latin-Slavic world?

Let them deny and lessen the significance of this last fact. Let the haters of Jews relative to the second point as well find it natural that such an unfit and unscrupulous nation renounced and killed Christ; but then let them also explain why Christ belonged precisely to this nation. On the other hand, if one finds to the contrary the first fact—Christ belonging to the nation of Israel, predesignated and chosen for this from the beginning—to be comprehensible, then in this case how can we explain this chosen nation turning out to be unworthy of election *precisely in the purpose for which* it was chosen? Either way, the matter appears at any rate enigmatic and requires elucidation. We will begin with the first fact and the first question.

I. Why Were the Jewish People Destined for the Birth of the God-man, the Messiah, or Christ?

To the extent that appointment proceeds from God, it is a matter of absolute freedom. But one ought not to think of Divine freedom as resembling human arbitrariness or predilection; true freedom does not exclude reason, and according to reason such appointment or election, being the attitude of God to a certain subject, corresponds not only to the property of the one being elected, but also to the quality of the one who is electing. The *conditions* for the election of the Jews should be in the national character of the Jews. This character was sufficiently successful in defining itself over the course of four thousand years, and it is not difficult to find and indicate its individual traits. But the aggregate of these traits and their mutual connection has yet to be sufficiently understood. No one would try to deny that the national character of the Jews possesses integrity and internal unity. Meanwhile we find in it three chief features that apparently not only agree with one another, but are directly in opposition among themselves as well.

Jews are first of all distinguished by a deep religiosity, loyalty to their God to the point of total self-sacrifice. This is a people of the Law and the prophets, martyrs, and apostles "who, through faith, subdued kingdoms, wrought righteousness, obtained promises" (Epistle to the Hebrews 11:33).

Secondly, the Jews are distinguished by an extreme development of health, self-consciousness, and initiative. Just as with all Israel so too with each family in it and with every member of this family—all are permeated to the depths of their soul and the marrow of their bones by the feeling and consciousness of their national, family, and personal *I* and strive in every way to manifest in fact this feeling and self-consciousness, stubbornly and tirelessly working for oneself, for one's family and for all Israel.

Finally, the third differentiating trait of Jews is their extreme materialism (in a broad sense of the word). The sensual character of the Jewish *worldview* was expressed symbolically even in their writing (in restriction of the alphabet to consonants alone—to the body of words, whereas the spirit of a word—vowels—are either completely omitted or are signified only by dots and small marks). And with respect to the Jewish materialism of daily life, that is, the predominance of self-interest and utilitarian arrangements in their activity from vessels of Egypt to the bourses of contemporary Europe, it seems there is no need to elaborate upon this.

Thus, the character of this surprising nation identically manifests the force of Divine principle in the religion of Israel, the force of human self-affirmation in the national, family, and personal life of Jews, and finally the force of the material element that colors all their thoughts and deeds. But how are these elements that struggle against each other combined in one living individuality? What connects the religious idea of Israel with the human initiative of Judaism and with Jewish materialism? It would seem that total loyalty to God alone should annul or at least weaken both the energy of the human *I* and attachment to material goods. Thus, we see, for example, in Indian Brahminism a predominant sense of divine unity led religious people to a complete denial of both human individuality and material nature. In turn it would seem that a predominant development of the human principle—humanism in one or another form—would wring out the superhuman power of religion on the one hand, and lift the human spirit above crude materialism on the other, as we see in the best representatives of ancient Greece and Rome, and even in modern Europe as well.

It is just as clear that a dominion of materialism in views and endeavors is not compatible either with religious or with humanitarian ideals. And yet all this gets along together in Judaism, not at all violating the wholeness of the national character. In order to find the key to this enigma, one does not have to dwell on abstract concepts about religion *in general*, about idealism and materialism *in general*, but one has to examine more carefully the particulars of *Jewish* religion, of *Jewish* humanism and of *Jewish* materialism.

Believing in the unity of God, Jews never assumed the religious task of man to merge with Divinity, to disappear into His all-unity [*vseedinstvo*]. And they did not even acknowledge this kind of negative and abstract unity-of-everything or indifference in God. Generally speaking, Judaism always saw in God not an infinite emptiness of the universal substratum, but an infinite fullness of being, having life in itself and giving life to another (notwithstanding several mystical notions of the later Kabbalists, and the pantheistic philosophy of the Jew Spinoza). Free from any external restrictions and definitions, but not diffusing into general indifference, the God who exists defines Himself and appears as a perfect personality, or an absolute *I*. In conformity with this religion neither should there be a destruction of man in universal Divinity, but personal mutual activity between the Divine and the human *I*. It is precisely because the Jewish people were capable of such an understanding and such religion that they could become the chosen people of God.

The Living God made Israel His people because Israel also made the Living God its own. The forefather Abraham, living amidst pagans and still not having received direct revelation of the true God, was not satisfied and was not attracted by the cult of sham gods that was so appealing to all nations. Service to elemental and demonic forces of nature was contrary to the Hebrew soul. The forefather of Israel could not believe in what was inferior to man, and he searched for a personal and moral God, belief in which did not degrade him, and this God appeared and called him and gave a promise to his clan. "By faith, Abraham obeyed when he was called to go out to a place which he should later receive for an inheritance; and he went out, not knowing where he went" (Epistle to the Hebrews 11:8). The same thing that led Abraham out of the Chaldean land led Moses out of Egypt as well. Notwithstanding all the temptations of Egyptian theosophy and theurgy, "by faith Moses, when he was come to years, refused to be called the son of Pharaoh's daughter [. . .] and by faith he forsook Egypt, not fearing the wrath of the king" (ibid., 24, 27).[6]

Having separated from paganism and been elevated by his faith above Chaldean magic and Egyptian wisdom, the forefathers and leaders of the Hebrews became worthy of Divine election. God chose them, revealed himself to them, and concluded an agreement with them. The agreed upon contract or covenant of God with Israel constitutes the center of Hebrew religion: the sole phenomenon in universal history, for in no other nation did religion take this form of agreement or covenant between God and man, as two beings, while not of equivalent power, *morally homogeneous*.

This elevated concept of man does not violate Divine grandeur at all, but on the contrary allows it to appear in all its power. God finds a worthy subject of action for Himself in the independent moral being of man, otherwise He *would have nothing* to act upon. If man was not a free personality, how would it be possible for God to manifest His *personal* being in the world? The holy religion of the Jews is beyond all the naturalistic and pantheistic religions of the ancient world as much as the independently existing and self-defining God who reigns over it transcends the impersonal essence of worldly phenomena. Neither God nor man preserved their independence in these religions: man was a slave of unknown and alien laws here, and Divinity appeared as a plaything of human fantasy in the end (in the artistic mythology of the Greeks). In the Judaic religion, to the contrary, both aspects—Divine and human—are alike preserved from the beginning. Our religion begins with a personal relationship between God and man in the ancient covenant of Abraham and Moses, and is confirmed in the closest personal unity of God and man in the New Testament of Jesus Christ, in which both natures exist inseparably, but unmerged as well. These two covenants are not two different religions, but only two stages of one and the same Divine-human religion, or speaking in the language of the German school, two moments of one and the same God-human process. This single and true Divine-human Judeo-Christian religion proceeds by a direct and magisterial path amid the two extreme errors of paganism, in which first man is absorbed by Divinity (in India), and then Divinity itself is transformed into a shadow of man (in Greece and Rome).

The one true God, having chosen Israel and been chosen by it, is a God of power, an independently existing, Holy God. The God of power chooses for himself a powerful man who could struggle with Him; the independently existing God reveals himself only to self-conscious personality; the Holy God unites only with a man searching for holiness and capable of *active* moral exploit.[7] Human powerlessness seeks Divine power, but to a powerful man this is powerlessness: man, out of nature weak, is incapable of powerful religiosity either. Precisely in the same way an impersonal man, without character and with little developed self-consciousness, can not understand how necessary the truth of an *independently existing* Divine being is. Finally man, in whom the freedom of moral self-definition is paralyzed, who is incapable of *beginning action* out of himself, is incapable of a perfected exploit, achieving holiness. For this kind of man Divine holiness always remains something extrinsic and alien—he will never be a "friend of God."[8] From this it is clear that the true religion we find in the nation of Israel does not exclude but on the contrary requires the development of free human personality, its self-consciousness and initiative. Israel was great out of faith, but for great faith it is necessary to have great spiritual power in oneself. For its part, the energy of the free human principle is manifest better than anything precisely in faith. The prejudice that faith oppresses the freedom of the human spirit but that positive knowledge broadens freedom is very widely circulated. But it turns out to be the opposite according to the essence of the matter. The human spirit crosses the boundaries of the given present reality in faith, confirms the existence of subjects that *do not force* acknowledgment in it—it freely acknowledges them. Faith is an *exploit of the spirit*, revealing things unseen.[9] The believing spirit does not await the influence of an extrinsic subject passively, but boldly goes to meet it, it does not follow after phenomena slavishly, but anticipates them—it is self-actuating and free. As a free exploit of the spirit, faith has moral worth and merit: blessed are those who have not seen and believe [Jn 20:29]. Contrary to our spirit, empirical knowledge, being subordinated to extrinsic fact, is passive and inadequate: there is neither exploit nor moral merit here. Of course, this opposition of faith and knowledge is not absolute. For the believer always one way or another acknowledges the subject of his faith, and on the other hand positive knowledge always accepts on faith something that can not be empirically proved, and, namely, the objective reality of the physical world, the constancy and universality of the laws of nature, the non-mendacity of our perceptive faculties, and so forth. Nevertheless it is without doubt that the predominant trait in the sphere of faith is the activity and freedom of our spirit, and in the sphere of empirical knowledge—passivity and dependency. The independence and energy of the human spirit are not required in order to acknowledge and know a given fact from without: they are needed to believe in that which has not yet crossed over into a visible fact. The manifest and the present themselves *insist* on their acknowledgment, the power of spirit is in prefiguring what is to come, in acknowledging and pronouncing what is mysterious and secret. Here is why the higher energy of the human spirit is manifest in the Israelite prophets, not in spite of their religious faith, but precisely by virtue of this faith.

This unification of a most profound faith in God with a very elevated exertion of human energy was preserved even in later Judaism. For example, it is expressed quite sharply in the concluding paschal prayer about the arrival of the Messiah:

Almighty God, create Your temple soon and near, today, soon, as near as possible in our days, create it today, create it today, today, create it, today create Your temple! Merciful God, great God, kind God, God most-high, blessed God, dear God, infinite God, God of Israel, create Your temple in a time near, soon, soon, in our days, create it today, create it today, create it today, today, create, create Your temple soon today! Powerful God, living God, stalwart God, glorious God, blessed God, eternal God, terrible God, excellent God, reigning God, wealthy God, amazing God, true God, restore Your temple today without delay, soon, soon, in our days, without delay soon, create it today, create it today, create it today, create it today, create today Your temple soon! (From the Latin translation of Buchstorff)

Apart from sincere faith in the God of Israel and the persistent human will directed to Him, yet another important particular is noted in this characteristic prayer: those who pray do not want their God to remain in a super-worldly sphere: seeing in Him the idea of all perfection, they absolutely require that this ideal be embodied on earth, that Divinity give itself an outwardly visible expression, *create for Itself a temple*, a corporeal habitation of Its power and glory—and moreover, that this temple be created *now, as soon as possible*. In this impatient striving to embody the Divine on earth, we find a guiding thread for understanding Jewish materialism, and also for the explanation of the present situation of the Israelite nation.

In speaking of materialism, it follows to differentiate three classes in it: practical, scientific-philosophical and religious. The first class of materialism directly depends on the mastery in a given people of the lower aspect of human nature, on the predominance of animal impulses over reason, sensual interests over the spiritual. In order to justify in oneself such a predominance of the lower nature, the practical materialist begins to deny the very existence of all that is not accommodated in this lower nature, that is not possible to see or touch, to weigh or measure. In elevating this denial to a general principle, practical materialism crosses over into theoretical or scientific-philosophical materialism. The latter, by way of rational analysis, reduces all that exists to elementary facts of material nature, systematically denying all truths of a divine and spiritual order. Just as practical materialism has always existed everywhere that there have been morally unrefined people, so too theoretical materialism passes through the entire history of philosophy, adopting various modifications, combining usually with the theory of atoms in its metaphysics, with sensualism in its theory of knowledge, and using for its ethics the doctrine about satisfaction as the highest goal (hedonism) on the one hand, and relying on determinism, that is, on the doctrine about lack of a free character in all our actions on the other.

Neither of these types of materialism are particularly pertinent to Judaism. Practical materialism in its pure form is very rarely found among real Jews: as was already noted, even their universal love of money is consecrated by a higher goal—the enrichment and glory of all Israel. In precisely the same way scientific-philosophical materialism grew not in Semitic soil, but in Greco-Roman soil and then in the soil of Romano-German education; only through the milieu of this education can Jews adapt to themselves a materialistic philosophy that is completely alien to their own national spirit. But then from days of old there had been a third, special type of materialism that was characteristic of this national spirit; it is radically differentiated from the first two, and for brevity's sake I will designate it with an altogether imprecise title: *religious* materialism.

Jews who were faithful to their religion and fully acknowledged the spirituality of Divinity and the divinity of the human spirit did not know how and did not want to separate these higher principles from their material expression, from their corporeal membrane and form, from their extreme and ultimate realization. Jews require a visible and tangible embodiment and salutary results for every idea and every ideal; Jews do not want to acknowledge an idea that is not capable of subjecting reality to itself and being embodied in it; Jews are able and ready to acknowledge the most exalted spiritual truth, but only for the purpose of seeing and experiencing its substantive action. They believe in the invisible (for every faith is faith in the invisible), but want that this invisible become visible and that it manifest its power; they believe in spirit, but only in that which permeates everything material, which uses matter as its membrane and its instrument.

Not separating spirit from its material expression, Jewish thought by the same token does not separate matter from its spiritual and divine source either; it did not acknowledge matter in and of itself, did not impart significance to corporeal existence *as such*. Jews were not servants and worshipers of matter. On the other hand, being far from abstract spiritualism, Jews could not relate to matter with equanimity and alienation and still less with the enmity that eastern dualism supplied it with. They saw neither devil nor Divinity in material nature, but only an *unworthy dwelling for the Divine-human spirit*. While practical and theoretical materialism is subordinated to corporeal fact as to law, and whereas dualism averts matter as evil—the religious materialism of the Jews forced them to turn greatest attention to material nature, yet not in order to serve it, rather in order to serve the Supreme God in it and through it. They had to separate in it the pure from the impure, the holy from the defective, in order to make it a worthy temple for the Supreme being. The idea of *holy corporeality* and concerns about realizing this idea occupy an incomparably more important place in the life of Israel than in any other nation. A significant part of Mosaic legislation concerning the distinction between the pure and impure and concerning the rules for purification belongs here. It is possible to say that the entire religious history of the Jews was directed at preparing for the Israelite God not just sacred souls, but sacred bodies as well.

If we now compare the striving of the Jews toward the materialization of the divine principle with their concerns about the purification and sanctification of our corporeal nature, then we will easily understand why it is precisely Judaism that presented the most concordant material milieu for the embodiment of the Divine Word. For both reason and piety require acknowledging that, apart from a holy and active soul, a holy and pure corporeality was needed to serve the purpose of making Divinity human.

Now it is clear that this sacred Jewish materialism does not at all contradict but, on the contrary, serves as a direct supplement to the two first qualities of this nation—its powerful religiosity and its energy of human self-consciousness and initiative. A believing Israelite wants the subject of his faith to command the entire fullness of reality, to be realized ultimately; for its part, the energy or activity of the human spirit as well can not be satisfied with the abstract content of an idea and ideals—it requires their actual embodiment, requires that the spiritual principle ultimately take command of material reality, and this assumes the capability of such inspiration in matter itself—assumes a *spiritual and holy corporeality*. The religious materialism of the Jews descends not from unbelief, but from a surplus of faith, thirsting for its fulfillment, not from a weakness of human spirit, but from its strength and energy, not fearing a defilement of matter, but purifying it and utilizing it for its aims.

Thus, the three chief qualities of the Jewish nation in its collective activity directly corresponded to the exalted mission of this nation and enabled the accomplishment of Divine deeds in it. Firmly believing in the Living God, Israel encountered divine phenomena and revelation; believing in itself as well, Israel could act in *personal* relation to

Yahweh, stand face-to-face with Him, conclude an agreement with Him, serve Him not as a passive instrument, but as an active ally; finally, by virtue of that same active faith striving toward an ultimate realization of its spiritual principle, through a purification of material nature, Israel prepared amidst itself a pure and holy dwelling for the incarnation of the Word of God.

This is why Jews are the chosen people of God, this is why Christ was born in Judea.

II. Why the Jewish People Rejected Christ and Shun Christianity

All that is good in man and in humanity is protected against distortion and perversion only in unity with Divinity. As soon as the God-human connection is violated, the moral balance in man himself is immediately violated (though at first imperceptibly).

We discerned three chief qualities of the Jewish character: first, a sturdy faith in a living God; second, a most powerful sense of its own human and national identity; and third an unrestrained striving toward the utmost boundaries of realizing and materializing their faith and their feeling, to give them flesh and blood as soon as possible. In their proper combination, with the second and third necessarily dependent on the first, these three qualities constituted a great advantage and glory to Israel; they made it a chosen nation, a friend of God, a helper for the incarnation of Divinity. With the violation of the necessary relation among them, with preponderance of the second and third over the first, these same three qualities become a source of great sin and calamities.

When an unreserved faith in the Living God and His works stands in the first place, both Jewish self-consciousness and Jewish materialism serve the work of God and substantiate a truly *Divine rule* (theocracy).

But as soon as these purely human and natural particulars of the Jewish character acquire preponderance over the religious element and subordinate it to themselves, then this great and premier national character in the world inevitably appears with the distorted traits that explain the universal antipathy to Judaism (though the enmity to it is not justified): in this distorted form, the people's sense of self is transformed into national egoism, in limitless self-adoration, with contempt and enmity toward the rest of humanity; and the realism of the Jewish spirit degenerates into the exceptionally businesslike, self-interested character that shrinks from nothing, and behind which the best traits of true Judaism are almost completely hidden for an outsider, and all the more from a prejudiced perspective.

Many events of Jewish history, in particular the fundamental event of Christianity, would be incomprehensible without this profound distortion of the national character in a significant part of the Jewish nation. True, we do not see a special Judaic character in the *direct* adversaries of Jesus Christ, but only universal human vices and errors: the embittered vanity of "teachers" unmasked in their pettiness in union with false patriotism and sham political wisdom of national rulers—phenomena quite well known everywhere both before and after Christ. The personal enmity and spite aroused by Christ were fully understandable, His direct adversaries did not possess anything mysterious in themselves—these were most common specimens of depraved human nature. That these people could not be convinced by the miracles of Jesus Christ is understandable as well. These miracles were good works for those who suffered, and not signs for unbelievers. People who had come to know about these miracles only through word of mouth could easily deny their reality, but those adversaries of Christ who themselves were witnesses of His wonder working did not find it difficult at all to reject their *divine* character and ascribe them to demonic forces.

But how could it be explained that the multitude of people attracted precisely by the divine character of Christ's teaching and deeds suddenly disavowed Him and gave their Messiah over to His enemies? I do not find it possible to agree completely with the generally accepted explanation of this fact among us. The matter is usually presented as follows: the Jewish nation, though it awaited the Messiah, due to its unrefined-sensual character, imagined the kingdom of this Messiah exclusively in the form of political triumph and the mastery of Israel over all nations; the Gospel preaching about a purely spiritual Kingdom of God had nothing in common with these expectations, and therefore the Jews could not recognize their Messiah-King in Jesus. It seems to me that such an explanation is lame in both respects, and is in need of a double correction for its substantiation. It is beyond doubt that the Jews incidentally expected a political victory of Judaism from the Messiah too; it is beyond any doubt as well that Christ preached first and foremost a Kingdom of God in spirit and truth; but just as the issue of the Messiah was not exhausted by his political victory in the expectations of the Jews, so too on the other hand the proclamation of the Kingdom of God by Christ was not exhausted by the worship of God in spirit and truth alone. With respect to the Jews, their messianic expectation was founded first of all on prophetic writings, and the coming kingdom of the Messiah is presented in these writings predominantly as the fullest revelation and triumph of true religion, as the inspiration of the Sinai covenant, as the confirmation of the law of God in human hearts, as the promulgation of true knowledge about God, and finally, as the appearance of the Holy Spirit of God in every creature:

> I have sworn by myself, from My mouth proceeds truth, and the word is true. Before Me every knee shall bow, by Me every tongue shall swear. In the Lord alone, they will say about Me, are truth and strength; all who have been in enmity against Him shall come and be ashamed. (Isaiah 45:23–24)[10]

> Listen to Me, My people, bend your ear to Me, my tribe. For from Me the law will go out; My justice I place as a light to the nations [. . .] Lift up your eyes to the heavens and look at the earth beneath; for the heavens will vanish like smoke, and the earth will wear out like an old garment and all who live on it, but My salvation will abide forever and My truth will not end. (Isaiah 51:4, 6)

> Behold, I gave Him (the Messiah) as a witness for the nations, as a leader and commander for the gentiles. Behold, you will call a tribe that you do not know, and nations that do not know you, they will run to you for the sake of the Lord your God and for the sake of the Holy One of Israel, for He will glorify you." [Isaiah 55:4]

> Let the impious forsake his path and the unrighteous his thoughts and let him return to the Lord, and He will have mercy on him, and to our God, for He is abundantly merciful. [Isaiah 55:7]

> My thoughts are not your thoughts, and your ways are not My ways, says the Lord. But as the heavens are higher than the earth, so are My ways higher than your ways, and My thoughts than your thoughts. (Isaiah 55:8–9)

> For behold, I create a new heavens and a new earth; now the former things will not be remembered, and will enter the heart. (Isaiah 65:17)

If you will return, O Israel, says the Lord, return to Me; and if you take your abominations from before My face, you will no longer go astray. And you will swear: the Lord lives in truth, justice, and righteousness; and the nations will be blessed by Him and in Him they will glory. For so says the Lord to the men of Judah and to Jerusalem: break up your unplowed ground and do not sow among thorns. Circumcise yourselves for the Lord, and remove the excess flesh from your hearts, men of Judah and people of Jerusalem. (Jeremiah 4:1–4)

Behold, the days are coming, says the Lord, when I will conclude with the House of Israel and with the House of Judah a new covenant, not like the covenant I made with their forefathers in the day that I took them by the hand to lead them out of the land of Egypt; that covenant of Mine they violated, though I remained in union with them, says the Lord. But here is the covenant that I will conclude with the House of Israel after those days, says the Lord: I will put My law in their minds and write it on their hearts; I will be their God and they will be My people. Now a man will not teach his neighbor or a man his brother, saying, "know the lord" because they will all know Me from the least of them to the greatest, says the Lord: for I will forgive their lawlessness and will no longer remember their sins. (Jeremiah 31:31–34)

I will give them an undivided heart and put a new spirit in them; and I will remove from their breast their heart of stone and give them a heart of flesh, so that they will follow My decrees and keep My laws and fulfill them; and they will be My people, and I will be their God. (Ezekiel 11:19–20)

I will no longer hide my face from them, because I will pour out My spirit on the house of Israel, says the Lord God. (Ezekiel 39:29)

I will betroth you to Me forever, I will betroth you to Me in righteousness and justice, in goodness and compassion. I will betroth you to Me in faithfulness, and you will know the Lord. And it will be that in that day I will hear, says the Lord, I will hear the heavens, and they will hear the earth, and the earth will hear the grain, the new wine and oil, and they will hear Israel. I will plant her for Myself in the land. I will forgive the unforgiven, and I will say to those who are not My people, You are my people, and they will say: You are my God! [. . .] For I desire mercy, not sacrifice, and knowledge of God rather than burnt offerings. (Hosea 2:19–23; 6:6)

These are the deeds you are to do: speak the truth to teach other; judge in your courts in truth and peaceful love. No one among you plot evil against your neighbor, and do not love false oaths, for all this I hate, says the Lord. (Zechariah 8:16–17).

From the rising to the setting of the sun, great will be My name among the nations; and in every place incense will be brought to my name, a pure sacrifice; great will be My name among the nations, says the Lord of Hosts. (Malachi 1:11)

And they will be Mine, says the Lord of Hosts, in the day when I make up My possession in that day, and I will spare them, just as a man spares his son who serves him. And then you will again see the distinction between the righteous and the wicked, between those who serve God and those who do not. (Malachi 3:17–18)

And you, children of Zion, rejoice and be glad in the Lord your God: for he will give you rains in measure and will send you abundant rain, both early and late, as before—And it will be afterward that I will pour out My Spirit on all flesh, and your sons and daughters will prophesy; your old men will dream dreams and your young men will see visions. Even on my servants, both men and women, I will pour out My Spirit in those days. And everyone who calls on the name of the Lord will be saved; for on mount Zion and in Jerusalem there will be salvation, as the Lord has said, also among the rest whom the Lord will call. (Joel 2:23, 28, 29, 32)

The part of the Jewish people that did not acknowledge the prophetic writings (Sadducees) did not expect *any* Messiah; and those

who expected him *on the basis of the prophets* could not exclude from
their expectations the religious element that was predominant in
the prophets. For Jews expecting it, the Messianic Kingdom did not
have to have an exclusively political character, but a *religious*-political
one, it had to be presented to them not in exclusively tangible, but
in *spiritually* tangible images. On the other hand, Christian teaching
never appeared as a preaching of abstract spirituality. The fundamental truth of Christianity—the incarnation of the Divine Word—is
a spiritually *tangible* fact. When Christ said: *he who has seen Me has
seen the Father* [Jn 14:9]—He certainly brought Divinity nearer to the
perception of a sensing human being rather than distancing it. At the
same time, both by His words and by His example, Christ sanctified
the practical foundations of religious life—prayer, alms, and fasting.
It is not surprising that the Gospel is silent with respect to the juridical and politico-economic decrees of Mosaic legislation on the eve of
approaching great revolutions; the most extreme zealots of Judaism
of that day could hardly think that the civil laws given by Moses
in view of seizing the land of Canaan, would remain changeless in
the kingdom of the Messiah, when the people of God would govern
all the Earth. Christ spoke about the destruction of the Jerusalem
temple, yet certainly not out of scorn for its sacredness, about which
He, on the contrary, concerned himself with the greatest zeal (driv-
ing out the merchants [Mk 11:15]), but solely because he foresaw the
very event that took place a short time later. And this foretelling of
the destruction of the Second Temple could not now be too insulting to the sensitivities of the Jewish people, which had endured the
destruction of the First Temple, immeasurably superior to the second
in grandeur and glory.

In general the teaching of Christ did not deny the tangible forms
of religious life, but inspired them; neither did it deny the fact that
the kingdom of the true God must conquer for itself the entire world.
If the Kingdom of Christ had been of the world, then it would not
have the right to rule the world, but precisely because it is not of the
world and is alien to worldly malice, it receives the entire world for
itself as an inheritance *by right*: blessed are the meek, for they shall
inherit the earth [Mt 5:5]. Christians, just as Jews (in the prophets)
not only strive for a renewal of the human spirit, but also hope for a
new heaven and new *earth* according to His promise, for truth lives
in them.[11] The kingdom of God exists not only inwardly—in spirit,
but also outwardly—in power: it is true *theocracy*. Christian religion,
elevating the human spirit to God, lowers Divinity to human flesh: all
its excellence, its fullness and perfection is in this manifest mystery.

Christianity is distinguished from pagan wisdom by the *goal itself*; it is distinguished from Judaism only by various *attitudes* toward this goal.

The ultimate goal is one and the same for Christians and for Jews—universal theocracy, the realization of divine law in the human world, the embodiment of the heavenly in the earthly. This union of Heaven and Earth, this new covenant of God with creation, this completed circle and crown of the universal enterprise is acknowledged by both Christianity and Judaism alike. But beyond this a *path* to the crown was also revealed to us in Christianity, and this path is the *cross*. And it is this path of the cross that Judaism of that time could not understand; it searched for a sign, that is, a straightforward and direct manifestation of Divine *power*. Jews strove directly to the ultimate conclusion, to the final deductions; they wanted to acquire by means of a formal *conventional* path outwardly that which is necessary to gain through suffering, that which is procured by means of a complex and difficult process, by a path of internal bifurcation and moral struggle. Being restricted formally by faithfulness to an ancient *agreement*—in order to receive the Kingdom of God *according to stipulation*—they did not want to understand and accept the path of the cross, through which the kingdom is not acquired directly from without but is *at first* adopted from within in order to become manifest *later* outwardly. They did not want to understand and accept the cross of Christ, and it is now eighteen centuries that they carry their own heavy cross unwillingly.

The cross of Christ, through which the Kingdom of God is acquired, required a dual exploit from the Jewish people: first, a repudiation of its national egoism, and second a provisional repudiation of worldly endeavors, of their attachment to earthly well-being. Preserving the *positive* particulars of its character, Judaism had to broaden and at the same time deepen the religion, to attach to it a fully universal importance and in particular to impart to it the ascetic spirit that it always lacked. Jews should have occupied for a while a position with respect to a hostile world such as that of the persecuted Christian church: they should have acted against the pagan empire not as insurrectionists, but as martyrs, for then they would have been victorious and would have united with Christianity in common triumph.

In order to embody the Kingdom of God on earth, it is *first* necessary *to withdraw* from the Earth; in order to realize the spiritual idea in material reality, it is necessary to be free, released from this reality. Slaves to the Earth can not rule it and consequently can not make a foundation for the Kingdom of God out of it. In order to make natural life an instrument and a *means* of a higher spiritual life, it is necessary to be released from natural life as a *purpose*. A meaningless union of spirit with matter needs to be severed in order to establish a true and holy conjugation between them.

The *higher* goal is not in an ascetic release from natural life for Christianity either, but in the purification and sanctification of this life. But in order to cleanse it, it is first necessary to be cleansed of it. The task of Christianity is not in the destruction of earthly life, but in its *ascent* to meet a God who descends. And just as a lever is needed in the physical world for lifting a great weight, that is to say the acting force must be at a certain distance from the point of resistance, so too an ideal life in the moral world must be at a certain distance from intimate life, in order the more powerfully to act upon it, in order the sooner to maneuver it and lift it. Only one who is free from the world can act on behalf of the world. A captive spirit does not have the possibility of rebuilding his dungeon into a radiant temple: he must first free himself from it.

The purpose of Christian asceticism is not the weakening of the flesh, but the *strengthening of the spirit for the transfiguration of the flesh*. Corresponding to this, Christian universalism too has as a purpose, not the destruction of each nation's natural particulars but, on the contrary, the strengthening of the national spirit through its purification from every egoistic leaven. These purposes were not alien to the Jewish nation. It concerned itself not only with the purity and holiness of its corporeal nature, but also with the *justification* of its national spirit. But the very process of this justification was examined by Jewish legal minds more according to form than according to essence. They searched for unification with God by means of extrinsic provisional agreement, and not by means of intrinsic worship through an experience of the cross, through moral exploit, through self-abnegation both personal and national. But this astonishing path, which leads to the goal by distancing oneself from it, was completely incomprehensible to the greater part of the Jews, who strove directly and quickly toward the ultimate result. Their intense drive rose up against Christian self-abnegation, their attachment to material life did not accommodate Christian asceticism; their practical mind-set could not reconcile this visible contradiction between end and means; they could not understand how willful suffering leads to good, how killing of the body serves its restoration, how repudiation of personal and national interests procures fullness of personal and national life.

If for these Jews the idea of a cross now appeared as a great temptation laid upon man, then a cross lifted by God himself became for them the temptation of temptations; and the same Judaic nation that prepared, through its best elements, the material and the medium for incarnation of God the Word, turned out to be in its aggregate the least sensitive to the mystery of this incarnation.

The *rudiment*, the necessary foundation and the center, is a *God-man*, that is, a union of Divinity with human nature in one individual person. The end and consummation is God-manhood (more precisely, humanity made divine), that is, a combination with God—by means of a God-man—of all humankind, and through it all creatures as well. Jews, searching for an ultimate practical result in all matters, thought only of collective union with God and did not understand the necessity of an individual rudiment and a means for the achievement of this common goal. Even those Jews who were ready to allow the possibility of the incarnation of a divine Person (Kabbalists), rejected the path of Christ as impractical and inexpedient. But in rejecting the God-man as the single rudiment of salvation for everyone in common, as a sign for the Gentiles, Jews by the same token distorted the meaning of God-manhood as well, making out of it an exclusive advantage for the Israelite people. This corresponded completely to the reality-based character of the Jewish worldview. For although the nation is collective, it is still a manifestly real entity, whereas humanity had been transformed from the time of Babel into an abstract concept, not at all existing as a real and unified whole in and of itself. Therefore the Jews, who had not subjugated the fleshly intellect to the mind of truth, naturally remained at the borders of their nationality in their image of the Kingdom of God, rejecting the whole of humanity as an abstract fantasy, removing from the Kingdom of God its actual foundation. Thus, Christianity, as the preaching of universal human brotherhood, on the one hand seemed to Jews somehow too broad, abstract and unreal; at the same time inasmuch as Christianity connects the matter of universal salvation with the single Person of Jesus, it represents to Jews something narrow, arbitrary, and insufficient. From both aspects, Christianity, having in view to gather all around one, and through one unite each with all, represents for Jews—for the pragmatist and for the realist—an unrealizable idea and for this one reason is already false. It is only possible to prove to Jews *factually* that they are mistaken—by realizing the Christian idea in actual fact, carrying it out consequently in real life. The more fully the Christian world would express in itself the Christian idea of spiritual and universal theocracy—the more powerful the influence of Christian principles on the private life of Christians, on the social life of Christian nations, on the political relations in Christian humanity—the more manifestly the Jewish view of Christianity would be refuted, the nearer and the more possible a conversion of the Jews would become. Thus, *the Jewish question is a Christian question.*

III. The Fortunes of Jewish and Christian Theocracy— Russia, Poland, and Israel

Christianity and the Jewish people have a common theocratic task—the creation of a just society. Since the source of all truth is in God, then a just society is a Divine-human society, a society where God is united with man. The whole human being willingly subordinates himself to God here, all people are unanimous among themselves and exercise complete command over material nature. According to Jewish conception such an ideal society must be embodied in the nation of Israel (in the kingdom of the Messiah), according to Christian conception all nations alike are called to it. This Christian universalism should not be understood in the sense that all nationalities constitute only undifferentiated material for a universal theocracy. All nations are equal only before the gospel law in the sense that, for example, all citizens in a state are equal before the law of a country; this does not interfere at all with various positions and classes of citizens having their own rights, which flow from the special obligations of their service (so in the most egalitarian country a physician receives special rights that agriculturalists do not have, and in the most democratic republic a minister has advantages over the night watch, and so forth, though all of them are equal before the law, which defines both the rights of all in common, as well as the special rights of each). Similarly, various nations can have various advantages in Divine citizenship (*in civitate Dei*) as well, according to special historical position and national calling, only if mutual love and common solidarity are not violated by this.[12] Thus, there is no absolute contradiction between the theocratic ideas of Christianity and Judaism. If Jews have claims to a special position and significance in a universal theocracy, then we do not need to reject this claim in advance, especially if we remember what the Apostle Paul says about this subject:

> Theirs is the adoption as sons and the glory, and covenants, and receiving of the law, and service and the promises; theirs are the patriarchs and from them Christ in the flesh, who is God over all [. . .] Did God reject His people? By no means! God did not reject His people whom he foreknew [. . .] but

so that you not be conceited, I do not want to leave you
ignorant of this mystery, brothers: Israel has been blinded in
part until the full number of the nations has come in. And
then all Israel will be saved. [Rom 9:4–5, 11:1–2, 25]

But how will it be saved, how will it enter into the city of God?

In order to recognize the theocratic situation of a certain nation,
it is essential to define the very content of theocracy more narrowly.

Until the time that God will be all in everything, until each human being is a receptacle of Divinity, until then a Divine administration of humanity requires special organs and guides for its activity
in humanity.[13]

Moreover a Divine administration must be promulgated across
all human life and can not be restricted to any partial realm of this
life; therefore the organs of Divine administration must be found not
only in the religious sphere proper, but also in the political and social
sphere. The religious sphere of life has as its special theocratic organ a
priest (or rather high priest, since a *priest* is not possible without a *prelate*); the political sphere has as its theocratic organ a *king*, as Divinely
anointed; finally, the social life of the nation has its theocratic organ
in the person of a *prophet*, that is, a freely independent preacher and
teacher. Each of these three representatives of theocracy has its independent sphere of action, but according to the very character of these
spheres they are found definitively in mutual relation to one another.
The priest organizes, the king governs, the prophet reforms. In the order
of Divine administration an *authority* founded on *tradition* belongs to
the priesthood, the king possesses *power* established *in law*, and the
prophet makes use of *freely independent personal initiative*.

The fullness of the theocratic ideal requires a balance and consonant
development of these three instruments of Divine administration.

If we take a look now at Judaic (Old Testament) theocracy, then
we will easily see that although it possessed both a priesthood (from
the time of Aaron) and a king (from the time of Saul), both these
offices, both the priestly and monarchic, were as if pushed into the
background and overshadowed by the prophetic office. The greatest
representative of the Hebrew people was not the high priest Aaron,
but the prophet Moses, and if David consequently occupied such a
preeminent place in the fortunes of Hebrew theocracy, this is because
he was not only king, but also prophet. In any case, it is striking that
just as the *prophet* Moses instituted the priesthood, so too the prophet
Samuel instituted the monarchy and anointed the first kings. It is
evident that among the Hebrews the prophetic office contained in

itself the source of monarchic as well as religious hierarchic power. Of the three kings of the undivided Hebrew state the first, Saul, notwithstanding his courage, and the third, Solomon, notwithstanding his wisdom, both turned out to be unworthy representatives of theocratic monarchy. The moral collapse of this monarchy (idolatry) was already made apparent under Solomon, and with its division into two under Solomon's son it loses its outward luster and power as well: enslavement to foreigners became only a matter of time for the bifurcated state. Thus, the view of the prophet Samuel was justified when he agreed so grudgingly to the institution of monarchic authority in Israel. He was correct, not because monarchic authority was superfluous for the Hebrew people (on the contrary it was unduly necessary for them), but a man of God, knowing his people well, foresaw that the monarchic principle would not graft itself onto Israel and through its unsuccessful realization would only multiply the people's calamities.

Just as the precariousness of state authority turned out to be ruinous for the political existence of the Jewish people, so too the insufficient development of the pontifical principle struck a blow at the religious life of Jews. The priesthood, reserved by custom to one clan and restricted by the formal obligations of the priestly office, could not vivify the nation religiously: its negative qualities sooner furthered the Pharisaic-Talmudic crystallization of Judaism, which preserved in itself a kernel of truth that was, however, enclosed in an unduly rigid, impenetrable shell. However, this crystallization was fully completed only after the priesthood disappeared with the destruction of the Second Temple, following the disappearance of the last phantoms of the monarchy, and the inspired prophetic office was ultimately regenerated in a rationally laborious teaching office (rabbinism) that placed its entire soul in the fulfillment of the paternal bequest: *erect a fence around the law*, and this fence was erected with such zeal and industry that soon an actual labyrinth came of it, in which it was difficult even for Jews themselves to find the path of true life.

From our point of view the fortunes of Jewish theocracy present first of all the instructive result that with all the great blessings that the Jewish nation received from God through their prophets, the prophetic office alone could nevertheless not compensate for the lack of a single strong state authority, on the one hand, and an authoritative and active priesthood on the other: the first of these deficiencies removed political independence from the Jews, the second halted their religious development.

Christianity appeared as a broadening and an embodiment of Judaic theocracy not only by the fact that it joined new national elements to it, but even more by the fact that it elevated and strengthened the formative principles of theocracy itself. First of all it gave to the world a genuine priesthood directly according to Divine morality, independent of any human office and establishment. We know that the priesthood was initially instituted in Judaism by human means, through the Divine prophet Moses. Thus, the Jewish priesthood was found to be genetically dependent on another office—the prophetic, which stood alone in Judaism in a direct connection to Divinity. In Christianity, to the contrary, the priesthood is initially represented by the Divine Person of Jesus Christ. The apostles received the mysterious gift of priesthood *directly* from him and transferred it to their successors through the laying on of hands. Properly speaking, Christ was and is the single true High Priest; but while the visible church has a separate existence on earth, the bearers of the priesthood of Christ need to be visible, serving as priests and witnessing, not on their own and not in the name of any man whatsoever, but only as surrogates of Christ, by His power and grace. Corresponding to this in the temporal order is the fact that the essential ecclesiastical hierarchy of a direct and unbroken chain of succession is tied to Christ himself without any extraneous means.

The intrinsic unity of the ecclesiastical hierarchy depends on its divine origin, and ecumenical councils and popes have served as the visible expression of this unity in the life of the church.

Christianity also elevated the monarchic element of theocracy along with this hierarchical element. Development of this element fell to the lot of Byzantium, the representative of the Hellenized East, which drew to itself the center of the Roman Empire. In the Orthodox emperor of the new Rome all the pagan elements of the monarchic idea were cleansed and regenerated by Christianity. The East brought its image of the sovereign as a supreme ruler, an unconstrained autocrat; Hellas introduced its idea of a king as a wise ruler, a pastor of nations; Rome provided its notion of an emperor as an embodiment of state law, Christianity tied all this together with the exalted mission of Orthodox emperor as the principal servant of true religion, as defender and preserver of its interests on earth. Acknowledging in Christ a special monarchic merit, our religion provides an exalted consecration for state authority and makes the Christian emperor fully independent, veritably a supreme ruler. Divinely anointed and reigning through Divine mercy, a Christian sovereign is independent of the popular will. While unrestricted from below, the authority of a Christian emperor is, however, restricted from above: being father and ruler of the people, a Christian emperor must be a son of the church. Moreover, not being tied to Christ himself by any actual succession, the emperor in the temporal order must be consecrated by the direct representative of Christ's authority, by the high priests of the church, which is accomplished in the sacred act of anointment and coronation of the monarch. This does not give the ecclesiastical hierarchy any rights in the realm of state authority, but this obligates the emperor to be a faithful son of the church and a faithful servant of the Divine enterprise; only under this condition does he have the significance of Christian emperor, one of the formative organs of true theocracy. The Byzantine emperors who expressed this idea of Christian monarchy more starkly than others and who always remained faithful to it in principle, notwithstanding certain deficiencies in the utilization of their power, were both in life and in death highly respected and glorified by the church. Such were Constantine the Great, Theodosius the Great, and Justinian. The respect that these great representatives of Caesarism received from the church clearly shows that the church values the principle of Christian monarchy and that it does not at all relate indifferently to one or another form of administration, as some maintain.

But the idea of a Christian monarch with all its significance is only a part of the theocratic idea, and its one-sided development at the expense of the other theocratic elements, its preponderance over them, can lead to ruinous consequences for the Divine enterprise on earth. And this is what happened in Byzantium. Most of its rulers thought that the supreme sovereignty over the Christian nation they received from Christ through the church extended as well to the very faith of Christ and to the very living foundations of the church, and that they could rule absolutely in the sanctuary itself; and instead of serving the church through their dominion, they compelled the church to serve their dominion. Great calamities for the Christian world proceeded from here—the patronizing of heresies, sometimes even contrived by the emperors (monotheletism, iconoclasm); the constant persecution of Orthodox bishops and stripping them of their power; the unlawful institution of toadies and heretics in their place; and many other abuses of power as well.

But the abuses of Byzantine Caesarism had still more profound consequences—they distorted the very life of Christian community in the East. With an insufficiently independent and firm spiritual authority in Byzantium, the imperial power was unrestrained in this quarter and came down with all its might upon the life of society, oppressing in it every energetic personal initiative, every independent action. All the strong departed for monasteries, all the weak became enslaved to crude willfulness. Despotism fed on moral weakness and begat societal depravity. The salvation of the soul was conceded to the monasteries, but the chief task of worldly life consisted in obliging the emperor and his servants. The theocratic task of Christianity—the creation of a just society—suffered a decisive collapse in Byzantium. True, thanks to good aspects of the Byzantine character—piety and attachment to church tradition—the Orthodox *faith* was preserved in the East, but these qualities turned out to be insufficient not only for the creation of a Christian society, but also for securing the Orthodox world against the victorious incursion of the Muslim world. The victory of Islam, having nearly eradicated Christianity in Asia and Africa, was first of all a matter of crude force, but it also had at the same time a certain moral justification. A Muslim who believes in his simple and not very elevated religious-moral law fulfills it in good conscience both in his personal and in his community life: he *judges* both civic and criminal matters according to the Koran, *makes war* according to the direct command of the Koran, and relates to foreigners and to the conquered again in conformity with the instructions of the Koran, and so forth. Meanwhile in the community life of the Christian world the Gospel never had the significance that the Koran occupied in the Muslim state and society. Therefore a Muslim committed to sensuality can live this way not going against his conscience, he has a law such that he can do so—everyone lives like this among them; but the believing Christian has to willy-nilly constantly violate his faith, for the community amidst which he lives is rarely guided by Christian law. In the last days of Byzantium, as a result of the exclusively ascetic direction of religiosity, this bifurcation between faith and life, between personal salvation of the soul and social activity was, it is possible to say, elevated to a steadfast rule. Thus, the triumph of the Muslims was a just punishment of the Christian East.

With respect to the West, although the theocratic task there was never forgotten and was not abandoned, its practical realization also turned out to be unsuccessful, but now for other and in part opposite reasons.

If in Byzantium the chief reason for every evil was contained in the inordinate predominance of the emperor's autocracy, then in the West the root obstacle of the theocratic enterprise was, oppositely, the weakness and splintering of state authority. Charles the Great was the first and *last* real, that is, autocratic, emperor in the West (where his name was merged with the sobriquet "great"—*Charlemagne*—whereas among the Slavs bordering the Western empire his name was made into a synonym for the sovereign—*carolus*—*korol'*). Only the idea of a "Holy Roman Empire of the German nation" remained after this classic representative of theocratic monarchy in the West. In reality it was not only the unity of the Roman Empire that disappeared, but also the unity of the German nation. With the destruction of imperial autocracy the Western church lost the chief instrument for fulfillment of its theocratic task. This church, united and centered in the Roman see, was not afraid of the *mighty* empire of Charles the Great, but on the contrary, made use of its might: a weak and splintered empire turned out to be harmful and dangerous to the papacy. Having remained the sole representatives of order and community interests in the chaos of feudalism, the popes had before them a leaderless and disconnected multitude of semi-barbaric aggressors, with respect to which papal authority had to take on the character of coercive force against its will. Since the Roman bishop was the sole authority generally recognized throughout the European world, he had to adopt for himself the functions and imperial authority that only nominally belonged to German kings. By the same token, the popes not only awakened against themselves the enmity of the semi-barbaric potentates they had to bridle, but more particularly evoked a rivalry of the German kings. Not knowing how to cope with their immediate vassals, these German kings strove to realize their imperial pretensions with respect to the pope and the Italian city-states, in order to re-compensate themselves in a defenseless Italy for their weakness in Germany and the rest of Europe.

The tragic struggle between papacy and empire exploded and continued for three centuries along with its epilogue in France, striking a decisive blow to the enterprise of Christian theocracy. First, the spectacle of this struggle between the two predominant powers created a profound demoralization among Christian nations, undermined in their eyes the authority of both the ecclesiastical and the imperial administrations, and through this prepared the soil for the Protestant movement. Second, even without this, the struggle in the end exhausted the insufficient forces of the German Empire, so that over the course of the Middle Ages, during the rule of Emperors Friedrich II and Maximilian, the emperor's authority amounted to complete vanity. Finally—and what is most important—this ill-fated struggle compelled the papacy to don "the wretched weight of earthly armor," which was also the direct or indirect cause of many ecclesiastical abuses, many errors of spiritual authority. But these abuses and errors served as a pretext and justification for anticlerical action. Meanwhile an imperial authority now reduced to vanity—notwithstanding its later union with the papacy—could not stop this revolutionary movement and restrict the egoism of the second-rate potentates who sponsored the revolution. They found a dual benefit for themselves in it, since Protestantism, firstly, placed all church and monastic property at their complete disposal, and secondly, conceded to them supreme rights in the sphere of religion itself in conformity with the principle *cujus regio, ejus religio*, in view of which, as is known, many German princes introduced Protestantism into their realms *forcibly*.

With respect to the essence of Protestantism, it consists in the abuse of the third principle of Christian theocracy—the principle of prophecy or freedom of the individual spirit in matters of religion. The *abuse* here consisted, firstly, in the fact that the principle of prophecy, that is, the freedom of individual inspiration, is acknowledged not in third place, that is, not under condition of faithfulness to the two other principles of theocracy, which have the advantage of positive Divine institution, but is acknowledged as the first and in essence the only principle of the Kingdom of God. For the inordinate authority in religious matters that Luther ceded to the sovereigns adhering to him has the character of a practical and temporary concession; wherever Protestantism developed its principles freely and consistently—in Switzerland, among the English and Scottish Puritans, in American sects—it appears deeply hostile to the monarchic idea. With respect to the apostolic priesthood, its complete negation both in theory and in practice constitutes indisputably the distinctive character of Protestantism, according to which every believer is now also a priest. The priesthood here is confused with the prophetic office, and the latter is acknowledged, not as a special office or *obligation of certain* people who are called to this by God, but as a natural *right of all*. According to true Christianity, just as according to Jewish understanding, the prophetic calling requires a high degree of righteousness and special moral exploits (Elijah, John the Baptist); however, Protestantism denies the significance of human righteousness and exploits and reduces all religion to the single status of faith, thus ceding to every believer the absolute right to act as a self-appointed and peremptory arbiter of religious matters.

Veritably, all who truly believe will be Divine prophets in the end times with the appearance of a church triumphant, when all will be kings and priests as well. But this is still a long way off, and turning the end into the beginning is a method that does not promise success.

A true prophet in Judaism and Christianity does not *revolt* against priestly and monarchic authority, but *harries* them and assists them by means of denunciations and admonitions. The true prophet does not acknowledge his calling as a natural right he has in common with everyone, nor in any way as his personal privilege either, but as a special Divine gift that requires moral cultivation on his part. Having rejected these two necessary conditions of true prophecy—subordination to legitimate authorities and striving to be worthy of a higher calling—Protestantism essentially distorted the third theocratic principle: in separating prophecy from priesthood, it did not bequeath to the world true prophets either.

The great success of Protestantism depended more than a little on the discord that had preceded it between the two predominant authorities in the Christian world. Without this discord, which came at a time when equality and mutually appropriate actions of the ecclesiastical and imperial authorities were needed, there could have been found neither such seemly pretexts for the beginning of an anti-ecclesiastical movement nor such favorable conditions for its promulgation. The power of Protestantism arose from the ruins of the theocratic edifice of the West. The fragility of the edifice depended on an improper attitude of the two major theocratic authorities, and this improper attitude in its turn was directly conditional on the division and the antagonism between the imperial East and the pontifical West. An overarching imperial authority—the main instrument of the theocratic enterprise—could not have any authority amidst the willful and self-confident nations of the West. For the papacy, this rickety empire turned out to be the cane about which the ancient prophet speaks: in wanting to lean on this cane, the spiritual sovereign of the West both broke it and pierced his own hand. It would have been another matter if he could have leaned on the unshakeable Caesarism of the East, which, passing from one country to another, never lost its autocratic power and might thanks to the patriarchal character of the eastern nations. Then one power would have balanced and made up for the other. Eastern emperors, faithful to the traditions of Constantine and Theodosius, would have appeared as the main servants and trustees of the church—its ostensible bishops. Then, that is, if there had been no division of the church, the bishops of the Eastern church would have made use, just as now, of the protection of an Orthodox emperor. Additionally, they would have fortified their authority with all the concentrated power of its Western servants, and the Western bishops, having behind them the entire pious East in their difficult struggle with anticlerical and antireligious elements of those countries, and ceding the outward aspect of this struggle to the friendly power of an Orthodox Caesar, would not have needed to add the petty traits of official state politics to the exalted image of its spiritual authority. Then the private abuses that are placed in reproach to the historical activity of Catholicism, more or less justly, would not have appeared; then there would not have turned out to be any proper cause for the anti-Christian movement in the West, and if this movement would have nevertheless occurred (for it resembles past heresies as well), then it would not have been able to attach to itself any higher principles and ideals, it would not have been able to adopt the broad dimensions that it did and to achieve such lasting successes as had now fallen to its lot.

The division of the church, having violated the balance between the two first formative principles of Christian theocracy—priesthood and monarchy—by the same token made possible an illegitimate manifestation of the third theocratic principle—the prophetic. But Protestantism was not only an illegitimate manifestation of the prophetic principle, it was also a reaction of the German national element against the Latin. In this respect too a real, even if distant, cause of Protestantism was the division of the church, which undermined the universal character of Christianity and gave the upper hand to national and tribal contention.

In its turn, the German world too put forward its *particular* theocratic idea of Catholicism. Standing under the banner of a liberated prophetic office, Protestantism appeared to be to a certain degree a return to Judaism. But there was at the same time in this respect a huge difference between them in favor of Judaism. For, in the first place, Jewish prophets, as we know, did not revolt against the legitimate priesthood as the Protestants did; and in the second place, the Jewish prophets preached justification by faith and *deeds*, and not by faith alone. After the dispersion of Israel, when the prophetic office was substituted by a teaching office (rabbinism), the new representatives of Judaism, the rabbis, placed themselves the task of "making a fence around the law," that is, securing observance of the law in all aspects of life. This practical task remained the dominant one in all Talmudic literature. In Protestantism, just as in Judaism—but even more quickly—prophecy was substituted by teaching. (If [Martin] Luther and [Huldreich] Zwingli could be called prophets of the new confession, then [Phillipp] Melancthon, Luther's learned friend, sooner resembled a rabbi than a prophet.)[14] The well-spring for Jewish and Protestant teaching was the same—the Bible; both the former and the latter were scholars but they related to their book in completely different ways. Jewish rabbis saw in the book first of all Law, that is, a norm of life, and they directed all their efforts to consolidate this vital law by means of an impenetrable fence of tradition and interpretation. This kind of attitude to the holy book flowed from the *Jewish* national character; the national genius of the *Germans* related to the Bible otherwise. For Protestant German teachers the Bible became not so much a norm of life, as a *subject of theoretical study*. Less than anything did they concern themselves with a practical fence of tradition but, to the contrary, they intensively strived to exclude any traditional element from an understanding of the Word of God. Protestant teaching of the Bible passed to criticism, and criticism passed to repudiation. In our day, the Bible is no longer a point of faith for progressive teachers of Protestantism, but only a subject of negative criticism, and if they nevertheless continue to impart to it exclusive significance and occupy themselves with it more than anything else, then this is only a matter of habit. At first the leadership of the Protestant world crossed over from prophets to teachers, now the religious teachers in their turn give way to scholastic learning of a predominantly anti-Christian tendency. Not even a trace now remains here of the original, albeit false, theocratic idea that inspired the first leaders of Protestantism. The current violators of biblical texts have *nothing* to say to the world and *nowhere* to lead it.* In order to have direct influence on national life, Protestantism gave away too much to the authority of local states from the very beginning in its struggle against papacy and empire. And now at a time when the representatives of religion indulge in ruinous pedantry, the life of nations remains entirely in the hands of secular politics, in the power of private interests, vacillating between military despotism and the supremacy of plutocracy.

This decline of the Christian idea was not restricted to the German countries in which Protestantism triumphed. Although in the Latin or Roman part of Europe the religious movement of the Reformation did not have success, the practical result of this movement was universal secularization, that is, the separation of all spheres of human activity—of politics and of national leadership, of science and school, of art and social life—from religion and church; this universal secularization was promulgated across Latin Europe as well. Following the example of Germanic countries, the Romance countries, in the person of their ruling classes, repudiated the theocratic idea as well. One could have despaired in the fortunes of Christianity had

---

*The book "Die alte und der neue Glaube" (by a certain Strauss) can serve as sufficiently instructive confirmation of what has been said.

not fresh forces been saved in universal history's reserves—the forces of the Slavic peoples.

Both nations that represent the two opposite poles in slavdom—Russia and Poland—have not yet disavowed the principle of Christian theocracy. The best people of Poland—as well as the masses of simple Polish people—remain zealous Catholics and assiduously support the theocratic idea of Rome. The best people of Russia and the mass of the Russian people abide true to Eastern Orthodoxy and hold to the theocratic traditions of Byzantium. Amidst these two religious nations, each having its own theocratic idea, history has thrust a third religious nation, possessing as well an authentic theocratic idea—the nation of Israel. Notwithstanding the enmity that separates the three to this day, a question arises: Is this a fact of chance, or is the extrinsic connection of three theocratic nations preparing their spiritual union in a single all-encompassing theocratic idea? The answer to this question depends on how the theocratic ideas, the bearers of which are these three nations, are related to one another *according to the very essence of the enterprise*, whether these ideas exclude one another or, on the contrary, coincide among themselves.

In general theocracy has the aim of realizing religion (i.e., a union of God with man) in the totality of national life. Three conditions are necessary for the successful fulfillment of this task: (1) *A full independence of the religious principle* in society, for the essence and the main interest of the entire enterprise is in this principle, and if the religious element occupies a subordinate or dependent position in community life, then theocracy does not have any meaning; (2) *A proper segmentation of the societal corpus and a sound orderliness* in its administration, for without this religion does not have the steadfast and goal-oriented *means* to realize its influence in life and direct it in a theocratic sense; (3) finally, *a free and dynamic activity of individual energies*, for without such activity the very best societal organization will remain empty form.

Now we will return to the existing structure of life in Russia, Poland, and in the contemporary Jewish people centered in these two countries, in order to examine to what extent these nations satisfy the indicated conditions of true theocracy, for the realization of which each of them is called both by its national genius and by its historical fortunes.

We begin with Russia, with its system of life in the ecclesiastical, state, and social spheres.

The historically constituted system of Russian life is expressed in the following distinct traits: a church represented by a *council* of

bishops and resting on *monasteries*; a government centered in an autocratic *emperor*; and a people living by agriculture in *rural communities*. Monastery, palace, and village—here are our social foundations,
which will not be shaken as long as Russia exists. These elements
of our system of life contain great advantages in themselves, but at
the same time they can not conceal certain important shortcomings.
Thus, the *monastery* attracts, shelters and edifies believing souls; but it
can not awaken, support, and protect faith wherever it is weak—for
this a steadfast activity uncharacteristic of the monk is needed in
the world. Eastern asceticism, although modified in part by Russian
national character, nevertheless remains chiefly *contemplative* and
consequently is not at all called to prepare ecclesiastical functionar-
ies and administrators. Asceticism is generally necessary for religious
life; but the special obligations of ecclesiastical administration require
other special moral and practical qualities apart from ascetic sanctity.
Indefatigable activity and an unshakeable steadfastness are needed
in the struggle with secular, anticlerical forces, which gradually arm
themselves against religion more and more. The whole point is in the
fact that the church on earth must not only *preserve* the sanctuary of
faith, but also relentlessly *struggle* over it with external enemies, it
must strengthen, protect, and amplify religious life. And neither the
monastic character nor the synodic form of ecclesiastical administration present favorable conditions for such an active struggle. A fully
independent, centered, and energetic ecclesiastical authority is needed
for the struggle. The dependency of spiritual authority on secular
authority and the absence in it of a special centeredness paralyzes
the external activity of the church and undermines its influence on
the life of the people and society. It is thanks to God that the Russian
church makes use of the guardianship of an Orthodox emperor who
is autocratic and consequently independent of the godless elements
of contemporary society. But apart from this negative condition that
we have at present, that is, apart from the politically boundless imperial authority, a positive condition is still required for its successful
service to the Divine enterprise: it is necessary that the authorities
of a Christian state be guided by the directives of an independent
spiritual authority, as the manifest representative of Christ's church on
earth; for this it is necessary that the spiritual authority, personifying
the religious element in society, have full independence. The church,
bereft of fully independent representation, can not have real influence
either on the government or on society. And here we see that notwithstanding the piety of the Russian people, notwithstanding the loyalty
of our sovereigns to Orthodoxy, notwithstanding the many excellent

qualities of our clergy, our church is bereft of the significance befitting it and does not guide the life of Russia. Our people place Divine justice [*pravda*] above everything, they are theocratic to the depths of their souls, but they are bereft of the first substantive condition for the realization of theocracy, thanks to the root shortcomings of our ecclesiastical system.

With respect to the *political* system of Russia, its great strength is in tsarist autocracy and in the unanimity of the people's attachment to the tsar. The weakness of this system consists in the fact that there is nothing stable at present between the tsar and the people, there is no well organized and disciplined society, there is no ruling class. Since times long past, in particular since the times of Peter I to Alexander II, the civic structure of Russia rested on two distinct organizations, adjoining one another and in part overlapping one another, but never fully congruent with one another: the landed gentry and bureaucratic officialdom. The latter was the direct instrument of state authority, the gentry stood nearer to the people and to a certain degree represented the Russian land. Russia could not have been formed into the homogeneous and solid body that it is to date, despite all its decay, without the help of these two organizations. The main shortcoming of this dual organization consisted in the fact that, being a reliable instrument of state authority, it was not at the same time a faithful conduit of the people's needs from the land to the tsar. A *change* in our civic order became a necessity. This order was *demolished* by the reforms of the sixties. The gentry, bereft of independent significance and having grown cool to the land and become ravaged significantly (in part their own fault), formed the main contingent of a contemporary intelligentsia that can not have any state and civic significance, for in their routine opposition to the government, in their alienation from the people, it in no way can serve as a link between the tsar and the land. But, along with the gentry, a decisive blow was also struck by the old bureaucracy, which should have divided its sphere with new institutions of another character. Apart from this, the solid state spirit and civic discipline of the old officialdom was at root undermined by the influence of a new intelligentsia armed with the liberalism of servants of the press. With respect to the new institutions, they are on the one hand turning out to be completely powerless due to the insolvency of the societal element that dominates among them (the remains of a "scattered" gentry in local institutions); on the other hand, other of these institutions are accused—and not without foundation—of a *spurious* tendency, by virtue of which they serve not so much the tsar and Russia, as the "liberal" intelligentsia and its civic opinion—a service that is all the more fruitless in that there can be neither a real intelligentsia nor an actual civic opinion in Russia because of the absence of a civic society itself, because of a lack of defined social groups that are organized for collective activity. The societal elements among us that constitute the active part of society are decidedly weak and insolvent. The previous class of service people, consisting of the gentry and officialdom, lost its distinctiveness and its significance. Next, there exists among us a certain number of educated and even thinking people—apart from scholars and litterateurs by profession—who in any case do not constitute a society, and do not represent an important social force in Russia; but in the absence of a unifying principle and a clear goal of action their social significance is completely insignificant. Then there remains a rather large and continuously increasing semieducated multitude, at times capable of good turns and impulses, but for the most part given over to coarse and petty instincts. Neither does this milieu provide any actual elements for social organization. Organized activity exists among us, but only of a destructive tendency, and here the better people of the multitude appear as unconscious victims of deception.

In light of such a situation, even if the uppermost level of government were inspired by the most exalted and holy ideas, it would not be able to find any suitable instruments for its realization in Russian society. Everyday heroes and selfless administrators will always be found among our people for any undertaking, but where is there in our society a ruling class capable of and habituated to acting in solidarity? Thank God that there are enough social forces present among us for even just a so-so maintenance of the ordinary functions of the state's mechanisms.

Meanwhile such an insolvency of society is not just sad in a civic sense, but is even reflected in the economic situation of Russia in a very harmful way. Russia lives by farming, and in today's terms the entire economic system must be defined by agricultural interests. Exhaustion of the soil means the ruin of Russia, and meanwhile everything is leading to such an exhaustion. Farming goes on in today's Russia, with a population of a hundred million, using the same means as three hundred years ago when the population was one tenth of that. But if rapacious management was the only possible way at that time, it now gradually becomes more and more dangerous with each passing year. The natural productive forces of the land are not limitless—people sooner or later *devour the land*. Only a transition from a management rapacious in its origin to a synthetic or rational management can prevent such an outcome, or at least put it off. But it is not possible to even imagine that the people will on their own change the system of management. Fathers and grandfathers taught the old method—who will teach the new one? An entire class of educated and skilled people who would dedicate themselves to this task is needed. We do not have such a class. On the other hand a rational agriculture is a very complex matter in a material respect as well, it requires active support on the part of industry, it is in need of technical invention and discoveries. The *village* does not live without the *city* under such conditions. Village life in and of itself falls into routine and stagnation—galvanizing activity belongs to the city: enterprise, initiative, invention are singular to it. The city must assist the village, must be in solidarity with it in the common interest. But neither do we have this. We do not have an enterprising and active industrial class, which, utilizing the natural riches of the country, would assist the rural economy with its industry. The urban element among us is not connected organically with the life of the land, does not take any positive part in it: it is occupied exclusively with its own *personal* advantages. And precisely because it is generally a rural country Russia has great need of the assistance of the city with its concentrated economic and spiritual forces.

But our urban class turns out to be too weak, uncoordinated and not intrepid enough to fulfill its assignment successfully. The growth of our cities (especially in the last thirty years) has given rise only to a particular bourgeois civilization with artificial needs that are more complex, but by no means more elevated, than simple provincial people have. Meanwhile the greater part of our industry exists only for the satisfaction of these artificial (and sometimes also perverted) needs of urban civilization. Industry does not serve the land but the city, and yet this would not be a disaster *if* the city itself served something good. But instead of being premier nerve centers of the social organism, in reality our cities instead sooner resemble harmful parasites, exhausting the national body. Our urban civilization takes everything from the land and does not give anything to it in return. The most important inventions and discoveries that our century is so proud of—for example, railroads and steamships—bring more harm than utility to the land. The seeming advantage that is obtained by them for the entire country (facilitated market access for agricultural products) is decisively outweighed by the harm that they inflict on agriculture itself; in saying *harm*, I use an expression that is too feeble, for soon it will become clear to all that the promulgation of these very convenient means of intercourse are the *ruin* of our agriculture. Railroads relentlessly devour forests, and without forests our huge continental plain sooner or later (and sooner rather than later) will turn into a barren wasteland. The striking depletion of our rivers and multiplying droughts—are not prophecy now, but fact. In other countries irrigation is secured either by the proximity of the sea or by high snow-covered mountains. But we keep only forests and marshes, out of which flow our great rivers and by which they are fed. And now, not confining ourselves to the destruction of forests, we have set about assiduously draining marshes.

Thus, the basis of our economic life—farming—will be ruined by spurious civilization, that is, by a civilization that turns means into an end, makes idols out of instruments and sacrifices for the convenience of some that which is necessary for everyone. Enthralled by this kind of civilization, instead of assisting the village, the city threatens it with ruin, and the village cannot save itself from this ruin. The economic activity of our rural community is eternally defined by a routine that is completely defenseless against the new and elaborate disasters threatening farming. It is precisely only that which we lack among us that can avert these disasters: the dynamic and convivial activity of individual strengths, inspired by an understanding of the common good directed at a common, *creative* goal. Our society, or the so-called intelligentsia, has decisively proved its incapacity for convivial action and solidarity for the common good, and in the popular masses the personal element is weak and suffers.

Summarizing what has been said, we arrive at the following conclusion. All the historical advantages of our system of life that indicate to us the original and great calling of Russia are decidedly paralyzed by material deficiencies such that the fulfillment of this calling is made very difficult. First, we possess a most important Divine gift—the Orthodox and holy church, *but the church does not possess us.* Ecclesiality, represented by the spiritual authority, is bereft of practical independence among us and can not freely act upon and guide the life of the nation and the society: we participate in a holy and blessed body—the church—but the prime condition for the *growth* of this body in us is absent.

Second, we have yet another great advantage—a holy and autocratic tsarist authority, but we also make poor use of this good. What with the civic insolvency of our society, with the extreme disorganization of societal forces, with the absence of an actual ruling class, the supreme power is bereft of the necessary instruments to forge the destiny of Russia. Finally, even our third treasure—a deeply pious nation, with manifest state importance and dedicated to the most real and healthy occupation of farming, a patient, peaceful and self-sacrificing people—is a good that is of no use to us. Without the convivial work of individual initiatives in the social-economic sphere, the popular masses, with all their good qualities not only are not capable of re-creating the land and making it a humble instrument of the human spirit, but also are not capable of securing for themselves the necessary means of existence; they can hardly feed themselves by means of the land. Rural strength without the assistance of urban rationality remains a blind and defenseless strength against all kinds of possible disasters. But where among us is there an urban (i.e., civilized) rationality capable of really assisting the village, capable of teaching and guiding the people in the common work?*

Under such conditions—that is, better to say in the absence of necessary conditions for true progress—the great advantages of our national-historical system are only good *rudiments* or possibilities that await other conditions and new elements for their salutary action. Russia, left to itself, is *alone*, weak. It is not good for man to be alone: we apply this Divine word to collective man as well—to the entire nation. Only in union with that which it lacks can Russia make use of that which it has, utilize it in the fullest measure both for itself and for the entire world. Then our faith in Russia will be justified in the positive forces by which it lives as well: in the Orthodox church, which stands on tradition and is crowned with the ideal of ascetic holiness, in the holy and autocratic authority of an Orthodox tsar; by virtue of the Orthodox people, attached to the land, but not forgetting about God, searching for higher truth more than the goods of daily life; a people not making an idol out of itself, not a democratic people, but a theocratic people. Here are our great positive strengths that await for their creative action and manifestation the practical factors they lack.

Moving from Russia to the historical system of Poland, we meet here traits of a directly contrary character. If the major deficiency of our system in a civic respect consists in a weak sense of society, in the absence of an independent and active higher class, then the higher class in Poland to the contrary was and is everything. Poland and the *szlachta* [nobility] are one and the same. (If the word "Pole" elicits a definite and distinct image in our mind, then this is absolutely an image of a member of the nobility, and in no way a peasant or a merchant.) In the absence of a national urban class in Poland, and

---

*Splendid ventures are well known—rare people who dedicate their lives in self-sacrifice to the people's good. Their noble activity does not remain fruitless, but does not change the general situation.

with the suppression of the rural class (and what's more half of it not of Polish descent), the *szlachta* constituted the entire nation, and with the vanity of royal authority, the entire *state* was contained in the *szlachta* as well. The exclusive development and predominance of the *szlachta* created for Poland its original society, its distinct and rather high culture. Thanks to this circumstance, Poles more than other Slavic peoples have a capacity, if not for *amicable* then for *martial* action.[15] But these social and cultural advantages did not prevent our Poles from godlessly and inhumanely oppressing the simple people and giving themselves over to unbridled willfulness instead of managing the state. The *entire* strength of Poland was in the *szlachta*, and Poland was lost. It was not lost because it possessed a strong nobility, for this was an advantage, but rather because its nobility turned into a class reigning without restraint, and containing the state in itself instead of being a social class organized for the service of the state and for the management of the nation. Based on the vanity of Polish monarchic authority and on the nation not having rights, it would be a great mistake to see in Poland an aristocratic republic. The distinctive character of this kind of republic is well known (for example, Venice) and represents the direct opposite of Poland's political system: the latter is no more than legitimized anarchy. It is known that the Polish *szlachta* represents the only example in history of a ruling class in which each member *individually* possessed the entire fullness of state authority [*liberum veto*]. This absolute independence of the individual person made impossible the independent existence of the entire Polish state.

Yet having lost its political independence, Poland was not lost: it still lives through its national idea, which carries (although often in a distorted form) a special theocratic character. The Poles, who for the most part fall within the boundaries of the Russian Empire, do not want to, and cannot merge and disappear in a sea of Russians, for they not only constitute a distinct national force, but also represent a particular spiritual idea—the idea of Catholicism. We know that one of the essential elements of Christian theocracy is contained in Catholicism, that the papal principle developed to an extreme degree in it; while we cannot go into a theological examination of the question here, we can not deny the fact that only Catholicism represents an *absolute* independence of the ecclesiastical authority before the state and society. In the East a united ecumenical church among us is gradually concealed more and more behind many national churches, the connection among which gradually weakens more and more. Either an exclusively or even just a predominantly *national* church inevitably becomes a *state* church. The state independence of a nation absorbs

the independence of its church. For the reinstatement of an independent sense of church in our imperial East, it must have a point of rest
outside itself, as at one time the Orthodoxy of the East found itself a
solid point of rest in the Western papacy. But the Western high priest
in turn is in need of the protection and advocacy of an Eastern tsar,
of the patriarchic piety of an imperial nation. A reunification between
Orthodoxy and Catholicism should liberate and strengthen the church
in the East, and in the West reinstate a Christian sense of state. And
since the state authority of the East belongs to Russia in its tsar, and
the spiritual authority of the West belongs to the Roman high priest,
then aren't our Poles natural intermediaries of unification, since they
are subjects of the Russian tsar and spiritual children of the Roman
pope, Poles-Slavs and close to Russia through blood, and in spirit and
culture adjoining the Romano-German West?[16]

At the present time Poles think of such a role less than anything;
all their efforts are directed not at a universal-religious task, but at a
national-political one—the restoration of a great Polish state. But for
anyone besides them themselves the fantastic nature of this goal and
the fruitlessness of their efforts are fully apparent. True, after the fall
of the Polish monarchy, Poles forgot something and learned something.
They forgot the boundlessness of personal willfulness, forgot their "I
will not permit it" [*liberum veto*] and learned to act and organize collectively; now an active part of the Polish nation, that is, the *szlachta*,
represents a rather united and disciplined collective force. Nevertheless
the Poles do not have enough of the most basic necessary conditions
for their political reconstitution. Without any of the rudiments of a
strong state authority, with the exceptional suffering of the rural class
and with the absence of an urban class, all of Poland is represented by
the *szlactha* alone. While the *szlachta* in the best instance can serve as
a useful and important organ in a state and national body, in no way
can it serve as the body itself. Poles should understand (and the best
among them are already beginning to understand) that this striving of
a particular organ to become *in its separateness* the whole organism is
a striving that is both immoral and insane. They want to liberate and
exalt the Polish nation and for this goal look upon all the rest as upon
a means and an instrument. But what if the Polish nation itself is only
a means and instrument? What if the true essence and assignment of
this nation is in it itself and not in who it is represented by, that is,
not in the *szlachta*, but in *what* it represents, that is, in Roman Catholicism? In truth it is thus. In truth all the meaning and all the power
of the Polish people is in the fact that amidst slavdom, in the face of
the East, it carries and represents the great spiritual principle of the

Western world. The Polish state was lost, and Polish nationalism will
be lost, and all the designs and undertakings of the Poles will turn
into nothing. But a Poland called to sacred service was not and will
not be lost. To serve Catholicism—here is the exalted mission of the
Polish nation. Both the first and the greatest service is—reunification
of Catholicism with Orthodoxy, conciliatory mediation between pope
and tsar—the first principle of a new Christian theocracy.

If Christianity is not doomed to lethargy, then it should show
the world its moral power, justify itself as a religion of the world
and of love. I am not speaking about a love indifferent to all and to
everything, I am not speaking about reconciliation with everyone and
with everything. I know that the church on earth is a militant church,
but let civil war be damned! Let the long deception that feeds the
illegitimate enmity and is fed by it be exposed and dispersed! Let a
new flame be kindled in the coldest heart of the Bride of Christ! Let
all the obstacles that separate that which is created for the unification
of the universe be brought to dust!

The day will come that a Poland made whole from long madness will become a living bridge between the sanctuaries of East and
West. A powerful tsar will lend a helping hand to a persecuted pope.
Then true prophets will arise out of the midst of all the nations and
they will be witnesses to king and priest. Then the faith of Christ
will be glorified, then the nation of Israel will be converted.[17] It will
be converted because it will see with its own eyes and will recognize
the kingdom of the Messiah in power and in fact. And then Israel
will not be superfluous amidst Egypt and Assyria, amidst Poland
and Russia.

Is it true that even now the Jewish people constitute a completely
superfluous and even uniquely harmful, parasitic element in the place
of its greatest increase—on the Russian-Polish border? This border,
in particular the lands of White and Red Rus, represents a striking
phenomenon: social elements here are sharply defined according to
various nationalities—Russians comprise the rural farming class, the
upper class is represented by Poles, and the urban industrial class—by
Jews. If the Jews have been able, however, to seize so enduringly and
indivisibly western urban Russia not just in favorable conditions, but
for the most part in conditions unfavorable to them as well, then this
clearly shows they are more capable of forming an urban industrial class
than the Russian people or the Polish *szlachta*. If the industrial class
everywhere, instead of assisting the rural people, lives on its account,
exploits it, then it is not surprising that the Jews appear as exploiters
of the people wherever they constitute the entire industrial class. But it

is not they who have created such a situation. Far too long they were in the school of Polish lords who oppressed Jew and peasant alike. But isn't self-interested oppression of one class by another the general rule of societal life in all Europe, just as it is with those lords? If our peasants are in need of Jews and suffer from their oppression, then this is possible only by virtue of the helpless social-economic situation of these peasants, and this situation does not depend on the Jews. A needy peasant goes to Jews because *his own people will not help him*. And if a Jew, helping a peasant, exploits him, then they do this not because they are Jews, but because they are the masters of financial business, which is based on exploitation of some by others.

The misfortune is not in Jews and not in money, but in domination, the *absolute power of money*, and this absolute power of money is not created by Jews. It was not the Jews who placed profit and enrichment as the goal of all economic activity, it was not Jews who separated the economic sphere from the religious-moral sphere. An enlightened Europe established unscrupulous and inhumane principles in social economy, and then reproached the Jews for the fact that they followed these principles.

The deeds of the Jews are no worse than our own, and it is not for us to indict them. Indeed they are guilty only in the fact that they remain Jews, preserve their separateness. But show them a visible and tangible Christianity, so that they have something to attach themselves to. They are a people of enterprise—show them the Christian enterprise. Unite the church, harmonize it with the state through just deliberation, create a Christian state and a Christian society. Of course, Jews will not accept Christianity when it is repudiated by Christians themselves: it is difficult to fathom that they would unite with that which itself is divided. Do not answer that the Christian world was once united and yet Jews were not enthralled by it. For that was an involuntary, semiconscious, untested, and innocent unity. And when trials and temptations came, this unity did not hold up—to the shame of the Christian world, to the justification and exultation of the Jewish people. And it will be correct in its exultation, as long as we do not reinstate Christian unity freely and consciously. This duty first of all lays upon us—Russians and Poles, for in us the Christian East and West stand face-to-face with all the untruth of their enmity, with all the necessity of their reconciliation.

The unification of Christianity will mean a great division of Judaism: but if the division of Christianity was a misfortune for Christians, then a division of Israel will be a great blessing for Jews. The better part of the Jewish people will enter a Christian theocracy, and the lesser will remain outside it, but only in the end times, having received retribution according to Divine truth, will it be saved according to His mercy, for the word of the Apostle is sure, that *all Israel will be saved*.

And when the Jews enter the Christian theocracy, they will bring to it that which is their strength. Once the best forces of the Jewish people were the prophets; prophecy was the first manifestation of free and active personality; then the prophets were replaced by *teachers of the law*, prophecy passed over to rabbinism—a new manifestation of the same personal and active principle; finally, today the main strengths of the Jewish people are turned predominantly to economic activity—the last extreme manifestation and materialization of the personal principle. Jewish personality established itself initially in the sphere of divinity, then in the sphere of material human life. Here is the ultimate expression of Jewish strength and this sphere will remain with the Jews in a Christian theocracy as well. But it will have another character, another goal and another relation to the subject of activity. In today's unscrupulous and inhumane system of our life, the goal of economic activity is only gain both for Jews and for non-Jews: objects of material nature, although vital as well, appear only as *instruments* for the satisfaction of blind self-interested desires. In theocracy the goal of economic activity is the *humanization* of material life and nature, its construction through human reason, its inspiration through human sensibility. Thus, this nature, the Earth and everything on it—animals and plants—now enter into the very goal of human activity, and are not used just as its instruments: such use is abuse. When self-interest ceases to rule over human relations in society, it will cease reigning as well in the relations of man to nature. In a theocracy, material nature will serve man as well, and much more than now, but this service will be based on mutual love. Nature will subject itself lovingly to man, and man will lovingly look after nature. And which nation more than any other is capable and called to such a nursing of material nature, if not the Jews, who from the beginning acknowledged its right to exist, and, not resigning themselves to it as a blind force, saw in its lucid form the pure and sacred shell of Divine essence? And just as the flower of the Jewish people once served as a receptive medium for the incarnation of Divinity, so too the Israel to come will serve as an active intermediary for the humanization of material life and nature, for the creation of a new earth, where truth lives.

4

New Testament Israel

"Bethlehem," a house of prayer in Kishinev, will celebrate the first anniversary of its founding on the upcoming day of Christ's birth. No one would have believed it if someone had said several years ago that a Jewish house of prayer would appear in southern Russia in the name of Jesus Christ the Son of God, and that in it hundreds of Jews would listen to the preaching of the Gospel every week. The man through whom this establishment came about, Josif Rabinovich, awakened a powerful hatred and persecution against himself on the part of his fellow countrymen. At first they said that he is a deceiver, then that he is insane. But anyone who has listened to him without bias knows that there is in him a *true Israelite, in whom there is no guile*. In this is the entire story of his conversion. He came to Christ by way of the Law and the Prophets; he saw him and said: *Rabbi, You are the Son of God, You are the King of Israel.*[1]

Need it be said that for a natural born Jew, brought up on the promises of the Old Testament, this term *King of Israel* has a completely different meaning than for us? If a natural born Jew acknowledges the true King of Israel in Christ, then he will find in Him not only the fulfillment of his religion, but also the total satisfaction of his national-historical sentiment. And it is not just the expression "King of Israel," but even the more general name "Savior" as well that sounds different to a converted Jew than to us. We understand "Savior" as from the common sins and sufferings of human nature, but a Jew having come to Christ finds in Him apart from this a Savior from the particular historical disorders of his nation.

Here is how Josif Rabinovich expressed himself in private conversation:

> The suffering of my people has always weighed upon my heart. And I tried every remedy to help them, but all was—in vain. When a doctor comes to a sick person, he must first question and examine him before giving a

remedy for the disorder. He takes his pulse, then presses first one place then another on the body, each time asking: Does it hurt here? Is there pressure here? But only when the doctor finds the place where it hurts—does a really loud answer resound from the sick person, evoked by the feeling of pain: Don't press, it hurts!—So it was with me too when I devoted myself to the sufferings of my people. I carefully pressed in different places. Since I was not settling on the place that hurt, I received almost no answer. When I said,"The Talmud and all rabbinic additions do not at all come down from Sinai, as they say, but all of this—is only a human labor of which half has meaning and half is nonsense"—these words affected my people little. And if I said further that "Both the *Torah* (the Law) and the entire *Tanakh* (the Old Testament) contain only human institutions, dubious histories and improbable miracles," then here as well I nevertheless remained the *respected Rabinovich*, and my people knew no pain from these words of mine. My people also remained calm when I placed Moses on a level with contemporary magicians, when I called him a fraud. I could have even denied God himself, and my people would not have produced a painful sound. But when I returned from the Holy Land with joyful news: *"Jesus is our brother,"* here I settled on a painful place, and a shriek of pain echoed from everywhere: "don't press, don't touch, it hurts!"

Of course it hurts; but know my people that this is your disorder, it is only over Him that you suffer—over your brother Jesus. Your disorder is only in the fact that you do not have Him. Accept Him and become whole from all your sufferings.

In a sermon given on August 3 of this year, the founder of New Testament Israel develops this, his main idea, in detail. Since this sermon was published only in the Hebrew language, I will cite it here with some omissions and abridgements, utilizing the manuscript in the Russian translation* received by me from the preacher.[2]

Reading from the Old Testament the regulation about the establishment of a King (Deut. 17:14–20) and in the New Testament the

---

*Of course, I had to rework this literal translation a little from Hebrew slang [*evreiskii zhargon*] with respect to Russian style.

corresponding place from the Gospel of Luke (Luke 22:24–29), the preacher turned to the people and began to speak:

> Beloved brethren! Nation of Israel! Your name and the memory of you arouse all my feelings. Israel! This esteemed name of many meanings, in which important ideas and fascinating memories are included and hidden! And who is this people *today*, who possesses this name? Is Israel indeed your name? They call you *yid*, and you are scorned and hated in the eyes of all the world. Is this the same nation that God acquired before all others as His property? Is this the people to whom were given the Scriptures and prophecies that comprise the source of life for all nations in the world? Is this the Israel to whom verily 3000 years ago its faithful lawgiver Moses gave fundamental laws and institutions comparable to the best statutes of today's enlightened nations? And now what has happened to you, my people? What has made you change so much that nobody can recognize you? True, you are sick. Alas! How long your illness endures! To what can you be compared, my nation, to what can you be likened? You are like a shipwreck, long since having sunk with your cargo and crew, and on the surface of the sea only the mast is visible, tossing from side to side; many ships pass nearby on their voyages, some successfully, while others are wrecked and sink completely to the bottom of the sea. This ship alone is restless under the water and can neither make it to the surface nor be totally sunk. So it is with you, my people. Israel! Long ago you were already total wreckage, there is nothing whole in your body, your brain is paralyzed, all the organs of your senses are atrophied. In only one portion of your heart is it still possible to notice now and then a small throbbing, your limbs shudder, and the traits of your face attest that it is not yet possible to place you on the list of nations that have expired. Yes, you are still alive, the name *Israel* still flutters above you. You roll here and there amid life's abyss, you stand between life and death, you can not live and you can not die.

Then the preacher recalls various methods that were proposed for the healing of the Jewish nation from its many centuries of illness.

Thus, the Talmudists thought that the best means for healing consists in the *imitation* of health and replacing the actual fulfillment of the Law with artificial tokens (for example, the so-called *tefillin* [phylacteries], that is, bands on the forehead and arms with words of the law traced on them). When with the passing of time it turned out that similar remedies only aggravate the illness instead of healing it, and in addition consigning Jews to universal ridicule, then the nation of Israel began to rip the Talmudic plasters off itself, in hopes that the rising *spirit* of a new *time* arriving would waft over it and heal all its disorders. It was then that there appeared the enlightener of today's Jews, Moses Mendelsohn, who discovered for them a new means of healing. In his teaching, all the sufferings of Jews originate from the fact that they consider themselves a *particular*, separate *nation*. All Jews have only to repudiate this, only to acknowledge themselves as Germans of the Mosaic Law in Germany, Poles of the Mosaic Law in Poland, and so forth, and then they will merge with the rest of the enlightened peoples and will save themselves from their national calamities, that is, in other words, the ship of Israel along with everything, even its mast, will be plunged into the depths of the sea. But here a century has passed and the spirit of the new time, the conciliatory tendency of which enlightened Jews so hoped for, suddenly crossed over into the terrible breath of an anti-Semitic storm that raged across all Europe, smashing homes into smithereens and scattering over the wind the common property of all these Germans, Poles, and Russians—the Mosaic Law. New saviors of the Jewish people appeared in this unhappy time—social and political writers who declared, contrary to Mendelsohn, that the Jews do have a nationality, and that this nation is still capable of living separately, not merging with other peoples, and that it is necessary only to change its climate and to resettle in Palestine for its regeneration.

> Here before you is a dangerously ill person that is hardly breathing and incapable of movement, and three doctors gathered around him for purposes of consultation. The first of them began to discuss at length the movements and exercises that it would be useful for the sick person to do; the second began to inquire about the sick person's real name, assuming that without the precise rendering of this name on the prescription it is not possible to go to the pharmacy to get well; finally, the third began to show that it is necessary for the sick person first of all to change his locale and leave for distant lands. Such are your doctors, Israel! When will you finally comprehend their absence

of reason? You have apparently completely forgotten
the words spoken to you and written in your Torah, in
the same Torah that you read twice weekly in the original
and once in translation—the words: *I, your God, am a Healer*
(Ex. 15:26). Know, Israel, that while you await assistance
and healing from the hand of mortals, but not from your
God, you will remain unhealed eternally. *"He sent his word
and healed them,"* says the Spirit of God through the lips of
the psalmist. (Ps 107:20)

The prophet Isaiah, seeing in his prophetic vision that the God
of Hosts will accomplish a predesignated annihilation over the whole
land, and that the higher branches will be cut off and the exalted will
fall, took comfort and said:

"And there shall come forth a rod out of the stem of
Jesse . . . and the spirit of the Lord will rest upon Him" [Is.
11:1–2]. Brothers! These words have no need of any interpretation, but require only careful listening, a pure heart
and direct meaning. These words: a rod out of the stem
of *Jesse*—are ready to give us understanding about Divine
counsel at the foundation of His heavenly kingdom on earth.
When the Spirit of God rested upon the Man of God, Isaiah,
and exalted prophetic notions took hold of his soul, and
Divine banners from times long since past were presented
to him—he went into a rapturous and indescribable joy.
He saw the entire history of the Christ of the God of Jacob,
comprising the hope and glory of the nation of Israel, from
the events of the life of the first true King of Israel, David,
the *youngest* of the children of Jesse, a *herder of sheep*. In this
history was preserved the fulfillment of all the promises given
to this nation, through whose action at the end of time the
wolf will lie down together with the lamb, and the leopard
with the kid, and a *little child*, the Christ, the youngest son
in the flesh of the children of Jesse, a herder of Bethlehem,
will lead them as the good shepherd. The sixteenth chapter
of the First Book of Kings [1 Samuel] elucidates and explains
to us these two prophetic words: *little child*.

The preacher continued after recounting the biblical story of
how the prophet Samuel, against his own desire and in spite of all
appearances and all human considerations, anointed for kingship the
little shepherd David, whom God himself chose:

The goal of the Lord in such a selection, as is apparent from
the next chapter (17:41-47), was that through the battle of
this sheep herder with the Philistine Goliath *all the earth
would know that Israel has a God*, and that the Lord saves
neither by the sword nor by the spear. This terrifying Philistine, relying on his fleshly strength and on his gigantic
weaponry, which is described in detail in the holy book,
cursed the Israelite army, saying: "give me a *man* to fight
in single combat." Marking the fear and confusion of Saul
and all the Israelites, Scripture relates to us further that
the eldest sons of Jesse followed Saul to war, but David,
the youngest, did not cease tending his father's flock of
sheep in Bethlehem. He finds himself in military service
only *by chance*—only because his father Jesse sent for him
to bring food to his eldest sons. Brothers! It merits noting
this circumstance, that even today in its exile the entire
Hebrew nation does not stop recalling in its prayers the
elevation of David to King of Israel, a kingship on which
are based its most treasured and brightest hopes: *David
the King of Israel is alive eternally*, as it is said: "the scepter
shall not depart from Judah"—it merits noting, I say, that
this grandiose event of Jewish history followed as if in
an *oblique* and *accidental* manner. This is because, as it is
said: "Truly You are a secretive God, the God and Savior
of Israel," you give to man the free will to attribute one
or another occurrence to the work of God, or to a simple
accident, and through that experience a believing heart.
Thus, having landed unforeseeably in the ranks of service
and having heard the insulting challenges of the Philistine,
David clothed himself with zeal for the God of Hosts and
cried out to him: "Who is this uncircumcised one, who
so abuses the army of the living God?" And when they
presented him before King Saul, and he said to him: "You
can not go against this Philistine, for you are still a boy,
and he has been a man of war from his youth,"—David
answered simply: "Your servant slew both the lion and the
bear, and so it will be with this foreigner. I will go and
defeat him, and take away the abuse from Israel: for who
is this uncircumcised one to destroy the army of the *living
God*."[3] With these words the future King of Israel wanted
to say that only the Spirit of God inspires and fortifies a
man, and without this, a man is like a beast of the field

with only his own strength. And therefore he added with
full confidence: "The Lord, who saved me from the claws
of the lion and from the claws of the bear, will also deliver
out of the hand of this uncircumcised one." Then David,
dressed in Saul's battle armor, both helmet and sword,
removed all of it, and, taking his shepherd's staff and
putting into his bag five smooth stones (a stone rejected
is the cornerstone), he approached the Philistine, saying:
"You come at me with sword and spear and shield; but I
come to you in the name of the Lord of Hosts, the God of
the armies of Israel, whom you have abused, and this day
the Lord will deliver you into my hand—*all the earth shall
know that there is a God in Israel*. And all this assembly shall
understand *that the Lord does not save with sword and spear*."
Here is the longing: not to show one's own power, but the
power of the living God, so that all the Earth would know
that there is a God in Israel—this is the marvelous desire
that God in advance saw in the heart of the little shepherd
of Bethlehem, and it was this that made this shepherd the
chosen one of God.

Such was the mission of the first founder of the
Kingdom of God on earth, of the first king from the house
of Jesse, and this is the mission of the final king of Israel,
of the clan of Jesse—of the eternally existing Son of God,
Jesus Christ—and, namely, to show the world *that there
is a God* and to give all believers in Him eternal life, as
Christ himself said: "this is life eternal, that they might
know You, the only true God and Jesus Christ whom You
have set" (Jn 17:3). And just as David, the shepherd of
sheep and the least of all his brothers, was chosen in spite
of all human appearances, so also the Son of David, our
good shepherd. Having made himself low and adopting
the mark of a servant, he teaches us not to judge according to our fleshly eyes. He also said to His disciples: "he
that is greatest among you. let him be as the younger, and
he that is chief, as a servant: only to such is promised the
kingdom" (Lk 22:24–26).

The God of Israel mandates such a king, saying: "Set
over you a king whom your Lord God will choose—he
shall not multiply horses for himself and multiply wives
for himself, and place his hopes upon gold and silver, but
only on God and on the teaching of the Lord, that his heart

not turn away—then he and his sons will remain in their kingship amidst Israel" [Dt 17: 14–20].

God fulfilled just what he said. He found Himself such a king according to His heart, David, and in order that he and his sons always remain as kings amidst Israel, the throne of David, His father, was given by God to Jesus, to our Messiah or Christ (i.e., the Anointed One, the King), the son of David and the Son of God, and he acceded to the throne over the house of Jacob for ever, and of His kingdom there will be no end (Lk 1:32, 33). Yes, brothers! He is the shoot cut from the stem of Jesse and the small child that leads together wolves, sheep, lambs, leopards, kids, cows, and bears (i.e., all kinds of people and nations, civilized and wild), as the prophet Isaiah saw it. And if we will follow Him with completely sincere repentance and enter into the kingdom of this seed of Jesse in the flesh, then *He*, in conformity with the prophecy of Isaiah, *shall judge the poor* (i.e., us) *with righteousness and shall smite the earth* (rebelling against us) *with the rod of His mouth* [Is 11:4]—with the Holy Gospel, for our Heavenly Father promised His kingdom to Him, and only those believing in Him will inherit together with Him.

Brothers, put all these words into your heart, remove from your midst all love of falsehood, approach and draw near to your Messiah, to our King Jesus. He will heal you of blindness, which the prophet noted, saying to us: "Who is as blind as My servant?" (Is 42:19). Yes, you, Israel, are the blind one about which the disciples of the Lord Jesus asked: "Who sinned, he or his parents?"—and Jesus answered them: "neither he nor his parents, but this was in order that God's works be made manifest in him" (Jn 9:2–4). Yes, Israel! You are blind, for you the light of the world is dark, and on all your roads lie stumbling stones. Some (the Socialists) say that *you* have sinned, others (anti-Semites) say that it was your *parents*, but only what the Lord and Savior said is true: "*in order that God's words be made manifest in him.*" For this you became blind, for this you are defeated and oppressed, and for all that you are *still* alive, in order that God's works be made manifest in you. If only you turn to *Yahweh*, to your *God*, if you love Him and believe in His Son Jesus Christ, the redeemer of all human sins, and you gain sight as the blind man in

Jerusalem: through this faith in Jesus, the light of life, under which all enlightened peoples walk, will also be opened to you, and you will be raised again to the level of the renowned peoples in this world.

This Messiah Jesus, who descended into the abyss and ascended to heaven, will also descend upon you, in order to cast all your sins into the depths of the sea, and will lead the sunken ship of Israel out of the sea of sorrows, and you again will become the people of God. The Prince of life and peace created peace between Israel and the nations! And the word of the prophet will be fulfilled: and the wolf will lie down together with the lamb, and the leopard together with the kid, and a *little child*—our Lord Jesus Christ—will lead them. And blessed be his name for ever and ever. Amen . . .

Here is the spirit in which the founder of the new Israel preaches. "Every spirit that confesses that Jesus Christ came in the flesh is from God" [1 Jn 4:2]. It is clear that our preacher has the faith of Christ. It is only possible to ask: by which path or *way* did he achieve it? Christ himself is the Way, the Truth and the Life. And although Christ as the Way, or the Way of Christ, is one in its moral essence, which is humility and obedience to the higher will, in its visible manifestation this Way is very diverse depending on *whence one comes*. If for us, those born in the church, the Way of Christ consists in free subjection to this church in all its definitions, then for Jews, born outside the church, the lawful Way of Christ, indicated by Christ Himself and His Apostles, is the attentive and sincere following of the Old Testament's prophetic meaning.

There is a great difference and even a direct contrast between Christian sects that have separated themselves from the *defined* church and those who have gone and left—some nearer, others farther, for the endless wasteland of rationalism—and this New Testament Israel, beginning from ancient traditions and attaining the One in Whom is the final fulfillment of every truth. And if the fullness of Christian truth has yet to be definitively displayed in the consciousness of this newly born community, if much and even all that is here appears in unsure and unclear characteristics, then this is the very same as it was with the entire Christian church at the beginning of its history. All truth was given in Christ, but not all of it was immediately revealed to the Christian consciousness. Only with a total lack of caring for historical truth is it possible to maintain that all the dogmas of Orthodoxy that are adopted by us today were confessed explicitly and definitively by the whole church from its very beginning, from the times of Christ and the apostles. In actual fact, the original Christian religious teaching was not at all a mechanistic aggregate of separate dogmas, but was the living seed of truth, out of which a complex and extensive system of Orthodox dogma gradually divided and spread. This living seed of Christian faith presents to us as well a New Testament Israel in its *Credo*, which in essence is identical to the ancient Apostolic Creed: here is this *Credo*.*

1. I truly believe that our Heavenly Father is the living, true, eternal God, who created heaven and earth, all that is seen and unseen by His Word and the Holy Spirit. He is one, everything comes from Him and all is in Him, and everything is His.

2. I truly believe that our Heavenly Father, conforming to his promises to our Father, to the prophets, and to our king, David, the son of Jesse, raised a savior for Israel, Jesus, born from the Virgin Mary in the city of Bethlehem in Judea, that he suffered, was crucified, died and was buried for the sake of our salvation, that he rose from the dead, is living and sits at the right hand of the Father in heaven, and from there will come to judge the living and the dead on earth. He is King over the house of Jacob forever and His kingdom will have no end.

3. I truly believe that according to righteous condemnation and Divine Providence our fathers were struck with hardheartedness and impiously opposed their Messiah, the Lord Jesus, and through that awakened a great zeal in other nations of the Earth and reconciled all of them through faith in Christ, according to the word of His Gospel, so that the Earth would be filled with the knowledge of the Lord, and the Lord would become king over all the Earth.

4. I truly believe that every man is justified without works of the law, by faith alone in Jesus the Messiah, he is the Word of the Heavenly Father, eternally begotten of the Father, and that the very same God alone justifies Jews, circumcised of faith, and Gentiles, not circumcised of faith, and there is no

---

*Josif Rabinovich composed two confessions of faith: an extensive one of twenty-five articles and a short one of seven articles. We cite the latter, supplementing it from the extensive version in only one place.

difference between Jews and Greeks, slave and free, man and woman, but all together are united in Christ.

5. I truly believe in the single Holy Apostolic Church.

6. I confess one baptism for the forgiveness of sins.

7. I look for the resurrection of the dead into eternal life. Amen.

In this confession only the truth of the promised Messiah appears vividly and distinctly; all the rest is either in shadow or in embryonic form. But it was precisely this Truth as the Messiah that constituted the entire content of the original apostolic preaching, as we see in the Book of Acts. Just as then, every believing Jew now has to begin precisely from this messianic faith, in order to consciously accept Christianity on their religious-historical soil. Every other attitude to Christ on the part of Judaism would be useless and fruitless. And is it only for Jews alone that Old Testament promises have decisive significance? Does not the Church rely as well chiefly on these messianic promises in its articles of religious faith? True, these ecclesiastical definitions have an independent meaning and absolute authority for us now. But to require that a conscientious and religious Jew immediately adopt for himself all the dogmatic resolutions of the universal [church] councils would be unfounded and extremely unjust. We know that the definitions of the Universal Church were called forth by certain necessities and inquiries that had appeared in history. Each of these dogmatic regulations were a definite response to a *definite question*. But if I do not ask a certain question, if this question is foreign and incomprehensible to me, then what kind of significance can the answer to it have for me, even if this answer were absolutely faithful and true in and of itself (which all the dogmatic definitions of the Universal Church are)? If I *myself* do not ask, then an answer to the questions of others will be an empty sound that passes me by. If, for example, I never occupy myself with metaphysical questions about the forces and actions of the Divine and the human essence, if I do not note a distinction at all between natural will or desire (*thelesis*) and moral will (*gnome*), then will I really suffer any harm from the fact that the dogma of the sixth universal council concerning two natural wills and actions in Christ presently remains as mute words to me?

The divine significance of Christ as the *Word*, eternally begotten of the Father, is expressed in the creed of New Testament Israel. The triune Divinity (Father, His Word and the Holy Spirit) is expressed there as well. True, we will not find a formal definition of three co-existing *hypostases* [persons] in this creed, just as we will not find it in our creeds: the Apostolic, Nicene, and Constantinople. But if the whole Church could exist for several centuries without this formula, then why can't a small community of Jewish Christians exist without it several years? And what is to be done if the distinction between essence and hypostasis is unclear to the Jewish mind? That distinction was not elucidated even in Christianity itself. What a great temptation occurred in the Church, when at the end of the fourth century Miletius of Antioch first utilized the expression "three hypostases"! Since the Greek word hypostasis was literally translated into Latin by the word substantia, Western Christians began to accuse Eastern Christians of an apparent worship of three gods. Only thanks to the scholar Hieronymus [St. Jerome], who knew both the Greek and Latin languages very well, did an elucidation of the misunderstanding succeed and calamitous discord in the Church was averted. But, it will be said, let these New Testament Jews not utilize Greek terms that are incomprehensible to them, but let them only directly acknowledge the perfect Divinity of the Word and the Spirit. We will not respond to this ourselves, but will cite what St. Gregory the Theologian said in a similar case, and precisely when the question was with respect to Christians who had refused to acknowledge the Holy Spirit as God.

"The syllables trouble you, the expression alone, and it is a stumbling block and a stone of temptation for you, which Christ was for some as well. This is—a human infirmity. Let us come together among ourselves spiritually, we will do better in fraternal love than in self-love. Acknowledge the power of Divinity and we will make an indulgence in expression for you. Confess nature under other terms that you respect more, and we will treat you as infirm, *even concealing something for your satisfaction*. For it is shameful, literally shameful, and rather foolhardy, to be healthy in soul and to fix sounds prominently, to conceal treasure, as if in envy of someone, or to be afraid of consecrating a word. *But it is even more shameful for us to subject ourselves to that which we accuse another, and in judging disputes with respect to sounds, we ourselves stand for the letter.* Confess a single Divinity in the Trinity, or, if it suits you, a single nature, and I will petition for you the Word of God from the Spirit. For I know very well that he who gives the former will also give the latter, and all the more, if the reason for dispute is some kind of spiritual timidity, and not devilish stubbornness. I will say still more clearly and briefly: if you do not indict us for the more exalted expression (for one must not envy exaltedness), neither will we judge you for the expression *that you are in the meantime able to achieve though by another path*, until you attain the same refuge that we have. We strive not for victory, but for the return of brothers whose separation torments us."*

We will be bound by the admonitions of the great prelate. New Testament Jews do not indict us for our exalted expressions (in the dogma of the Holy Trinity), neither will we judge them for the true, though incomplete as well, understanding of this subject, until which time it be in their power to attain, though by another path, a refuge in common with us. It is one thing to diverge from a full definition of truth, it is another thing not to arrive at this definition. Protestant rationalism strives for an artificial simplification of Christianity, but New Testament Israel proceeds from the natural simplicity of the initial Messianic fact, and can enter into a complete fullness of growth in Christ given favorable conditions. It was not Protestantism, but the Universal Church that was produced out of the primitive simplicity of the Apostolic community. Meanwhile among us, due to the single superficial impression of outward likeness, it is desired to forcibly tether New Testament Jews to Protestantism. Two trains going in opposite directions can meet and sometimes stand together on one and the same station: does it follow from this that it is necessary to connect one with the other forever? Seeing that the train of New Testament Israel stands at the present moment side by side with their own, Protestantism cries: you should ride together with us! On their part, this is, of course, understandable; but what foundation and what interest does our government have in removing the independence of a Jewish community that came to Christ by way of its law, having accepted its Messiah on its own and on His own native soil, on the soil of a three thousand year old historical tradition? What foundation, what interest is there to subordinate such a community to an alien and unsound confession of an unfavorable tendency. Is there any sense in giving over as sacrifice a people who confess a positive religion, founded by God himself, to people who confess only arbitrary human *opinions*? It is not possible to point to a single position that would express a personal opinion of Josif Rabinovich in the confession of New Testament Israel. Is this Protestantism?

Remaining a Jew absolutely, the founder of New Testament Israel acknowledged his close connection with Russia and expressed himself very sympathetically with respect to the Orthodox Church. Here is what he writes, incidentally, in a private letter:

. . . I see that the guardsman of Israel does not doze and does not sleep. He began to work mercifully and keenly

---

*Works of St. Gregory the Theologian (Moscow, 1844), IV:12–13.

in the hearts of my Russian brothers in Christ for the sake
of an unfortunate and nearly dead Israel. In actual fact it
is time as well for Russian Christianity, which possesses
an immeasurable supply of faith in Christ, not to consider
this only its own, belonging only to it alone. The Lord said:
"Whoever believes in Me, as the Scripture has said, out
of his heart will flow rivers of living water" [Jn 7:38]. . . .
Every *Christian* state must know that the unfortunate Jewish question does not consist in: What is to be done with
the Jews? How can their rights be broadened or limited to
acquire earthly blessings amidst the Christian population?
The question is rather How can they be made into, not wily,
but true Israelites, that is, How can they be brought to the
rivers of living water that flow from the heart of believers
in Jesus Christ. Only then will they stop being loyal to the
prince of this world and the sons of the *father of falsehood*, that
is, the Talmud. . . . Yes! Yes! Tell all brothers in Christ who
grieve about the blindness of Israel that its return to its true
Messiah is inevitable, for God imprisoned all in disobedience,
in order to pardon all. Oh, the fathomless richness and wisdom and vision of God! The finger of God—the complexity
of the Jewish question in all Europe—shows us that now
is the moment of labor for Jews obstinate to this day, and
precisely in Russia, where God's Providence has packed them
in such large numbers. Western Christianity gave Jews the
possibility to become familiar with the Gospel—it is there
that it was translated excellently into the ancient Hebrew
language, and Eastern Christianity, the defender of which
stands Russia, is foreordained, in my belief, to give them
the possibility of building a Church.

We will not be troubled by this desire to build a Church instead
of simply joining with the Church that has already been built. New
Testament Israel wants to be grafted onto the trunk of Christianity as
a small but living branch. Many branches have already withered and
broken off, but the trunk is sturdy and indestructible. It is capable of
giving to this small branch as well all the life-giving sap it needs in
order that it increase in its fullness. It is clear that New Testament Israel
is an embryonic phenomenon. In any case it is found on the path to
the true goal. Why would we place a stumbling block for it on this
path? Wouldn't it be better to show that "We strive not for victory,
but for the return of brothers whose separation torments us."

5

The Teaching of the Twelve Apostles

Since the middle of this century the number of sources for the history of the ancient Christian church has been enriched by three discoveries. The one that has perhaps elicited the greatest hopes and expectations among them has justified them least of all: I have in mind a Gnostic composition found in the Coptic language, known under the Greek title Πιστις Σοφια [*Pistis Sophia*].[1] We knew about Gnostic teachings only what was reported by those who laid them open with the goal of refutation, and individual works of these heretics were, as is known, ruthlessly extirpated by pious zealots. Therefore the interest that had to have been aroused by the discovery of Πιστις Σοφια, in which the Gnostics' own voice was expected to be heard for the first time, is understandable. Unfortunately, this voice turned out to be of very little importance in terms of its content. This is simply a collection of several monotonous and pretentious hymns and lamentations, connected to the legendary conditions typical of all apocrypha. The author of this work certainly thought least of all to set forth any Gnostic teaching, and our knowledge about the subject was essentially not enriched at all by the discovery of Πιστις Σοφια.

More important in this respect was the discovery of the extensive writings of St. Hippolytus [of Rome] on heresies; small excerpts that had been previously known were usually ascribed to Origen under the title φιλοσοφουμενα [*philosophoumena*].[2] Although even now we still do not have this work in complete form, the greater and most important part of it, however, has been discovered; it sheds a clear new light on certain fundamental points of Gnosticism, such as on the teaching of the originator of all Gnostic heresies, Simon, on the teachings of the Ophites, and in particular on the system of Basilides.[*3]

---

*For a detailed evaluation of Hippolytus' work, see the excellent book of elder priest and professor A. M. Ivantsov-Platonov on heresies and schisms of the first three centuries.

For all that, the newly discovered work of St. Hippolytus without doubt yields interest and significance to the third, final discovery in the sphere of ancient Christian writing, the so-called teaching of the twelve Apostles (Διδαχη των δωδεκα αποστολων). This artifact, small in volume but great in content, does not illuminate and elucidate for us any particular aspects in the development of Christian or pseudo-Christian ideas, but rather depicts Christianity, the living body of the church itself, at one of the most interesting moments of its existence.

After the totality of Divine gifts was manifested in a concentrated and intense development of spiritual life in the Apostolic church, the slow and complex process of elaborating permanent forms of the church's objective existence had to begin. These permanent forms were to insure the natural health and growth of the body of Christ on the foundation of the supernatural gifts of grace. At the very beginning of this formative process, we must confront a brief but significant period of the simplest church existence, when the marvelous inspiration of the first witnesses of the New Testament ended and the complete structure of the church had yet to be defined. Before the original surge of Christian life turned into the definite, wide conduit of the historical church, for a while it arrived in lands as a shallow and formless streamlet. However, disregarding the scantiness and indeterminacy of its characteristics, it is precisely this streamlet that passed on to us the living water of Christ, and this discovered artifact gives us anew his full and faithful image. This simple and befitting image of the church in its most pure, embryonic form immediately shatters two conceptions about this subject, both false and mutually opposed to each other, and it completely confirms the proper conception about the development of the church. Before validating these thoughts of ours about the significance of the newly discovered artifact in the content of the entire Διδαχη [henceforth: Didache], we must briefly impart some information about it and then set forth the grounds on which we ascribe the time of its composition precisely to the period that directly followed the activity of the most immediate disciples of Christ.

In the study of church history the existence of the Didache was known through the implications and citations of various ecclesiastical writers, beginning with Clement of Alexandria (at the end of the second century) and ending with Nicephor Kallistos (who lived in the fourteenth century). Among the ancient writers, the aforementioned Clement in his Stromata, while not naming our artifact directly, cites an entire maxim from it as *Holy Writ,* υπο της Γραφης (ειρηται); Eusebius Pamphilus points to it directly under the title των αποστολων αι λεγομεναι διδαχαι; finally, St. Athanasius the Great refers to our artifact Διδαχη καλουμενη των αποστολων in one of his epistles together with the noncanonical books of the Old Testament (Wisdom of Solomon, etc.) as of one of those writings that was read publicly in the church by enactment of the fathers.

Although, as was stated, the church historian Nicephor Kallistos mentions the Didache in the fourteenth century, it was in all likelihood only in someone else's words. Another Nicephor, the Patriarch of Constantinople (who died in 820), should be considered the last ecclesiastical writer to have seen and had in hand the text of Didache. He reports about the length of our artifact, presuming two hundred verses to be in it, which nearly corresponds to today's discovered text. It can be concluded with great confidence from the fact that Didache did not land in the "library" of Photius, who read everything, that it also disappeared from circulation in the ninth century soon after Patriarch Nicephor. In any event, when the study of church history through sources then began with the renaissance of knowledge in the West, the Didache appeared to be among the number of artifacts of Christian antiquity that had vanished without a trace.

The glory for the discovery of this treasure belongs entirely to Metropolitan Philotheos Bryennios of Nicomedia. He found a manuscript that contained the synopsis of the Old Testament of St. John the Golden Mouth [Chrysostom] and several other minor works, and among them a complete and substantially corrected written text of Didache in the Jerusalem court of Constantinople. Having created in 1883 an excellent edition of the artifact discovered by him, this capable hierarch completely vindicated the good fortune that had fallen to him. With the appearance of this edition all doubt vanished that the discovered work is the same one about which Eusebius, Athanasius, and Nicephor spoke, and which Clement of Alexandria cited as authoritative *Holy Writ*.

His Holiness Philotheos who justly noted at the beginning of his "Prolegomenon" that the work discovered by him is proximate to the Apostolic era, that it is an artifact of ancient times, unfortunately defined the time of the composition of Didache too precisely between [AD] 120 and 160. The esteemed editor demonstrated superbly that Didache could not have been composed later than the time indicated by him, but he did not show that it could not belong to a much earlier period. The German researcher of Didache, the well-known scholar Harnack, earnestly strove to prove this.[4] But with all due respect to this distinguished representative of German scholarship, it must be said that his argumentation on this point is extremely unsuccessful.

Harnack brings in one extrinsic reason and several intrinsic ones for the opinion that Didache could not have been written directly after the Apostolic era, but must be attributed to the second or even the third quarter *of the second century*. The extrinsic reason (presupposed also by Metropolitan Philotheos Bryennios) consists in the fact that the author of Didache allegedly utilized the well-known Epistle of Barnabas. That the first chapters of Didache have many sayings in common with (and sometimes even literally identical to) the second half of the Epistle of Barnabas is not subject to any doubt. But the question about who borrowed from whom is obviously not resolved by this at all. Neither Bryennios nor Harnack introduce any kind of valid reason in favor of the primacy of Barnabas, which remains only an arbitrary presupposition. On the contrary, in comparing these two artifacts, it is easy to become convinced of Didache's primacy.* The Epistle of Barnabas is bereft of any intrinsic consistency and integrity and consists of heterogeneous arguments and remarks that easily could have been collected from various sources. And it is precisely the second half of this epistle, which coincides in many places with Didache, that is connected with the first half in a completely *extrinsic* manner, by means of this phrase: Μεταβωμεν δε και επι ετεραν γνοσιν και διδαχην (Let us proceed to other knowledge and teaching). In contrast to this Didache, as even Harnack acknowledges, is distinguished by the integrity and consistency of its account. Is it possible to allow that the author of such a composition wrote out his fundamental thoughts directly from someone else's work, work of incomparably lower merit than his own? Of course, for an absolutely reliable solution of such a problem no rationale can replace direct factual evidence, which is absent in the given case. But *all probability* inclines in favor of Didache preceding the Epistle of Barnabas. Having conceded this primacy, we necessarily must move the period of Didache's composition to the era directly adjoining the beginning of the church. For the Epistle of Barnabas could hardly have been written later than the ninth decade of the first century, and consequently the most probable period of Didache's composition must be accepted as *the eighth decade of the first century*.

The intrinsic bases that induced Harnack to attribute the composition of Didache to a much later epoch are shaky to the extreme. In the first place, he indicates that our artifact witnesses to a certain disorder in the moral life of the Christian community. Even if it does

---

*As we learn from a brief note by Harnack, the German scholars Pap and Funk support this opinion. Unfortunately, we were not successful in obtaining their articles prior to the present essay's composition.

so witness, then it does so in no way more than the epistle of Apostle Paul to the Corinthians does, the authenticity and antiquity of which is not contested even by unfavorable criticism. If there could be both contention and occasions of coarse dissipation among Christians in the sixth decade of the first century, then why could not similar phenomena take place thirty years later? The Christian church was not safeguarded from the evil passions and sins of humanity in a single moment of its existence.

Further, Harnack indicates the decline of the prophetic office, which follows from the precautionary measures against false prophets that we find in Didache. But the Apostles themselves warned the faithful against false prophets and all kinds of false teachers in their epistles; false Christs are spoken about in the Gospel, false prophecy is indicated in the Apocalypse. Just as Moses gave the Israelites a rule for differentiation of true prophets from false ones in the Old Testament church at its very foundation, so in a similar manner Christ and the apostles acted at the foundation of the New Testament church, and our Didache in this respect immediately follows the directions of the initial Christian revelation.

In one obscure place of our artifact, which Harnack interprets in his own way, the expression *ancient* prophets (οι αρχαιοι προφηται) is used. Harnack proposes understanding by this the prophets of the apostolic epoch, for otherwise *his interpretation* of the entire obscure place that is in question would not have any meaning. But for this reason, having forgotten the conditional and presumptive character of such a consideration, he forwards it as a positive argument in favor of a comparatively late period of Didache's composition; for, he says, if this artifact names prophets of the apostolic century as ancient, then this means it must be separated from them by a significant interval of time. But it follows in response to this that the Harnackian interpretation of the indicated obscure place, which requires understanding αρχαιοι προφηται as prophets of the apostolic century, does not have any advantage over other interpretations of the very same place that do not require such an understanding of this term at all. Even here "ancient prophets" all the more naturally connotes Old Testament prophets (as even Bryennios accepts), and in such case the expression can tell us nothing about the time of Didache's composition.

Neither do the citations from the Gospels that are found in Didache and that in the opinion of Harnack must prove the late period of this artifact have anything to say about this time. But, in the first place, in order to attribute the writings of our synoptic Gospels (for the author of Didache evidently did not make use of John) to the second century, it is necessary to have stronger faith in the consideration of a certain critical school, which, moreover, is itself not in agreement in this respect. And, in the second place, it is in no way possible to say with confidence that the author of Didache made use of our Gospels *in the form* in which we have them. He does not rely on one or another gospel as on a particular book but speaks in general about the Lord's "good news." And with the exclusion of the Lord's Prayer, which of course was well known in the church from the very beginning, all the remaining Gospel citations in Didache are so brief (for example, "give not that which is holy to dogs" [Mt 7:6], or: "love your neighbor as yourself," etc.) that their literal coincidence with the corresponding texts of our Gospels does not prove anything precisely. These brief aphorisms could have been taken by the author of Didache from the "words of the Lord" (Λογια του Κυριον) that later entered into the body of the Synoptic Gospels thoroughly.

Speaking in the final chapter about the Second Coming of Christ, Didache does not place this future event in any connection with the destruction of Jerusalem and the destiny of the Jewish people. Harnack also sees in this an "intrinsic basis" for relating our artifact to the second century. However, all that one can possibly conclude by right from the indicated circumstance is only the fact that Didache was written after the destruction of Jerusalem and the decisive separation of the Christian church from Judaism. But nobody doubted this anyway.

Finally Harnack sees the mark of a comparatively late epoch in the weakening of the Gospel requirements for complete self-denial, especially with respect to possessions. The Gospel says: give away all your possessions to the poor, but Didache charges giving to the poor only a part of one's possessions, and selectively at that. But here Harnack, in the first place, confuses the commandment of perfection with a positive instruction, and in the second place, he forgets that in the apostolic church as well commandments of Gospel perfection were realized only at the very beginning, when everyone had one soul and property in common. And later, already in the period of the Apostle Paul's activity, we do not find any suggestions of common possessions. If such an accomplished scholar as Harnack could not find any better arguments for the support of his opinion, then no particular audacity is necessary to cast this opinion aside as based on nothing.

Thus, nothing obstructs us from relating the time of the composition of Didache directly to the post-apostolic epoch, that is, to the end of the first century.* But several considerations decidedly force us to dwell precisely on this time.

---

*The boundary between the apostolic and post-apostolic period of church history is defined usually independently of the tradition regarding the uniquely long life of St. John the Divine.

If we compare the picture of church relations that Didache presents to us with the data that we find in the epistles of St. Ignatius the God-Bearer [Theophorus]—of course, in those among them whose authenticity is acknowledged by the most dispassionate and established critics*—then what strikes us is the huge change that must have transpired in the church in the interval of time between the appearance of Didache and the epistles of the holy bishop of Antioch. In "the teaching of the twelve apostles" all attitudes and practices of the church are depicted *in statu nascenti*, in an indeterminate and formless shape; in the epistles of Ignatius all that is essential appeared already crystallized and strictly delimited; not only does the common hierarchical principle of the church (having existed from the beginning) obtain a more distinctive definition, but also particular forms of church structure come out clear and precise as well. Whereas Didache shows us at the head of the church at once apostles, prophets, teachers, bishops and deacons—among which there is nothing to connect some of these ministries between themselves or others—all holy ministry and church governance in the epistles of Ignatius turn out properly centered in a single clearly partitioned hierarchical structure with three separate and defined degrees of bishop, presbyter, and deacon. We think that there is not the smallest possibility of conceding such a significant and successful achievement of a distinct and fixed church structure in the confines of one and the same generation. Thus, we must presuppose that twenty or thirty years certainly passed from the time of the writing of Didache to the appearance (of the authentic) epistles of St. Ignatius the God-Bearer. And since we know with sufficient confidence that the period of the latter coincides with the year 107, then this points to *the eighth decade of the first century* as the most probable (in our opinion the only probable) time of the composition of Didache.

One can introduce yet another circumstance in support of this. In our artifact there is not the least indication of any kind of persecutions or torture of Christians on the part of the pagan state and people. If, as we are convinced, Didache was written in the eighth decade of the first century, then such a silence is completely understandable. For Nero's persecution, the only one having taken place up to that time, had an absolutely unique character and could not evoke any general instructions. Moreover from the first years of the second

---

*As is known, a whole series of epistles, among which several are doubtlessly spurious, is ascribed to St. Ignatius; the authenticity of others, on the contrary, was argued only by glaringly tendentious critics. For essential information about this, see the foreword of St. Ignatius in the priest P. A. Preobrazhenskii's Russian translation of works by apostolic men.

century legal criminal persecutions of Christians had already begun in broad dimensions in the entire Roman Empire, in view of which such an all encompassing guidance of Christian life as Didache, if it was written in the second century, in no way could have avoided any instructions or admonitions.

If the two considerations introduced above are joined to this, to wit: (1) the borrowings from Didache that we find in such an ancient work of Christian writing as the epistle of Barnabas; and (2) the huge difference in the picture of church structure, as it is presented in our artifact, on the one hand, and in the authentic epistles of St. Ignatius the God-Bearer on the other; then it becomes more than probable that the time of the composition of Didache must be attributed to the end of the first century, more specifically to the eighth decade of that century (80–90).

And with respect to the place of Didache's composition, there are grounds to acknowledge that this work originally appeared in Egypt. The *doxology* that is repeatedly utilized in our artifact differs by the omission of the word *kingdom*, and this omission is precisely the distinguishing mark of the Egyptian church.

Turning to Didache's content itself, we find first of all that in the face of the extreme simplicity of the ecclesiastical life reflected in this artifact, all the formative elements of the Christian church were already fully present here, but only in an embryonic, amalgamated form. Although the attention of apostolic teaching is turned predominantly to the commandments and instructions of Christian morality, at the same time we see here also the principle of universal hierarchy and the foundation of dogmatic teaching, and finally the initial mode of the most important *sacraments*.

So-called *apostles* appear at the head of the ecclesiastical holy orders in Didache. A correct understanding of this term will give us the key to comprehending the entire ecclesiastical system of that time. The answer to the question What were apostles? is made easier by the fact that we can say with confidence what they were *not*. In the first place, they were not simple preachers and interpreters of the Word of God, because there were special people in the church for this ministry—*teachers* (διδασκαλοι). In the second place, apostles were not absolute possessors of a special personal gift—prophetic inspiration—for the bearers of such inspiration—prophets—are clearly distinguished from apostles. Finally, in the third place, apostles were not special stewards of local churches, administrators of ecclesiastical matters, because, again, special persons—bishops and deacons, who

can hardly be confused with apostles—were selected for this ministry.*
Without doubt insofar as apostles preached the Word of God, nothing
interfered with their prophesying as well, if inspiration from above
was found to be upon them; and Christian communities probably
also turned to them for higher guidance in all ecclesiastical matters.
In other words, they could perform all other holy ministries, they
could replace teachers as well as prophets and bishops, but the point
was that *nobody could replace them*. This, their distinctive and irreplace-
able character, did not consist in some kind of definite ministry, for
all ecclesiastical functions were assigned among teachers, prophets,
bishops, and deacons. If thus the differentiating property of apostle-
ship consisted not in a particular ministry, then it could consist only
in extraordinary authority. What kind of authority did the so-called
apostles have?

An apostle, that is, a *messenger*, assumes a sender, and it is clear
that the sender, who is above the one being sent, imparts to the latter
all his authority. If we find "apostles"—who nobody sent anywhere
and who were not authorized by any higher power—in the medieval
Waldensians or in the recent Irvingians, then this originates evidently
in the fact that "apostles" of these sects are only an artificial imitation
of such an office of the ancient church, the meaning of which is unclear
for the imitators.[5] But there could not be similarly artificial inventions
in the first century church itself. If messengers are being spoken of here,
then they probably somehow in fact were sent and were empowered.
It is just as sure that higher authorities in the church of Christ could
descend either directly from Christ or from those whom He Himself
made participants of His power in the church, that is, from those of
His disciples that are called apostles in the strictest sense of this word.
If our artifact was composed in the eighth decade of the first century,
then among the "apostles" (in the broad sense) that are being spoken
about there could also be direct disciples of Christ from among the
seventy: but the greater part of these "apostles" certainly consisted
of those having received their authority not from Christ himself, but

---

*In the fifteenth chapter of Didache where it speaks of the installation of bishops and
deacons, it is said that they also perform the ministry of *prophets and teachers* in the
church (υμιν γαρ λειτουργουσι και αυτοι την λειτουργιν των προφητων και διδασ-
καλων), but it is not stated that they could replace apostles. Only a Russian translator
in "Works of the Kievan Ecclesiastical Academy" places "apostles" in place of "teachers"
with surprising daring, to which can be compared only his translation of the words:
ου παντων δε—by the words: "but that is still not everything." We will have to return
to these two oddities of the translation, which is in general rather correct.

from the twelve by whose authority our Didache consecrates its instructions at the very beginning.

Thus, we see that the continuity of the consecrated path of Christ, or the plenitude of hierarchic power going successively from Christ through the twelve apostles, existed as well in the era that is shown in Didache. The hierarchical principle had its actual implementation as well in the church of that time, even if the particular methods of this implementation had not yet become established, had not entered into a monotonous system and were very much distinct from current forms. The chief distinction consists here in the fact that the aggregate of current bishopric power and ministry were not yet then centered in the hands of one person for each local church: the higher and universal aspect of hierarchical ministry was represented then by so-called apostles, and the lower and local functions were performed by elected persons who carried the title bishop, which thus corresponded to the current significance of this word only in part. But if as a result of this we do not have the right to identify the bishops of that time with those of today, then it would be equally unjust to maintain that at that time there was no higher prelate power, which is today represented by bishops, at all: this power also existed then, but it only belonged to persons with another title, namely, with the title apostle, since only the lower attributes of hierarchical ministry corresponded to the calling of bishop. Similar to the way that the title of imperator belonged at first to ordinary commanders, and subsequently came to signify higher power, so too the title of bishop, which expresses today a higher consecrated power in the church, originally belonged to ordinary delegated administrators or ecclesiastical overseers. But just as autocratic rulers existed under other names before they came to call themselves imperators, so too the prelates of the church existed under other names before they came to call themselves bishops.

It goes without saying that in cities where direct apostles of Christ themselves installed ecclesiastical representatives from among local Christians, such representatives combined in themselves both the power of prelate and the office of ecclesiastical overseer upon the departure of the apostles from their church, at which they certainly could not call themselves apostles (for they were not being sent anywhere, but remained in one place) and probably carried the title of bishop, which *in such cases* corresponded to the current usage of this word. In general there are neither grounds nor necessity to assume that the hierarchical connection of the church was manifested in an identical manner. There were cities (predominantly metropolises of the ancient world) where direct messengers of Christ themselves installed bishops, who were also made successors of their prelate power. In other cities or entire regions they left their disciples with full plenary power to build a legitimate ecclesiastical administration (for example, Titus, left by the Apostle Paul on the island of Crete). But there were also local churches (and probably they were the majority) where the business took place otherwise, and namely, as it is described in Didache. Messengers (αποστολοι) arrived who had their authority from the direct disciples of Christ and carried from them the blessing of the Lord to a local church, and set about using it just as the Lord himself. Having instructed the church by their counsel, these traveling prelates then continued on their way that very day or at the latest the following day, and the church consecrated by them continued to be governed on its own by means of bishops and deacons installed by the entire community. We have no trustworthy information about how, in the time that followed, prelate power was transferred from "apostles," who were consecrated from above for universal ministry, to the hands of ordinary bishops elected by local communities of Christians. There is no doubt only that in the second century this transition was already an accomplished fact. With all the importance of this fact it does not, however, follow to overexaggerate its significance. The point was not at all in the creation of a new hierarchical power, but only in the *securing* of that which was continuously done in the church from the very beginning. Peripatetic prelates of the first century settled in places and united their higher universal authority with the office of local ecclesiastical administrators, having received from the latter as well the title bishop, as more corresponding to their new manner of life. And since bishops could already in the era of Didache replace prophets and teachers, then, having received higher prelate authority through the uniting of their office with apostolic plenary power, the newly formed episcopate naturally could all the more concentrate in itself the prophetic and teaching ministry, that is, the work of the moral and intellectual upbringing and guidance of Christian people. But the more the significance of bishops as chief pastors of the church was elevated and became more complex, the more necessary became the education of other lower degrees of pastorship. And special hierarchical degrees of elders and deacons, which in the apostolic church acquired only *initiating authority*, appeared more clearly, stood out and, so to speak, congealed out of the common form of pastoral ministry, by measure of how the first ecclesiastical "overseers" were installed in place of apostles and prophets. Nothing at all is said in our artifact about elders, and deacons are mentioned alongside and inseparably with bishops as two ministries of one form and significance.

Thus, the data of our artifact lead us to the following conclusions with respect to the ecclesiastical establishment:

1. *A continuity of hierarchical succession and a universal bond of local churches was preserved* (in the period of Didache's composition) *by means of peripatetic apostles, which were actual prelates of the time;*

2. *The hierarchical structure of the church was found in embryonic form, differing, on the one hand, by an insufficiency of centeredness, for prelate power was not connected inseparably from the power of ecclesiastical administration, but existed also on its own, and, on the other hand, differing by an insufficiency of partition, for the degrees of elder-ship and deacon-ship had not yet been established and were not separated clearly out of the common office of ecclesiastical administration.*

Crossing over to the dogmatic content of our artifact, we find here, apart from faith in a living personal God, a completely distinct confession of the Lord Jesus as Christ (Messiah), a son of David and the son of God, who communicated to people a principle of new spiritual life, who founded the church as a rudiment of the Kingdom of God, and who would have to come a second time for the full realization of this Kingdom of God before the demise of the earthly world and the resurrection of all dead saints. Thus, we conclude in this respect that in the era of Didache's composition:

3. *Christian teaching was by no means limited to moral instructions or rules of the good life alone, but were founded upon a positive dogmatic truth about Christ-the-Savior, and in Him and through Him about the resurrection of the dead and eternal life;*

4. *Dogmatic teaching of the church existed then only in its original simple basics and, in the absence of more particular or detailed dogmatic definitions, free opinions and interpretations were ascertained in which more or less important mistakes were possible for believers.**

Finally, with respect to sacraments, in speaking about baptism and the Eucharist the author of Didache undoubtedly has in view

---

*One such mistake is found in Didache itself, as we will see further on.

actual mysteries. This is apparent already from the place where it is instructed to allow only those baptized in the name of the Lord to the holy table, for the Lord said concerning this: "Give not that which is holy to dogs" [Mt 7:6]. If the unbaptized are compared to dogs, to which one must not give what is holy, then it is clear that baptism could not represent an ordinary rite or symbol. At the same time, since by this holy thing that is forbidden to cast to the dogs we understand precisely the Eucharist, then it is evident that this was not simply a table, and consequently Eucharistic prayers were not a simple thanksgiving for food and drink. However, it must be noted that the manner of celebration of these sacraments represents an extreme degree of simplicity in the exposition of Didache. In particular the method of celebration of the Eucharist has little outward likeness to our mass [*obednia*]. Our artifact still speaks of penance and confession of sins in the church, but whether any kind of mystical significance is ascribed to this—or only purely moral acts are understood—is difficult to resolve. Thus, we conclude that at the time of our artifact's composition:

5. *Special sacred acts (baptism and the Eucharist) existed in the church, through which a mysterious blessed meaning was acquired and which had exceptional importance in the life of Christians;*

6. *The celebration of these sacred acts does not represent in this era the fullness that it acquired in subsequent times.*

Generally speaking, we find that in the ancient church that is described by our artifact:

7. *There existed all the positive principles of church life that later grew into a complex system of hierarchical relations, dogmatic definitions and sacramental sacred acts; but all this existed only in primary contours and did not have the complete and fixed form that the later church presents.*

Two views on the character of earliest Christianity are decisively undermined by the data found in the newly discovered artifact: first, the view that wants to reduce Christian religion to a single teaching of morality without any dogmatic foundations and claim that the sacraments conforming to this view are only later artificial additions; and, second, the contrary view that maintains all the sacraments as well as the forms and hierarchical and dogmatic definitions that exist today in the church have existed unchangingly from the very beginning *in the very same form* and with the very same significance as now. Both these views—both rationalism and ancient belief*—are concordant among themselves in that they both *resolutely deny any development in the church*; for, in accordance with the first of them, the fullness of ecclesiastical forms, existing historically, did not develop from within the Christian religion itself, but consists of arbitrary (according to some even malevolent) inventions of individual ecclesiastical people; in accordance with the second view, all the fullness of ecclesiastical forms and definitions was given from the beginning in a prepared form and did not therefore require any inward increase and development.

Our artifact testifies in a dazzling way against the tendency of the first, rationalistic view, which strives to extract from Christianity its very soul and leave a visible body of dead works alone; it so testifies when it situates the sacraments of baptism and the Eucharist in such a prominent place, when it places at the foundation of all its teaching the truth of a Messiah who has come, and assumes as the crown of its hopes the very same Messiah coming in a *miraculous* manner, not for the purpose of establishing a peaceful and satisfactory life on earth, but for the purpose of destroying this world, gathering His church of the living, *resurrecting* His church of the dead and creating on their foundation a new miraculous and mysterious Kingdom of God. Our artifact testifies in a dazzling way to the superrational character of ancient Christianity as well, and the Gospel formula of baptism in the name *of the Father and the Son and the Holy Spirit* adopted by it—a higher teaching of Christian theology, unattainable to ordinary reason is predetermined in it. Didache even includes an element hostile to reason in the realm of moral instructions and rules of life—namely, the *ascetic* element, formally defined at that (fasts on certain days of the week).

But our valuable artifact just as eloquently also testifies against the old believer view of the church as an absolutely immobile disposition of once and for always determined forms and attitudes; it so testifies by the indication of a completely different hierarchical *organization* (with an identity of hierarchical *principle*); it so testifies by the indeterminacy of its dogmatic concepts; it so testifies by an extreme simplicity of celebration of the sacraments set forth by it.

And the immutable and indisputable testimony of our Didache is so much against both aforementioned views that the adherents of

---

*Unfortunately, we encounter the latter as well among those who do not consider and do not call themselves old believers.

the one and the other, not having any hope to reinterpret this testimony in their favor, had to resort to desperate means for the sake of self defense—to the distortion of the artifact itself expressly in a false translation of it. So the anonymous translator of Didache in one Moscow journal, striving to exclude from this work all that is sacramental and sacred, arrived at the point that he rendered the prohibition to receive the Eucharist by the unbaptized as a prohibition to sit down to eat with those that had not washed.

Another translator handled it much more subtly and skillfully (in "Works of the Kievan Ecclesiastical Academy," No. 11, 1884), obviously holding to a certain teaching about the church's absolute immobility. His translation is generally subtle and satisfactory, nor would it be possible to publish a "willful travesty" of a historical artifact in an academic organ. All the changes the academic translation permitted itself was one word in place of another in a single place, and then a single phrase in place of another. It seems to us that in reading Didache it must be clear for anyone having any kind of ecclesiastical-historical and theological conceptions (and all the more for the learned theologians of the Kievan Academy) that in the church of that time prelate authority belonged to peripatetic "apostles," and bishops were only elected overseers of local churches. But if there was a bifurcation of hierarchical power that does not exist anywhere now, then this means that a rather significant change took place in the hierarchical structure of the church, and it is this that the theory does not want to allow. What do we do here? The Didache truly says that bishops (and deacons) performed the ministry of prophets and teachers. But did prophets and teachers really have the authority of prelates? This would mean that something is incorrect. Only one thing remains: to put "apostles" in place of "teachers"; everything will then apparently be here as it should: apostles were undoubtedly prelates, and if bishops (of that time) could always replace them, then this means they were also actual prelates, which was what was necessary to prove.

However, the inventive translator dropped two things from view in this: in the first place, in ascribing to bishops of the time the prelate authority of apostles, one must ascribe the very same to deacons, for it is said about them in Didache that they can fulfill the ministry of prophets and teachers (that is, according to our translator—of apostles) indivisibly with bishops. And in the second place, something even more inconvenient occurs as a result of this spurious word in the translation; for here in Didache it is said that the community itself laid hands directly on bishops, that is, simple souls did this (χειροτονησατε ουν εαυτοις επισκοπους κτλ); if the bishops of that time possessed prelate authority as apostles, in accordance with the translator, then it comes out that they received these apostolic plenary powers from the local community, from their own flock, from simple souls(!!!). Thus, in wanting to assert an absolute invariability of hierarchical forms, our academic translation unnoticeably throws overboard the very hierarchical principle of the church, and in straining gnats it unnecessarily swallows a camel [Mt. 23:24]. Another gnat, against which the Kievan translator used means just as impermissible, is presented in the three small words οὐ πάντων δὲ at the end of the last chapter, where a future resurrection of the dead is spoken about: "but not all of them," notes our artifact, "and as it is said: the Lord will come and all the saints along with him." The words introduced present some real difficulty for purposes of an antihistorical theory denying any development of dogmas and maintaining that all points of dogmatic teaching accepted today had an obligatory designation from the very beginning. And so? Should one repudiate the theory because of three paltry words? It is much easier to put others in their place: in place of "but not all of them" say: "but this is still not all." It is somewhat similar; moreover, it has a different meaning, and yet almost no meaning at all. But then the theory regarding the same points in ecclesiastical dogma being obligatory once and for always for everyone is salvaged in the eyes of the majority of readers not inquiring of the original. It is possible to sacrifice historical truth as well as Greek grammar for purposes of such an excellent aim.*

If two contradictory theories that both deny the development of the church are exposed in falsehood with respect to the newly discovered artifact—as resorting to a distortion of the artifact itself in order to be saved from such exposure—then they themselves sign their own death sentence by this. On the other hand, a theory that finds for itself in the newly discovered artifact only confirmation and not the slightest contradiction of exclusive significance, by the same token obtains the best justification and testimony of its truth. The eastern church's theory of the development of the church as a living organism is just such a theory. This theory confirms an absolutely essential changelessness of dogmas, sacraments, and the church hierarchy, and at the same time allows for diverse changes of all particular definitions of ecclesiastical life in all three of its chief spheres—but only changes that descend from within in accordance with given common forms,

---

*Even more points stretched in favor of an antihistorical view about the immobility of ecclesiastical life are presented in the article of Fr. Soloviev, published in January of this year in the volume "Readings of the Society of Devotees of Spiritual Enlightenment."

by the path of organic growth and increase of the church itself. In accordance with this theory, at the critical period that is described in Didache, the church had to present precisely the very picture that we actually find in our artifact.

There was an essential hierarchy—consecrated from above—in the succession of authority of peripatetic apostles. But the particular forms of hierarchy did not then resemble the current ones—there was neither an actual integrity nor an actual partition in them. Thus it comes out according to our theory, and thus it turns out to have been in actual fact. Further, there was a fundamental dogma of Christian revelation, and it was already possible to distinguish in it certain particular vital truths, but even more was clouded and indeterminate. Here, too, our theory completely conforms with reality. There were, finally, actual sacraments—baptism, the Eucharist, perhaps penitence—but far from such defined forms as are now celebrated in the church.

There are people who can in no way reconcile in their minds the idea of an acorn with the idea of an oak. Some of them clutch the acorn and cry out that it alone is the actual plant with which it is possible to be fed, and that the oak was thought up afterwards for someone else's use. Others are struck to the contrary by the grandeur of the oak, and in no way want to concede that such a powerful tree arose from such an unimportant little thing as an acorn. They even cry out that this contradicts Orthodoxy, that all this is a fabrication by ungodly Protestants and Catholics.

The sure knowledge of the fact that the great oak came from a small acorn does not hinder us from residing under its blessed shade.

6

The Talmud and Recent Polemical Literature Concerning It in Austria and Germany

We have frequently happened to read and hear opinions such as the following one: "The Jewish problem could be easily resolved; it would be possible to reconcile with the Jews completely and to give them full civil and social rights if only they would renounce the Talmud, which feeds their fanaticism and segregation, and if they would return to the pure religion of the Mosaic Law, as, for example, the Karaites profess."[1]

Imagine that in some country where the Orthodox Church does not enjoy the favor of the government and of the majority of the population—let's say in Austria—words such as the following were propagated in the press and society:

> We will reconcile willingly with the Orthodox and will not restrict their rights, but only if they decisively repudiate their ecclesiastical rules and customs, the ancient scholastic trash of theirs called "teachings of the fathers of the church," and finally, such monuments to superstition and fanaticism as the "Lives of the Saints"; let them return to the pure teaching of the Gospel, as, for example, the Herrnhuters or Molokans profess."[2]

Adversaries of our church would be able to find points in our traditions to support them in justifying such a requirement, just as adversaries of Judaism find in the Talmud. Anyone who has looked into, for example, the so-called Kormchie [*Books of Canon Law*], by which our church governed itself over the course of many centuries, knows what kind of absurd and ignorant inventions fed the enmity of Orthodox toward other professions of faith. And, if in modern

121

times the Russian government found it necessary to compile for the leadership of our church the so-called Book of Rules, from which all the wild fables of the ancient Kormchie have been excluded, then similarly the antiquated portions of the Talmud lose their authority and compulsory character for truly faithful Jewish people as well. However, it is much easier to get rid of antiquated traditions and laws than the old and bad habit of measuring everything by two different standards and finding for oneself only mitigating circumstances and for others only onerous ones. In the evaluation of the Talmud and Talmudic Jews that follows below, we have attempted, first of all, to hold to the highest rule of Judeo-Christian morality: treat another as you would want him to treat you.

The Talmud is the literary expression of an organic model that was produced by the life of the Jewish nation over the course of many centuries after it lost its political independence. When the kingdom declined and the prophets fell silent, the sole foundation of national life remained the holy teaching (Torah), given to Moses on the holy mount. Three directions of religious-national life were embodied in the three well-known parties (sometimes incorrectly called sects) in the Jewish nation, namely, the Sadducees, Pharisees, and Essenes, and the different attitudes that they had to the holy relic they held in common developed with an intrinsic logical necessity. The particulars of these parties are all known, but their all-round profound meaning and their relationship to Christianity are often represented in a single light. The Torah was for the Sadducees a foundation upon which they did not want to build anything. Taking the religion mainly from its ritualistic, priestly aspect, they saw in it a fact of the past that was necessary to acknowledge and to preserve immutably, but that did not obligate one to any kind of further action. For them the established ancient teaching was a matter accomplished once and for always, an immutable relic, immovable and inviolable. But when religion is thus reduced to archaic rituals and sacrifices, to a memory of the past alone, then real life is betrayed and sacrificed to bad passions and interests that have nothing in common with religion. And the Sadducees, these guardians of the foundations, these zealots of ancient piety, in fact really turned out to be a party of self-interested oligarchs who abused religion and deceived the people. Depending on circumstances, they now awakened national fanaticism, now slavishly served and gratified the Romans, provided that they could preserve their ruling position in the Temple and Sanhedrin.

But apart from the obvious self-interest and dubious patriotism of the Sadducees, the very principle of this party was undermined by internal contradiction. Displaying as its standard the preservation of the Torah without any additions, Sadduceeism had at the same time to acknowledge the significant part of the Torah as a dead letter, not allowing any application to reality. But the greater part of the social-juridical and economic enactments of Mosaic legislation required completely different arrangements in social life than those that were maintained in the era of the second temple, under the dominant influence of the same caste of priests out of the midst of which Sadduceeism was formed. Thus, the latter became corrupted and succumbed to its own principle of preservation: religious conservatism requires the devout oversight of Torah's ancient revelation, but social conservatism forced the maintenance and defense of an order that was resolutely opposed to both the spirit and the letter of Mosaic legislation. Either extreme inconsistency or extreme lack of principle was necessary in order to stand at one in the same time both for the inviolability of the Mosaic Law and the inviolability of the order of things that was maintained during the reign of the Idumaeans [Edomites]. Here is why the more consistent or more sincere of the Sadducees left the faith of their fathers and openly put themselves under the banner of a foreign power and pagan ideas. Such were the Herodians, which the Gospel mentions, and the Epicureans, which are often spoken about in the Talmud.

With respect to the people who felt sincere loyalty to the national religion, they had to search for another way out and found it in Phariseeism. The Pharisees, together with their opponents, the Sadducees, acknowledged Torah as the immutable foundation of religion, but for them this Torah was not only just a fact of the past alone, which was necessary to revere, but also the law of the here-and-now, one that had to be fulfilled. The Pharisees did not want to allow a contradiction between the requirements of the religion and actual life; for them all life should go according to religious law, but the Divine commandments must be realized in all human affairs. At the same time that the Sadducees were establishing the Divine Law only in a *mechanistic* connection with a reality that was alien to it and valued it only as an extrinsic safeguard of the Jewish nation—as some kind of palladium of Jerusalem—the Pharisees, on the contrary, related to the religion *organically*, saw in the Mosaic Law an essential and integral form of national life. However, it was not easy to realize this view. In their simple, literal meaning, many statutes of Torah turned out to be not easy to fulfill in different historical circumstances, while, on the other hand, many newly arising vital complications were not provided for by Mosaic legislation. Meanwhile, either leaving any of the God-given laws unfulfilled or basing a situation's solution on any foreign principle identically meant undoing the law. Thus, in order to protect the law in a positive manner from ruination, in order to preserve it not as a dead and unnecessary letter, but as an actual principle of life here-and-now, it needed to develop by means of a complex system of elucidations, commentaries, and casuistic distinctions. Through this the higher authority of the ancient law was preserved as well, and at the same time, being adaptable to the changes of the living milieu, the law was preserved from extinction, and acquired the sturdiness of a living force for all times.

Phariseeism adopted as its motto a certain saying of the great Sanhedrin: *it is necessary to build a wall around the law.*

Thus, if for the Sadducees, as we noted, the law was the foundation on which they did not want to build anything, then for the Pharisees, on the contrary, it was the point of origination for an entire series of exegetical, casuistic, and legendary constructions—in appearance as fantastic and incoherent as life itself. These constructions, accumulating over the course of six or seven centuries, were, ultimately, assembled by the work of later gatherers of information into the single huge labyrinth of the Talmud.

But there had to appear side by side with the two Judaic parties that we just examined amidst religious Jews yet a third.[3] If for the Sadducees the word of God was only a concluded *fact of the past*, if the Pharisees made out of it a law of present life, then there had to be found also people who saw in it first of all an *ideal of the future*. These people, who took the name Essenes, did not search in religion for an extrinsic buttress for self-interested endeavors, nor for practical guidance in daily life, but for higher perfection and blessedness. If the Sadducees valued only the power of fact in their worldly wisdom, if the Pharisees elevated every fact to its moral-legal basis, subordinated life to law in their endeavors at formal justification, then the Essenes concerned themselves neither with the force of fact nor with the formal basis of action, but solely with the higher *goal* for which both facts and actions exist. If the first Judaic party related to religion mechanically and the second organically, then the third held to a *purely spiritual* understanding of religion. However, an absolute advantage of this religious party before the others was not at all confirmed by this. Exclusive spirituality and unilateral idealism could be even less fruitful than the worldly wisdom of the Sadducees or the moral-juridical formalism of the Pharisees. The place of higher goals is the Kingdom of Heaven, it is not given freely, but is taken by force.[4] Therefore, those who find themselves on the earthly path must willy-nilly ponder the factual buttresses and the formal foundations across which it is possible more surely to arrive at the goal. The axiom "he who wants a goal, wants the means" is fully applicable here; these are: right and force, law and power. And if he who chases after these proximate means forgets the higher goal and deserves judgment, then he who only dreams about ideal perfection, not making a practical step in order to draw nearer to it, is extremely pitiful.

The origin and fortunes of the Essene party comprise a question that has not yet been resolved by historical research. In any case it is without doubt that at the same time that the Sadducees divided their life between temple rites and political intrigues, at the same time that the Pharisees built innumerable fences around the law with an arduous zeal and a stubborn love of the task, more than a small number of Israelites who had retreated to places in the wilderness and had built their life on communal principles gave themselves over to occupations of another kind: they prayed, fasted, sang psalms, and awaited the Kingdom of God. The latter characteristic makes the Essenes, without doubt, harbingers of Christianity. In other respects Christianity has its historical roots not in the Essenes, but in Pharisaic rabbinism. It is not subject to any doubt that the predominant form of evangelical preaching (the parable) does not have in itself anything specifically Christian, but is a typical form of Talmudic *haggadah.** Further, the reader will see that the affinity here is sometimes confined to the form of exposition alone. In general, there was no need to invent new material at the creation of the temple of the new covenant; Christ and His apostles utilized the bricks that they had at hand for the task. Even the very plan of construction was not new in its parts, but in their unification, in the *whole* of the religious ideal. The evangelical idea united in itself in the closest way that which was positive and true in the three Hebrew parties. The principle of religious power and worldly wisdom, which the Sadducees held to and which they abused, was not repudiated by Christ, but received higher sanctification and confirmation from Him ("All *power* has been given unto Me" [Mt 28:18], "be as *wise* as serpents" [Mt 10:16]), just as the Pharisaic principle of law and justification by works was decisively confirmed in the teaching of Christ, who came not to destroy the law but to fulfill it, and who required from His disciples fruitful actions of true faith. Thus, that which was true in the ways of the Sadducees and Pharisees was in agreement with the way of the Gospel, and the same thing that the Essenes dreamed about—the Kingdom of God and His truth—was elevated as the goal of the Way.

---

*Everything in the Talmud that does not relate directly to the law, but has a religious-instructive and poetical character is called *haggadah.*

But it is precisely through such a synthesis of these diverse religious ideas and principles that their negative aspects were destroyed, and everything that was false in them. In this respect we find in the Gospel a relentless denunciation of all three Hebrew parties. Here is denounced the materialism of the Sadducees, who, resting on earthly power, lost any receptivity to the forces of a higher order ("in error, not knowing the scriptures, neither the power of God" [Mk 12:24], etc.); here is denounced the formalism of the Pharisees, which forced them to forget the spirit and goal of the law itself in their striving for legality and righteousness of action; and with respect to the Essenes, the one-sidedness of their contemplative and ascetic idealism is not denounced by words, but by the entire active character of the earthly life of Christ, His struggles and exploits.

The fact that the Gospel is especially occupied precisely with the Pharisees, and that entire chapters are filled with strong polemics against them, does not at all prove that Christianity was some kind of antithesis to Phariseeism, as it is usually presented. The issue was that the Pharisees were chiefly leaders and teachers of the people, and therefore the new religious teaching collided with them, first of all, as soon as it turned to the people. Neither the Sadducees nor the Essenes, generally speaking, appeared as preachers and teachers on the street and in the synagogues. In order to argue with the Essenes, it was necessary to go into the wilderness, and in order to denounce the priestly aristocracy (apart from exceptional occasions), it was necessary to go into its palaces. If at present someone wanted to develop some kind of religious social idea in Christian society, then he would not have to argue mainly with highly placed persons of spiritual and worldly rank—not with Athos monks, but with journalists, litterateurs, and professors—in a word, with the representatives of the so-called intelligentsia, which the Pharisaic teachers were at the time of Christ. Only when it came down to a matter of blood did the experts of blood sacrifice—the Sadducees—come to the fore; and, combining the holy mystery of the chief priest with the manifest wisdom of secular politics, they prominently announced: *it is better for us that one man die* [Jn 11:50].[5]

With respect to the Pharisees, it is fully apparent that Christ's denunciations were directed against the exclusive and one-sided development that yielded the principle of formal legalism in Phariseeism, which in practical application unavoidably led to falseness and hypocrisy. But then it is easy to become convinced of the fact that the Gospel does not subject to absolute condemnation the very principle of Phariseeism in general, but on the contrary, fully acknowledges its positive content, if one only recalls the words the most powerful preaching of Christ against the Pharisees begins with: "The scribes and pharisees sit in Moses' seat. *All, therefore, of whatever they bid you observe, observe and do that,* but do not their works, for they say but do not" [Mt 23:2–3].[6]

Thus, the Gospel, reproaching the Pharisees first of all in the fact that they do not carry out their teaching *in actions,* by the same token justifies Phariseeism's principle, which consists precisely in requiring *the enactment of law.* Christ does not say: acts are not necessary; on the contrary, He says: acts are necessary, but you do not do them. How many times would these reproaches be amplified if one were to address them to contemporary Christian society? Christ required from His disciples that their righteousness be greater than the righteousness of the scribes and Pharisees. But for us even the latter apparently constitutes an unattainable ideal. The Pharisees, at least in principle, did not allow the separation of religion from life, law from activity. On the contrary, their constant efforts were directed at all human acts being a fulfillment of the Divine law. They taught the observation of it, and Christ said about it: observe and do. Since that time, we have succeeded in elevating to a principle the contradiction between the requirements and conditions of societal life, between the Divine commandments and all our reality. Here is why Phariseeism, which was consolidated in Talmudism, was not and could not be abolished by historical Christianity to this day.

After the Essenes were absorbed by the new religion, and the Sadducees, who lived by temple and sacrifice, disappeared with the destruction of the temple and with the cessation of sacrifices, the Pharisees alone remain the representatives of all the Jewish nation, and the collection of their teachings, the Talmud, becomes the religious-national codex of all Jews. It is striking that, just as after the Babylonian captivity the first act of Jews was the editing of the Bible, after the final Roman blow too, hardly having collected themselves, the Jews immediately dedicate themselves with zeal to the collecting and editing of the Talmud. The national calamities that overtook them prompted Jews to hold to their religious law more firmly and to learn it more deeply, for they saw the true reason for all their calamities in the insufficient knowledge and fulfillment of this law. And if at the time of Ezra the religious law consisted only in the Torah of Moses, then at the time of the Roman pogrom, as a result of increasingly complicated understandings and attitudes, an entire collection of interpretations and supplements of ancient teachings and wise men (*amorim* and *shannaim*) was required for the religious-moral construction of the private and community life of the Jews—that is, the Talmud was required. And here, soon after the revolt of Bar-Kochba and the final destruction of Jerusalem, Rabbi Jehuda ha-Kadosh gathers together the basic part of the Talmud—the "Mishnah"—and commits it to writing.* And later, when on the stage of universal history the fierce struggle of paganism with Christianity was supplanted by the even more intense and fierce struggle within Christianity itself (the great heresies of the fourth and fifth centuries), and the external triumph of the church reinforced its internal troubles—at this time an outwardly dispersed but inwardly concentrated Jewish people, having concealed itself in dark corners of Palestine and Mesopotamia, unearthed for itself a distinctive instrument for self-defense: two huge collections of further casuistic interpretations and legendary supplements; the Jerusalem and Babylonian *gemara*† were joined to the Mishnah, and thus was completed the sure fence around the Jewish nation that was called the "Talmud."

The religious-national segregation of the Jewish nation was insured by the Talmud for many centuries. Was this segregation necessary, were the Jews correct, separating themselves from the entire world by a wall of Talmudic law? Before essentially answering this question, we want to give readers who are not at all familiar with the Talmud some practical idea about the normative spirit of this monument. Here for a start are several Talmudic sayings and parables:

A Gentile who occupies himself with the Divine Law (Torah) is equal to a high priest.

One who is illegitimately born, if he is learned, is more respected than an ignorant high priest.

One of the gentiles came to Shamai and said: "teach me, but only under the condition that you communicate to me the whole Torah in the time that I am able to stand on one leg." Shamai hit him with a yardstick, which he had at hand, and threw him out. The gentile turned then to Hillel, who fulfilled his desire, saying: "do not do unto another what you do not want done unto you,—in this is the source of the entire law, the rest is only detail; now go and learn."

A man must not say: "I will begin to study the law so that they will call me wise; I will learn the Mishnah in order to be called

---

*"Mishnah" means reiteration (i.e., reiteration of the law); it consists of sixty-three treatises, arranged according to six sections, which embrace all the religious and life attitudes of the Jewish people in unbroken connection.

†"Gemara" means completion or complement.

Rabbi and stand at the head of the school." He must not view learning either as a crown to be decorated with, or as an axe by which
sustenance is attained.

The goal of wisdom is good deeds and the improvement of life;
and for those who do not do good out of love of good, it would have
been better if they were not created.

Another saying: let a man occupy himself with the Torah and
good deeds, even if it is not for their sake alone, for with time he
will do this for their sake alone.

All is predestined by the Lord, however, the actions of a man
are free. The world is governed by goodness, and the will of man is
recognized by the abundance of his good deeds.

No one can harm even a finger, if it is not destined by God.

In the other world it is not as it is here. There they do not eat
and do not drink and do not give themselves over to any sensual
enjoyment; there is no envy, no hate, no discord, but righteous men
with crowns on their heads rejoice in the reflection of Divinity.

Whoever fulfills even one obligation will acquire for himself a
defender, and whoever commits even one sin will call forth upon
himself an accuser.

Do the will of God as your own in order that He make His will
yours. To His will bring as sacrifice your own, in order that He bring
the will of others as sacrifice to you.

Whoever has a basket of bread to eat but worries about living
the following day belongs to those of little faith.

A man is obligated to thank God for evil as well as for good.

A man must speak before God only in few words.

Whoever can intercede for his neighbor in prayer and does not
do this is called a sinner.

Who is wise? He who learns from everything. Who is a hero?
He who conquers his passions. Who is rich? He who is satisfied with
his possessions. Who is respected? He who respects his neighbors.

An evil inclination resembles at first a pilgrim, then a guest,
and finally, a master.

God says to the haughty: we can not both live in the world.

Whoever humbles himself, God will extol, and whoever extols
himself, God will humble. Lordship will escape from him who strives
for it, and it will come unexpectedly to him who avoids it.

Whoever just raises a hand against a man in order to hit him,
even if he does not hit him, is nevertheless called lawless.

Whoever publicly shames anyone is the same as one who has
spilled blood.

It is better for a man to belong to the persecuted than to the persecutors.

A similar saying goes:

Whoever is offended and does not return offense, whoever hears an insult and does not respond to it, whoever endures with love and suffers with joy, to him is applied what is said: "the beloved of God will be as the sun, rising in their grandeur."

God forgives the sin of whoever forgives an offense borne by him.

Be meek and flexible as the reed, and not grim and proud as the cedar.

Let your *yes* be a real *yes*, and your *no*—a real *no*.

One must not deceive even a gentile.

The words of a slanderer are sins, crying to the heavens.

Hypocrites will not see God.

One must be cordial to all people.

According to importance, a benefactor of charity is equal to all other benefactors taken together.

Friendship is higher than charity.

Whoever scorns the obligation to be charitable to the poor must be considered the same as an idolater.

While the temple stood, the sacrifice atoned for the sins of people. Today when there is no longer sacrifice, an offering to beggars substitutes for the sacrifice and atones for sins.

Whoever has a wife that dies, it is necessary to pity him just as if the temple had been destroyed in his day.

If someone says to you: I searched and did not find, do not believe him; and if he says: I found and did not search, do not believe him either; if he says: I searched and found—believe this.

Whoever is able to calculate the course of heavenly lights and does not do it, to him is applied what is said: "they do not contemplate the creations of God and they do not see the works of His hands."

Rabbi Simeon ben-Levi said: The doors are open for whoever wants to be impure (immoral), that is, he will not have a shortage of convenient occasions, but whoever, oppositely, wants to be pure, will receive assistance in this. This situation was explained in the school of Rabbi Ishmael with the following parable. A man sold tar and balm. When someone came to buy tar, the seller said: the product is before you, weigh it out and take it. If someone wanted to buy balm, the seller said: wait, I will weigh you out, so that I smell good too.

Rabbi Isaac said that, although all are equal in the face of death, a special place has been prepared for each righteous man that conforms to his worthiness. This is illuminated by a parable. When the king with his servant enters into some city, then all of them come through one and the same gate; but when they stop there for a night's lodging, then to each is designated a place according to his rank.

Rabbi Eliazar taught: Repent of the day until you die. Then his students asked him: "Does a man know on what day he will die?"—This means—answered the Rabbi—that he must improve himself today, for he could die tomorrow; thus he will lead his entire life in repentance, as it is said: let your clothes always be white, and unction for your head not be spared. Rabbi Johannan added to this the following parable. A certain king invited his servants to a banquet, but did not announce its time in advance. The intelligent among them donned their best robes and awaited near the palace, supposing that everything is always ready there. The foolish left to take care of their affairs, thinking that long preparations are necessary for a kingly banquet. Suddenly the king called those invited. The intelligent appeared before him in clean and expensive clothes, the foolish rushed in their dirty robes. Then the king said: "Let those who appeared in clean clothes sit and eat; let those who turned out in dirty robes stand and gaze."

"When Moses ascended the mountain of God, archangels asked God: What does this one born of woman seek among us? He came—answered God—in order to receive the law—You mean—they continued—You are giving to a human being the treasure that has been preserved from the creation of the world over the course of 974 generations? What is man that You think of him, and the son of man that You look at him? Almighty is Your name, Lord, in all the earth, and Your grandeur shines in the heavens!—You retort—said God to Moses—I am afraid—said he—lest they burn me with the breath of their mouths—Take hold of My throne of glory and make them answer—Ruler of the universe—began Moses—What is found in the law that You want to give to me? Doesn't it begin thus: I am the Lord your God, who led you out of Egypt. But did you, angels, reside in Egypt or work for Pharaoh? Then why do you need such a law? Further it is said: There shall be no strange gods among you; but have you lived among idolaters? Later it is said: Remember the Sabbath day; but do you work so that you have need of rest? And again it is said: Do not swear falsely; but are there lawsuits among you? And it is also said: Honor your father and your mother; but do you have parents? And, finally, it is said: Do not kill, Do not commit adultery, Do not steal; but do such things exist among you?—and God approved of Moses, and the archangels came to like him."

This last parable gives us the dominant idea for the evaluation of the entire Talmud. The law is given to man, and not to angels. In other words, the law can not presuppose absolute perfection of those fulfilling it, for then the law itself would be unnecessary. The Talmud does not repudiate perfection as a goal, as a moral ideal. But precisely in order that this ideal does not remain an idle dream, it is necessary to concern oneself with the paths to its achievement, and these paths pass through the imperfect and wanton nature of man. Before realization of an absolute ideal man must learn to restrict his will, according to nature directed not so much to absolute moral perfection as to the satisfaction of his egoism. The restriction of will is the law, and here the Talmud and the rabbis put for themselves as a task to restrict the willfulness of man by the prescriptions of Divine Law everywhere and in everything, not leaving to personal arbitrariness any relationships in private and community life. They enumerated in Torah 248 positive prescriptions and 365 prohibitions, and then multiplied these 613 laws infinitely through their application to every possible personal circumstance. That all this multitude of laws is not a goal in and of itself even for Talmudists is clear now from the Talmud's instruction: the number of laws given on Sinai was reduced later by David to 11, by Isaiah to 6 and even 2, by Micah to 3 and, finally, by Habbakuk to one proposition: the righteous man shall live by his faith (*tsadik beemunato ikhei* [Hab 2:4]). Comparing this instruction with the above-introduced response of Hillel to a Gentile, it is possible to see that there is no contradiction *in principle* between the legalism of the Talmud and New Testament morality, which is founded on faith and altruism. The principal argument between Christianity and Judaism is not contained in the moral sphere, but in the religious-metaphysical sphere, in the question about the significance of the God-man and the atoning sacrifice of Christ. True, apart from this, one must acknowledge as well the fact that Talmudists and the people led by them in practice have forgotten or neglected the elevated ideal-moral views of their *haggadah* and have submerged themselves completely in the learning and application of the formal statutes of the Talmud (*halakhot*), a result of which in Judaism the principle of law or formal truth acquired decisive preponderance over the principle of mercy (*khesed*) and intrinsic truth (*emet*). Fully acknowledging this one-sidedness of Jewish development, we in no way will resolve to judge it absolutely in view of the opposite and still more pernicious extreme that the Christian world presents to us. If Talmudic Judaism transgresses proportion in its endeavors to reduce all details of community and personal life to religious law, then our pseudo-Christian world not only has effected in practice, but also has erected in principle a complete division between religious truth and real life, between religion and politics, between ideal norms, which among us turn into empty words, and practical relations, which we strive in every way to secure in their manifest abnormality. Talmudic Judaism rises up with all its essence against this godless principle, against this immoral division, and in this is its justification.

Religion is for Talmudists the law of human life—in this respect they stand wholly on the ground of the Mosaic Torah. *Ushmarshem et khukotai ota haadam vakhai bagem ani Yahweh* (Observe all My statutes and My ordinances, which if a man does, he shall live by them [Lev. 18:5]). This saying was manifestly justified in the national life of Jews. Only by observance of these statutes and ordinances, first given in Torah and then encompassed in the Talmud, is Judaism alive, unequaled in the world as to its durability as a nation. Anti-Semitism can serve as the best evidence of the national longevity of the Jews. The bitterness of this movement in any event testifies to the sturdiness of the Jewish nation. "Do not shove a drunkard, he will fall on his own," says a Talmudic proverb. Anti-Semites demonstrate by their intensified shoving the certitude that the Jewish nation firmly stands on its feet.

Logic, historical experience and the word of God teach us that the chief condition of *lasting power is truth*, that is, faithfulness to oneself, the absence of internal contradiction and bifurcation. Every kingdom divided against itself can not stand [Mk 3:24]. Struggle is a necessary element of life, but precisely only as a personal element that enters into the composition of a living unity. The Jewish nation is stronger than the contemporary Christian world because, although internal struggle undoubtedly exists within it, this exists only as a subordinate phenomenon, not abolishing the essential unity of the whole. But in the Christian world this unity has lost all practicability, has turned into an abstract idea, powerless against the quarrels of its separate parts. True, the difference here also partly depends on the fact that the Jews represent one nation, whereas the Christian world embraces a multitude of national elements. But where is the power of Christian *universalism*, which they usually contrast to the narrow national egoism of the Jews? If New Testament religion is powerless against the isolated action of nations, then the Jews are right to remain in the Old Testament religion, which directly and openly announces its national character. Thanks to this, they are saved from the internal contradiction that hangs over the majority of Christians, who confess a supranational religion and yet are absorbed by purely national interests, passions, and prejudices. It is striking, however, that the Jews are usually accused at the same time both of narrow nationalism and of cosmopolitanism. The point is that the national idea itself among Jews has a certain universal significance, which was announced to the biblical Abraham ("And all the nations of the earth shall be blessed in him" [Ge 18:18]); and if Jews do not want to acknowledge the realization of this worldwide mission of Israel in Christianity, then neither can we in conscience maintain that it has already been realized among us. And from our point of view the realization of the universal is still in the future; and in this future fulfillment of Christianity, according to the words of the Apostle Paul, a particular and special role will belong to the Jews. And it would in this respect be strange to place the Jewish nation—out of which, beyond the Mosaic religion itself, came both Christianity and Islam—side by side with one or another *separate* nationality. It is possible to compare the Jewish nation only with all the rest of humanity, to which it is related as a trunk to branches (of course, not from an ethnographic, but only from a spiritual-cultural point of view).[7]

Passing through the *entire* history of humanity, from its very beginning up to our day (which it is not possible to say about another single nation), the Jewish nation as if presents in itself *the axis* of worldwide history.

As a consequence of this central significance of the Jewish nation in historical humanity, all the positive, as well as all the negative, powers of human nature manifest themselves in this nation with particular vividness. Therefore accusing the Jews of all possible vices finds its basis in actual facts out of the life of the Jewish nation. But when they want to judge all the Jewish nation as a whole on the basis of these particulars, then it is possible only to be surprised at the boldness of the accusers. When national parties in various countries accuse the Jews of an insufficiency of patriotism, then it is decidedly impossible to understand how Jews, in remaining Jews, that is, a single nation, can combine in themselves the conflicting patriotisms of all the nations amidst which they live. True patriotism for Jews can consist only in the love of the Jewish nation, and in this, it seems, they have no insufficiency. And aren't reproaches of cosmopolitanism amusing, when directed against the single nation that has preserved all its national distinctiveness through horrific experiences since forgotten antiquity? They have preserved it to such a degree that the same ones who reproach this nation for cosmopolitanism are compelled to link this reproach to one that is directly contrary and, as has already been noted, to accuse cosmopolitans of narrow national isolation. And this last reproach is just as strange as the first. For where has there been a nation more receptive and open to foreign influences as the Jews, who, having learned the intrinsic spiritual essence of their own nationality, never valued it by its extrinsic natural properties, and even continuously changed their language: returning from Babylon, they spoke in Chaldean, in Alexandria they began to speak in Greek, in Baghdad and Cordoba in Arabic, and today they speak everywhere in a semi-German jargon, and moreover they have always and everywhere accepted the personal and family names of foreign nations and other faiths.[8]

Conservatives of various countries and faith confessions unanimously reproach the Jews for a special inclination to liberalism, and acknowledge them even as the direct originators and chief movers of the contemporary liberal movement in Europe. If so, then for our part it remains only to feel pity that Jews up to now have so poorly fulfilled their task in the country where truly liberal principles and systems would be especially needed both for the "people of the land" and the "sons of Israel" themselves. It is striking, however, that the Jews deduce their ideas of freedom and social truth from the Mosaic Torah itself—and not without reason. In such a respected antiquity, the progressive ideas of the Jews could with identical right be considered conservative and even retrograde, so that any of the parties into which civilized humanity is broken down can find for itself sympathetic elements in the Jewish nation; however, it is itself free from the irreconcilable contradiction among all these elements, but subordinates them all to its religious-national unity.

Due to the apparent groundlessness of the principal sweeping accusations against the Jewish nation, which contradict one another and are mutually invalidated, anti-Semites had to choose another more personal and concrete ground for their attacks. Ancient complaints have been renewed about the Jewish religious law contained in the Talmud; that it prescribes the chosen people to hate all those of other faiths, in particular Christians, and to inflict upon them all possible harm. In truth, there would be nothing surprising if there actually were such prescriptions in the religious books of the Jews. Is it really necessary to recall everything that Jews suffered at the hands of Christian nations in the Middle Ages, when the persecution against them achieved such atrocities that even such a strict zealot of militant Catholicism and resolute adversary of Judaism as Pope Innocent III had to publish a special edict in defense of the Jews (*constitutio pro*

Judaeis) where he, incidentally, prohibits Christians under penalty of excommunication from destroying Jewish graveyards and exhuming buried bodies *with the aim of extorting money?** It seems to us that all the accusations against Jews for their love of money and exploitation of Christians pale in the face of such evidence. But let us leave behind these acts long past. Let us recall something more proximate in time and place. It will probably be interesting, although hardly comforting, to many of our readers to point out that in Petersburg less than one hundred fifty years ago, in 1738, a Jew Leib Borukhov and a navy Captain-Lieutenant Voznitsyn were burned at the stake for the fact that the first of these converted the second to Judaism by means of discussion.†

Apart from the unaccountable antipathies and prejudices against the Jews, there still exist laws to this day in certain countries—Christian at least in name—that impose curses on the Jewish religion, separating the Jews from the rest of the population by means of an impenetrable wall, as if they were infected with pestilence.

In view of this, if decrees of a corresponding spirit with respect to Christians were contained in Jewish religious-historical codices then this would only be just. But are such decrees really found among the Jews? This question has been sufficiently elucidated thanks to the modern anti-Semitic movement. The point is that as long as the Jews themselves or their defenders among Christians maintained that there are no statutes in the Talmud prescribing hatred of Christians and harming them, it was possible to repudiate such protestations as biased. But now from amidst the anti-Semites themselves people who command more or less scholarly means for such a task, use all efforts in order *per fas et nefas* to track down that which they need, that is, laws that obligate Jews to hatred and enmity against Christians, in the Talmud and other religious-moral Jewish books. And if the result of all these researches and efforts is ultimately reduced to almost nil, then any unbiased person will be convinced that on these grounds at least the anti-Semites' undertaking is lost.

About fifteen years ago a bitter literary struggle (partly legal as well) began and has still not completely subsided to this day in Austria and Germany because of the Talmud. Two anti-Semitic works provided the chief cause for this struggle: *Der Talmudjude,* by a Professor Rohling, and *Der Judenspiegel, by* a Doctor Justus (pseudonym). An entire polemical literature for and against Judaism and, in part,

---

*Innocentii III, "Opera ed. Migne," v. I, col. 865.
†See *Complete Coll. of Legis.*, No. 7612.

for and against the Talmud, has grown around these two booklets.* The work by Justus, *Der Judenspiegel*, is especially interesting for us. Its author, who apparently has practical familiarity with Talmudic literature, tried to derive from it a whole series of positive statutes that prescribe and obligate, as he maintains, hatred and enmity for contemporary Jews toward Christians. He compiled a hundred of such "laws." True, their details were resolutely denied not only by Jews, but also by Christian scholars, including, incidentally, the well-known Hebraist and theologian Delitsch. But since more or less learned defenders also appeared for Justus, then readers who were not specialists could be placed in a very difficult position, not knowing whom to believe. Unfortunately for the anti-Semites, out of their midst a Doctor Ecker came forward as the most serious and reliable defender of Justus. Notwithstanding all the enmity toward Jews and all the bias displayed by him in favor of the author of *Judenspiegel*, Doctor Ecker was not able, however, to conceal the factual truth in this undertaking.† He verified all the references of Justus and reprinted all hundred of these "laws" of Justus in his booklet "Der Judenspiegel im Lichte der Wahrheit," and produced the corresponding texts literally in precise German translation after each of them. Thus, all that the critic later says from his personal point of view does not at all prevent an unbiased reader from making a proper judgment on all points. And, in the first place, it turns out that Justus did not at all take his laws right out of the Jewish religious-juridical codex (*Shul'khan-arukh*)‡ but compiled each law from several excerpts taken sometimes from various works of not identical merit and authority. For the most part, these excerpts are placed in Justus' work in a completely arbitrary connection among themselves, texts are confused with commentaries, generally

---

*We will name only those works that we were able to read: Dr. V. Hoffmann "Der *Schuichan-Aruch*" (1885); Dr. Joseph Kopp, "Zur Judenfrage" 2 (Aufl, 1886); Dr. Jakob Ecker, "Der Judenspiegeel im Lichte der Wahrheit" 2 (Aufl, 1884); Franz Delitsch, "Rohling's Talmudjude" 7 (Aufl, 1881); and "Zweite Streitschrift in Sachen des antisemitismus"; and "Neueste Traumgesich etc," (1883); and "Schachmatt den Blutlugnern etc" 2 (Abdr, 1883); Dr. M. Joel "Meine Gutachten uber den Talmud" (1887); Karl Fischer, "Gutmeinung uber den Talmud der Hebraer" (1883). Of these eight (counting Rohling and Justus themselves) authors *three* are anti-Semites, *two* Jews, and *three* Christians.

†The bias was so strong that a suspicion was voiced that Dr. Ecker gave only his name, and that the apologia was written by Justus himself. However, this suspicion appears to us to have little bearing to the truth.

‡*Shul'khan-arukh*, that is, a set table, composed by Rabbi Joseph Karo in the sixteenth century in Palestine and later reworked for European Jews by Rabbi Moses Isserlesom. This book relates to the Talmud nearly as our "Book of Rules" relates to the ancient "Kormchie."

obligatory statutes with particular opinions of Rabbis—and all this is transmitted only approximately, in his words: a poor method when the point *concerns laws*. But more striking is the fact that the strongest expressions of hatred toward Christians are simply inserted by Justus himself, and without any designation and without any proviso at that. We will introduce one from among the many examples. Under No. 23 in "Judenspiegel" we read this law: "Witnesses can be acknowledged only bearing a human name; but an *akum* (Christian), or Jew who has accepted Christianity, which is even worse than a natural Christian, absolutely can not be regarded as people, by virtue of which the evidence they show also has no significance." Here is a "law" that would be very dear to the anti-Semites, if only it were not false. In actual fact, the two texts of the Jewish codex on which Justus relies voice only the following: (1) a Gentile (*goi*) and a man not liberated (*ebed*) are not competent as witnesses. (2) false informants (*ha-mosrim*) and the godless (lit: epicureans—*ha-apikorosim*) and apostates are worse than Gentiles and are not competent as witnesses. Even if, in spite of the direct evidence of many authoritative rabbis, it is accepted that under Gentiles are understood Christians, then, in any case, there is not a word about the fact that they are not people in the adduced texts. We are prepared to concede that many centuries of inhumane attitude of Christian nations toward Jews succeeded in the eyes of the latter in obscuring the human worth of their persecutors and in squeezing out of the heart of Israel fraternal feelings toward the new Edom.[9] But the point here is not in feelings, but in positive law. We know, for example, that a hundred years ago Orthodox Cossacks, warring with the last remnants of "Rech Pospolita" [Poland] hanged together on a single tree everywhere they could a Jew, a Polish priest, and a dog with the inscription: "Yid, Polack, and dog—one faith."[*10] But who would decide to insert this saying into a citation from the code of laws of the Russian Empire or from the canonical decrees of the Orthodox Church without any provisos? But the inventors of pseudo-Talmudic laws act in precisely this way.

Turning further to the content of these hundred laws of Doctor Justus, we find among them an entire series of decrees that prohibits Jews to take any part, directly or obliquely, in the religious services of those of other faiths (of course, chiefly Christians) such as: obtaining water for baptism, selling candles for church, trading icons or holy books of Christians, greeting them or giving them gifts on their holidays, and so forth (nos. 58 and ff). Thus, guilt is placed on the Jews

*This fact is reported, incidentally, in *The History of the Fall of Poland*, by S. Soloviev.

even for the fact that, remaining Jews, they do not enter into religious intercourse with Christians! But will the latter even allow such contact? In any case, before placing a similar requirement on Jews, one would first expect the restoration of religious solidarity among those who confess Christianity themselves. Having just recently written these lines, I received from a Protestant missionary several issues of an American missionary journal, where it was stated, incidentally, that the chief obstacle to the conversion of Russians and Bulgarians to Christianity today consists in the fact that these nations consider themselves to be Christian!* On the other hand, an Orthodox spiritual orator from the ecclesiastical faculty contrasted the Russian cross [*krest*] and the Latin *cross* [*krzyz*] as two hostile principles. Under such conditions Jews have a prepared response to every reproach of ours about religious-national isolation, and to every one of our requirements concerning broad religious toleration: physician, heal thyself [Lk 4:23], or even: hypocrite! First take the log out of your eye and then you will see, how better to remove the speck out of your brother's eye [Lk 6:41].

It is difficult to believe that "Judenspiegel" reproduces, inciden-tally, as an accusatory document against the Jews, laws that prescribe great caution in contact with Christians, so that they not be exposed to death or some kind of serious harm. It would be a strange thing as well to prove that these laws, which were formulated in the sixteenth century, had more than enough foundation and cause; but in that case *for whom* are these laws prejudicial and shameful?

This is a rather sad theme. But there are also amusing places in the "Judenspiegel." Among this number, undoubtedly, belongs law no. 76, which prohibits Jews from taking their children to any kind of Christian schools. What a pity that our Ministry of National Education knew nothing about such a law (according to Dr. Justus's assurance, obligatory at present as well): this would have saved it from the task of allotting a standard percentage of Jews for Russian schools.

Ultimately, if one were to eliminate from the indictment examined by us everything that is false, inaccurate and incongruous, then there would remain seven or eight laws that anti-Semites, with a certain semblance of truth, could make use of for their goals. Decrees that permit a Jew not to return something found by him if it is lost by someone of another faith, or that give permission to a Jew to use

---

*If the point were about the poor fulfillment of Christian commandments in the life of the nation, then such a reproach would be just, though it would be applicable more or less to all confessions of faith. But the honorable missionary does not see our paganism in this, but simply and only in the fact that we belong to the Orthodox confession.

the errors of someone of another faith in monetary calculations, or, finally, that allow usury to those of other faiths (which is prohibited with respect to Jews).

It would be very surprising if the Jewish codex of the sixteenth century acknowledged an obligatory equality for Jews and Christians, when in the most enlightened Christian countries this equality was acknowledged only several dozen years ago, and in the country where the greatest amount of Jews is now found, they do not have full rights of citizenship to this day.

The Talmudic law that permits usury only with respect to those of other faiths is taken directly from the Mosaic Torah. But from which religious source do our pseudo-Christian states borrow the decrees that legalize usury for *all* without distinction? In any case, isn't it strange to require of Jews that they relate to us better than we relate both to them and to one another?

However, it must be noted that the decrees referred to have a negative character, expressing in themselves only a juridical boundary of immoral action, and in no way a positive moral requirement. The Talmud only allows but in no way prescribes and approves of the seizure of a thing lost by someone of another faith. And if the inventor of the hundred laws sometimes converts permission into prescription, then this is only one of his forgeries, as judged even by critics biased in his direction (for example, no. 36). In actual fact laws of this kind express only an extreme juridical-obligatory *minimum* of moral acts. But, containing in themselves only the least juridical requirement, these decrees do not exclude the greater moral requirement. On the contrary, such a moral requirement finds in the Talmud itself a positive basis in three definite principles that Jewish ethics can be proud of: in the principle of the "blessed name" (of God)—*kiddush ha-shem*, in the principle of "abuse of the name"—*khillul' ha-shem*, and in the principle of "paths of peace"—*darke-shalom*. *To bless the name* means to do good works, in order that true faith be glorified in them, to do more than the formal law prescribes, to do good not out of fear and not for one's honor, but for the glory of the God of Israel. Students of Rabbi Simon ben-Shetakh—as it is related in the Jerusalem Talmud—bought him an ass from a certain Saracen. There turned out to be an expensive pearl on the harness of the animal. "Does the seller know about this?"—asked the rabbi—"No,"—answered the students. "Then go quickly and return the treasure to him." When this was fulfilled, the Saracen exclaimed: "Glory to the God of the Jews!" This exclamation of the Gentile—it is moreover noted in the Talmud—was dearer to Rabbi Simon than all the treasures in the world. "Once, our elders"—related Rabbi Khanina—"bought a bag of wheat from Roman soldiers who were passing through and found in it a purse with gold. They hastily caught up with the soldiers and returned the find to them, who then exclaimed: "Glory to the God of the Jews!" Rabbi Samuel ben-Suzarti left for Rome and found there an expensive adornment, lost by the empress. It was proclaimed to the entire population that whosoever returned the find over the course of thirty days, would receive a large reward, and that the one who was found in possession of it after thirty days would be punished. Rabbi Samuel brought the ornament on the thirty-first day. The empress asked with amazement: did he not know what was proclaimed? "I heard of it"—answered Rabbi Samuel—"but I brought the find not out of desire for reward and not out of fear of punishment, but solely out of a fear of God." And the empress exclaimed: "Glory to the God of the Jews!"

But if the positive principle of *kiddush ha-shem* is an ideal requirement, being realized only by righteous men, then the negative principle corresponding to it, *khillul' ha-shem,* places an absolute obligation on every Jew. By virtue of this principle, if a certain act that in itself is permitted by the law appears in given circumstances to be scandalous and could call forth abuse upon Israel and upon its God, then such an act, notwithstanding its abstract legality, becomes the greatest sin and crime. The broad application of this important principle more or less obviously depends not on Jews but on the nations amidst which they live. So, for example, if usury and other similar professions were considered as absolutely reprehensible and dishonorable in Christian society, then, by virtue of the principle *khillul' ha-shem,* Jews would be required to refrain from such professions.

Finally, the third principle—of the paths of peace—requires that certain actions, not obligatory according to law, for example, showing kindness to those of other faiths, giving burial honors to their dead, and so forth, be fulfilled by Jews for the preservation and establishment of peaceful and friendly relations with all—*mipne darke-shalom.* For, according to the Talmud, peace is the third (after truth and justice) pillar, upon which the universe is supported; and friendship is the greatest of virtues.

Thus, in the Talmud there are none of those bad laws that anti-Semites want to find. From the point of view of a contemporary ethics that has been freed to a certain degree from nationalism, a few individual statutes that may seem unjust lose all their practical force thanks to the principles of *kiddush ha-shem, killul' ha-shem* and *mipne dare-shalom.* Anti-Semites have to reluctantly return to a general indictment of the Talmud in principle. As a collection of religious-national tradition, which has in the main a strictly juridical character, the Talmud is that which strengthens the Jewish nation in its isolation; it is a stronghold, fencing off and separating Jews from the rest of humanity, that is, first of all from the Christian world, with which history has tied them in the closest way. The Christian world has now turned both its material and its spiritual weaponry against this stronghold of the Jewish nation for fifteen centuries. This weaponry has noticeably lost its edge, but the hostile stronghold stands as before. We are deeply convinced that its strength lies not in the stubbornness of Jews alone. Talmudic Judaism contains in itself a practical *religious-national law of life*. It is not possible to contrast abstract ideas of a common human civilization to *this kind of law*. These are completely heterogeneous subjects that can neither exclude nor substitute one another. Jewish tradition does not negate the ideas of contemporary enlightenment at all. The Talmud does not impede Jews at all in making use of all the goods of contemporary civilization and even in actively participating in the creation of these goods. The exclusive power of Talmudic Judaism's isolation is directed not outwardly, but *inwardly*. Consequently, it is possible to overcome this isolating power as well only from within.

The Talmud contains in itself the *religious-national law of life* for the Jewish people. If you do not like the fact that this law has a religious character, then attack religion in general directly: it goes without saying that if the whole Jewish nation loses its religious convictions, then the Talmud is out of the question. If you yourself stand on religious ground and you loathe only the national exceptionalism and indolence within Talmudic Judaism, in that case you must contrast (and not in words alone, but in deed) to this religious-*national* law of life another religious-*universal law of life*. Meanwhile, representatives of orthodox [*pravovernoe*] Christianity can come forth against orthodox [*pravovernoe*] Judaism only by preaching abstract theological truth (in the rare and the best cases accompanied by good hopes and wishes). But religious and conscientious Jews can respond to such preaching with something like the following:

"In your theological debates about the truth of Christianity you forget two things: the nature of religion and the special Jewish character. You forget that Christianity, *as religion*, must be a *system of life*, and not a system of theological ideas alone, and that, consequently, it is necessary to judge it not on theoretical foundations alone, but mainly on practical ones. At the same time you forget that Jews are also distinguished by this from Greeks, Indians, Germans, that for them speculative truth *in itself* does not have meaning, but assessing oneself only in one's application to life, assessing oneself according to one's useful action or according to one's actual utility. We Jews judge a tree not by the size of the trunk, not by form of leaf and beauty of color, but by the taste and the nourishment of the fruits. And not only Jerusalem but Galilee thinks thus as well; your Teacher also held to this view, and in your Gospel is written a saying, that every tree will be known by its fruits [Mt 12:33, Lk 6:44]. Thus, let us not speak about the foliage of Christian theology, but about the fruits of Christian life. I do not want to insist that these fruits were always bitter for us Jews. Perhaps this fever originates not with Christianity alone and even not with evil Christians. Perhaps Israel is still not strong enough in the commandments of its God, and He continues to test His people to this day, as He tested them by means of Mithraim and Assur, Javan, and Edom before as well. But what have Christian nations themselves taken from Christianity for their life? I am not speaking about saints and righteous men: they exist in Christianity as well as outside of it as a rare exception, but neither does Christianity chase an impossible goal—to improve all people *one by one*—it is not restricted to the preaching of personal morality, it takes the form of a collective whole, it appears as a church.

A church exists not just for the purpose of creating a holy man or creating holy people one by one, but for the purpose of building a social life *according to God's way*, in order that social truth and personal righteousness could mutually support and nurture one another. You Christians maintain that your religion is the highest and final stage of divine revelation, that it introduced into the world new and vital principles that Judaism did not know. If so, then these new principles should have renewed and re-created the entire life of Christian humanity, they should have introduced higher truth into all the social, civil and international relations of the Christian world. We want clear evidence of the *social* successes of Christianity. They usually point to the fact that the preaching of the Gospel destroyed the major ulcer of the ancient world—slavery. It is striking, however, that over fifteen hundred years prior to the appearance of Christianity, Mosaic legislation took much more real and general measures against slavery (namely, the institution of Sabbaths and Jubilees) than those ameliorating palliatives we meet in the church canons. It is without doubt that the moral *idea* of Christianity undermines slavery, but the point here is not in an idea, but in deed, and the deed of slavery continued to exist in one or another form during the entire time of the predominance of the Christian idea and was finally abolished only in the eighteenth and nineteenth centuries, that is, precisely in an era of religious decline and the rule of unbelief. Exactly the same must be said about the amelioration of criminal justice, the elimination of torture, and so forth. The successes in social morals that were achieved by Christian nations in the last two centuries are not found in direct connection with Christianity. And in any case these improvements of social morals are too superficial and change too little the overall picture of our social life, which is decidedly alien to the Christian ideal. Our Jewish nation *has seen* how pagans lived, now sees how Christians live, and finds no essential difference between the one and the other. The vital foundations are one and the same in both. In both one and the other social life is not based on universal moral solidarity, but on mutual opposition and the mechanistic balancing of private interests and forces; oppression of the weak by the strong and a struggle of the strong among themselves exists in both one and the other. Indeed has Christianity subjected the economic structure of society to any moral law, has it introduced rational goals and justice in the assignment of labor? Isn't today's economic exploitation the same coercion and today's competition the same struggle for *spoils*? You pray to the God of truth and love, but serve—the god of power and success, the very same golden calf that you reproach us for (the injustice of this reproach is unmasked by your Christian literature: in it the typical servant of the golden calf is not the Jew Shylock, but a miserly knight).

If the Christian society amidst which we live did not place money above all else, then we would have no reason to occupy ourselves with financial affairs. Financially, the Jewish nation is a product of your civilization: when we were independent, we glorified ourselves with our religion, and not with money, with the Temple, and not with the bourse. That which is good in our nature comes from our forefather Abraham; that which is good in our daily life comes from our lawgiver Moses, and everything that is bad both in our nature and in our daily life is the fruit of our accommodation to the society amidst which we have lived and live: first to pagan society and then particularly also to Christian society. Notwithstanding, however, this willing and unwilling 'accommodation to habitat' that has distorted our original nature, we nevertheless preserve our chief traits, elevating us over pagans as well as Christians, and, namely: steadfast attachment to our religious law, close solidarity among each other and good family morals. Merging with contemporary Christianity society would mean for Jews losing our moral foundations and not receiving anything in return.

Do not tell us that the bad organization and meager life of Christian society do not annul the intrinsic advantages of Christian religion, that religious truth has its own special realm. We know this, and our great Sanhedrin yet in ancient times pointed to the three bases of our religious life—teaching, service to God, and active love. But *in differentiating* among these three bases, we consider it impermissible and impious *to separate* them one from the other, to separate theory from practice, service to God from love of humanity. There is falsehood in this separation. Therefore, although we would acknowledge that your Christian teaching is true and your service to God is correct—but, seeing that your life and deeds are not governed by the law of love and truth, both divine and human—we consider your religion powerless and do not wish to join it.

If we Jews even could *comprehend* the essence of Christianity, we do not want to *take* your attitude toward religion as some kind of abstract truth.[11] According to us, truth can not be abstract, can not be separated from practical life. We are a nation of law, and truth itself is for us not so much an idea of the mind, as a *law of life*. According to you, on the contrary, truth—exists in and of itself, and practical life—exists in and of itself. Not only does your daily reality not realize your religious ideal (which is not possible to require), but it does not trouble you at all that the *law* itself of your life, for example, in the sphere of politics or social economics, directly contradicts your religious principle. You have people of the most diverse opinions who agree that religious-moral requirements do not have any meaning in politics and social economics, that everything is resolved here not through love of humanity and higher truth, but only through self-interest and love of self, of one or another nationality, one or another societal class. So it is and so it must be, according to you. Your religious ideal is an expression of higher sacredness, but the law of your life is and remains the law of sin and untruth. You are convinced that the ideal can not be practical, and the practical can not be ideal. We Jews, no matter how low we have fallen, do not agree to such a renunciation in principle of true life and living truth, to such an imposed bifurcation and contradiction between ideas and deeds, to an eternal powerless truth, to the eternal untruth of power.

It is one of two things: either your religion is really unrealizable, then this means it is only an empty and arbitrary fantasy; or it is realizable, and this means you are not realizing it only due to your evil will; in this case repent and correct yourselves before calling others to yourself. Learn to implement your New Testament just as we implement our Old Testament, and then we will come to you and will join with you. But now, if we even were to want to come to you, we can not, for we do not know which of you to come to. Your kingdom has been divided against itself and there is no unanimity among you. Show us a united and universal Christianity that would remove the fetters of national exceptionalism from us."

Any religious Jew could hold these or similar words up to us. And none of our retorts to his arguments would have the power of conviction for him, while the practical conclusion of his words remains irrefutable. We can not really think about the unification of the Jewish people with the Christian world while this world is divided against itself; we can not wait for Jews to sacrifice their national exceptionalism to us, when national enmity has predominated over universal unity among us ourselves; we do not have the right to demand that religious Jews abandon their dreams about a future kingdom of the Messiah; finally, we can not convince Jews to believe in Christianity when we ourselves believe in it so poorly. Those of us who think that Christianity will never achieve unity in itself and will never obtain power over our lives acknowledge by the same token the powerlessness of our religion, and they stand dumb before Jews.

Thanks to the Talmud, a Jewish nation preserved in its religious-national isolation has not yet lost the meaning of its existence. It stands to this day as a living reproach to the Christian world. It does not argue with us about abstract truths, but turns to us with the requirement of truth and faithfulness: either reject Christianity or decisively set to its realization in life. The trouble for us is not in the superfluous exercise of the Talmud, but in the insufficient exercise of the Gospel. The desired resolution of the Jewish question does not depend upon the Jews, but upon us ourselves. We can not force Jews to repudiate the laws of the Talmud, but it is always in our power to apply the Gospel commandments to the Jewish nation itself. It is one of two things: either Jews are not our enemies, in which case the Jewish question does not exist at all, or they are our enemies, in which case we must relate to them in the spirit of love and peace—here is the sole Christian resolution of the Jewish question.

7

On Counterfeits

I

Even in the very finest human undertakings the negative side usually lets itself be heard much sooner and more intensely than the positive. Our society's noticeable turn toward religious interests in recent years is very comforting; but even here we are seeing mainly the underside for the time being. The most proximate lamentable consequence of the observed turn consists in the fact that minds alien to true religion, or in any case insufficiently permeated by it, grasp at it under the influence of fashion and, not possessing the genuine article, are content with various counterfeits of their own and of others.[1] Among today's counterfeits, or substitutes, of Christianity the most innocent is, of course, the one that attempts to spread abstract morality of a partly philanthropic and partly ascetic quality under the name of Christian religion. Specious grounds are offered for such a substitution. That Christianity consists mainly in a life of virtue and in love towards one's neighbor is as true as the fact that wine made from grapes, chemically speaking, consists mainly of water. Moreover, pure morality, just as pure water, is not only very useful, but also constitutes an item of prime necessity. Why deceive oneself and others, however, by calling water wine and abstract morality—Christianity? The commandments of abstinence, of justice and of love of fellow man, as well as ascetic and philanthropic aspirations, do not belong exclusively to the teachings of any particular faith—all this constitutes, thank God, the common property of many religions and philosophical schools. And if the whole point is in these precepts in and of themselves, then nothing precludes setting them forth simply, in the name of their own intrinsic merit. Why then this special facade indicating subjects of another kind, completely alien and even unpleasant to the preachers of pure morality? Nobody forbids you to make do with water alone, but why do you pour it into bottles from a wine cellar and pass it off as the genuine wine itself?

Another substitution is at any rate much more malicious. Many people who justly acknowledge in Christianity other essential elements apart from pure morality, such as: dogmas, sacraments, a church hierarchy, imagine that the entire power of the Christian religion is comprised in these elements *in and of themselves*, separately and abstractly taken. Extending the previous comparison, it makes no difference if someone who knows that the chemical distinctiveness of grape wine from water consists in the absence of alcohol and several other substances thought on the basis of this idea to give everyone to drink, in place of wine, pure alcohol with a dash of tannic acid and dye. The deadly effect of such a drink on both the healthy and the infirm would not be subject to doubt. As history testifies sufficiently, a similar effect was always displayed when living Christianity was replaced by the pure alcohol of abstract dogmatics with a dash of hierarchic and mystical elements, not counterbalanced by principles of human enlightenment.

If you see in Christianity a living religion in which you yourself participate, with which you spiritually sustain yourself, then disputes about the predominance and advantages in it of one or another element have no meaning. It is very interesting and useful to know the chemical composition of our food, but no chemist will, as a result of his analysis, conclude by replacing bread with carbon, or meat with nitrogen. He himself—just as everyone else, even if they have never even heard of chemistry—is sustained only by concrete organic combinations of these elements.

With a living attitude to Christianity, an absolutely essential significance belongs not to one or another constituent element of this religion, but only to a single spiritual principle that forms out of them one distinct whole, in which and from which all the parts obtain their relative strength and importance. True and unfeigned Christianity is neither dogma nor hierarchy, neither church service nor morality, but the quickening spirit of Christ, actually, even if invisibly, present in humanity and acting in it through complex processes of spiritual development and growth—a spirit embodied in religious forms and institutions, forming the earthly church, its visible body, but *not exhausted by these forms*, not brought about definitively in any given fact. Traditional institutions, forms and formulas are necessary for Christian humanity, as a skeleton is necessary for a higher order living organism, but in and of itself a skeleton does not constitute a living body. A higher organism can not live without bones, but when the artery walls or heart valves begin to ossify, then this is truly a symptom of inevitable death.

I do not have it in mind here to examine the life of Christian societies themselves, but want only to indicate several theoretical counterfeits of Christianity, which also have, however, a practical significance as unfavorable symptoms of our social health.

II

Everyone agrees that truly authentic Christianity is that which the Founder of our religion himself advocated. What exactly did he advocate? If individual sayings are picked out of the Gospel according to one's particular taste, then there will be many different answers to this question. Some will find the essence of Christian teaching in nonresistance to evil, others—in the subjection to ecclesiastical authorities ("whoever listens to you, listens to Me" [Lk 10:16]), still others will insist on faith in miracles, and others still—on the separation of the divine from the worldly, and so forth. And texts arbitrarily pulled out run the risk of similarly arbitrary reductions, for, being read in full form and in context, they do not give the meaning expected. Leaving aside for the time being this exegetical enthusiasm, we note only that the many views on the essence of Christianity, very diverse among themselves but in equal measure fundamental (for each of them is based on some isolated gospel text), can in no way express the actual essence of Christianity; in the best case these are just particular points of teaching, which are possible to advance to the extent that individual sayings of Christ have come down to us. It is possible to understand the true meaning of these particular truths and to evaluate their actual significance only through their relation to a single central idea of Christianity. And for a determination of the latter it is not possible now to rely mechanically on the letter of individual texts, but it is necessary to resort to another, more sensible method. Is there no direct indication in the Gospel of what Christ himself and His closest disciples acknowledged as the essence of His preaching? Indeed, in the Gospel the teaching of Christ is spoken of in its aggregate, and the idea of Christianity expressed there as a unified whole. How is it then disclosed? Is it called his teaching about nonresistance to evil, or ecclesiastical authorities, or miracles, sacraments, the dogma of the Trinity, redemption, and so forth? No, all these points are found in the Gospel, but the Gospel itself, the good news itself of Christ, is not disclosed in these aspects. It does not call itself the Gospel of nonresistance, or the Gospel of priestly orders, or the Gospel of miracles, or the Gospel of faith, or even the Gospel of love: it invariably calls itself and acknowledges itself as the *Gospel of the kingdom*—the good news about the Kingdom of God.* The word of truth that the Son of Man sows is the "word of the kingdom," the mysteries revealed to Him are "mysteries of the kingdom," and His true followers are "sons of the kingdom," and so forth.

Thus, it is without doubt that the central Gospel idea, consonant with the Gospels themselves, is the idea of the Kingdom of God. Nearly all the orations of Christ are dedicated to its direct or oblique elucidation—both the parables, which were addressed to the people, and the esoteric discussions with the disciples, and finally the prayers to God the Father preserved in the Gospels. It is apparent from the sum total of the texts relating to this that the gospel idea of the kingdom is not exhausted by the concept of the dominion of God over all that exists—a dominion belonging to God as All-powerful and All-sustaining. This dominion is an eternal and constant fact, since the kingdom announced by Christ is something quick, approaching, arriving. Moreover, it has various aspects. It is within us, and it appears from without; it grows in humanity and the entire world by means of a certain objective organic process, and it comes by the free effort of our will. For worshipers of the letter all this can seem contradictory, but for those having the mind of Christ all this is combined in a single simple and all-embracing definition, according to which the Kingdom of God is a *full realization of divinity in human nature through the God-man Christ*, or in other words—*the fullness of natural human life, united through Christ with the fullness of Divinity*.

A perfect unity of Divinity with humanity should be reciprocal (unity in which one of the united elements is annihilated is not unity at all, and one in which it does not preserve its freedom is not *perfect* unity). The intrinsic possibility, the basic condition of unity with Divinity is found thus in man himself—the Kingdom of God is within you [Lk 17:21]. But this possibility must pass over into reality, man must manifest, disclose the Kingdom of God concealed in him, for this he must combine the explicit effort of his free will with the covert action of Divine grace in him—the Kingdom of God is taken by force, and applied efforts take possession of it. Without these personal efforts the possibility will remain just a possibility, a token of future

---

*Gospel of Matthew: 3:2; 4:17, 23; 5:3, 10, 19, 20; 6:10, 33; 7:21; 8:11; 9:35; 10:7; 11:11, 12; 12:28; 13:11, 19, 24, 31, 33, 38, 41, 43, 44, 45, 47, 52; 16:19, 28; 18:1, 23, 19:12, 14, 23, 24; 20:1; 22:2; 23:13; 24:14; 25:1, 34. *Gospel of Mark*: 1:14, 15; 4:11, 26, 28; 9:1; 10:14, 15, 23, 24, 25; 12:34; 14:35. *Gospel of Luke*: 4:43; 8:1, 10; 9:2, 11, 27, 60, 62; 10:9; 11:2, 20; 12:31; 13:18, 20; 14:15; 16:16; 17:20, 21; 18:16, 17, 24, 25, 29; 19:11; 21:31; 22:16, 18, 29, 30; 23:42, 51. *Gospel of John*: 3:3, 5; 18:36. *Acts* 1:3.

blessing is lost, the embryo of true life will die away and perish.*
Thus, the Kingdom of God, perfected in the eternal divine idea ("in
heaven"), potentially inherent in our nature, is necessarily at the same
time something *perfectible* for us and through us. In this respect it is
our *undertaking*, a *task* for our actualization. This undertaking and
this task cannot be confined to the isolated, individual existence of
separate persons. Man is a social creature, and the loftiest undertaking of his life, the ultimate goal of his efforts lies not in his personal
destiny, but in the social fortunes of all humanity. Just as the general
intrinsic potential of the Kingdom of God necessarily must cross over
into individual moral exploit for its realization, so too the latter for its
fullness inevitably takes up the social advancement of all of humanity,
joins one way or another at a given moment and in given conditions
with the general Divine-human process of universal history. If the
Kingdom of God is the combination of Divine grace with man, then
it is certainly not with man isolated in his egoism, but with man as
a living member of the universal whole. Such a man finds the Kingdom of God not only in himself, but also before him, in the objective
course and order of Revelation, in given combinations of Divinity with
the past and present of humanity, and also in an ideal anticipation
of other, more perfected combinations in the future. In all this there
is doubtless something predetermined, fateful, not dependent on the
personal will of each person. Individual freedom nevertheless is preserved, for every one is free to make use or not make use *for oneself*
of the general religious merit of humanity, to enter or not enter with
one's own life force into the organic growth of the Kingdom of God.
The latter in any case is not confined to the subjective moral world
of individual persons, but has its objective reality, its own universal
forms and laws and develops by means of a complex historical process, in which individual persons play in part an active and in part
a passive role. Hence, the important significance of the visible church
as a formal institution that symbolizes, and to a certain degree also
realizes, the universal whole in which individual persons participate,
the makeup of which they enter into, but which is not at all formed
from their arithmetic sum or mechanistic mass. At the same time,
only in the objective organic character of the collective Divine-human
process, assuming and including in itself our personal moral acts,

---

*It is striking in this regard that the words: "the Kingdom of God is within you" were
directed by Christ at the disbelieving Pharisees and scribes, among whom the majority probably remained just as disbelieving; consequently, here was understood only a
general *potential* of unity with Divinity stored in human nature.

though not composed of them—only in such a superpersonal (but not impersonal) character of this process—is the *suddenness* that is directly confirmed by the Gospel in the advancement of its ultimate results possible (for us).* Of course, this suddenness is only relative, fully combined with the unbroken and predetermined growth of the Divine-human organism, similar to the suddenness that also occurs in the outward appearance of inwardly prepared critical moments in purely physical growth. The sprouting and swelling seed in the soil suddenly puts out its shoot to the surface of the ground and just as suddenly the ripened fruit falls to Earth; in a similar manner too the most important phases of the Kingdom of God advance, though suddenly, yet in the *fullness of time*, that is, necessarily prepared by the preceding process. Thus, this suddenness does not exclude but, on the contrary, assumes the active participation of individual forces in the general growth of the kingdom of God.

Thus, at a superficial glance, contradictions, appearing between the intrinsic and extrinsic character of the Kingdom of God, between the gradualness and suddenness of its realization, are eliminated by themselves with a true understanding of the undertaking. As something that exists for us, the Kingdom of God must be our own spiritual state, namely, the state of intrinsic unity with Divinity. Such unity achieved its individual perfection in the person of the God-man Christ; but here it was revealed as superindividual. True *unity with another* cannot be only a subjective state; unity of the whole human being with God cannot be only personal. The Kingdom of God, or of heaven, cannot be only a psychological fact: it is first of all the eternal objective truth of positive all-unity. This truth is situated in natural man as well—in the social character of his life, in the universal all-embracing quality of his reason—situated, but not realized—not given, but only set. The fullness of all that exists in a perfected manner united with God through the Son of Man—this is the absolute ideal, the realization of which began and continues in universal history, as the common, universal undertaking of humanity; everyone works on it unconsciously and involuntarily and, moreover, it is the moral social obligation of the enlightened Christian to participate in it self-consciously and on his own initiative. In this respect, the Kingdom of God is formed not by a simple act of unity of the soul with God, but by a complex and all-embracing process—the spiritual-physical growth and development of the all-united Divine-human organism in the world. Just as with

*Gospel of Matthew 24:27, 29. Compare, on the other hand, the same chapter vv. 31, 33.

every organic growth, this growth represents not only a continuity of quantitative factors (as some crudely imagine, that the entire undertaking is in the accumulation of a certain sum of righteous souls for the kingdom of heaven), but also the division of qualitative degrees and forms, from which the higher, although also necessarily assuming the lower and predetermined by them (in a genetic order), can in no way be wholly deduced from them, and that is why they also appear as something new and miraculous.*

Having established the central idea of true Christianity, we will easily distinguish and expose the different counterfeits circulating today. We will note here only the most important and the most harmful among them.

III

Since the coming of the Kingdom of God does not appear as a deus ex machina, but is conditional on the universal-historical Divine-human process in which God acts only in union with man and through man, then we should acknowledge as a crude counterfeit of Christianity the view according to which a purely passive role alone belongs to man in the Divine undertaking; and all one's obligation relative to the Kingdom of God consists, on the one hand, in slavishly subjecting oneself to given divine facts (in the visible church), and, on the other hand, idly awaiting the approaching final revelation (the kingdom of glory), thus reserving all one's activity for worldly and pagan interests, which appear here in no way connected to the Divine undertaking. For the sake of plausibility, such a view alludes to the understanding that God is everything and man is nothing. But this false humility is in essence a revolt against God, who loved and exalted humanity in Christ, and Christians must not separate themselves from Him: "[He] gave to them power to become children of God" [Jn 1:12].[2] Sons of the kingdom of freedom are also called to conscious and independent participation in the undertaking of the Father. If there is spiritual immaturity among them, then this is only a fact that is necessary to take into account, but not raise to an ultimate and universal principle.

Followers of the indicated counterfeit to Christianity equate the activity of God in the gathering and building of His kingdom,

---

*But these new wonders are at the same time also new revelations, casting light on previous mysteries and enigmas. For from a truly theological point of view the lower forms and degrees already assume the higher as their goal, and that is why they are illuminated, they receive meaning, only with the manifestation of this higher goal.

in the increase and development of the Divine-human organism, to the display of God's omnipotence in phenomena of nature and the circumstances of earthly life. But they expose their speciousness by this very equation, getting tangled in internal contradiction. If they consider it impermissible to interfere in the fortunes of the Kingdom of God, as dependant on His will, neither must they interfere in any undertaking whatsoever, for everything depends on the will of God. However, they do not act this way, but concern themselves as energetically and enthusiastically as possible with the organization of every worldly undertaking possible, personal, national, and so forth. Where does this distinction come from? Why do they consider it necessary to assist God the Omnipotent so assiduously in their paltry little affairs, but do not want to assist in His great undertaking? Obviously, because they are interested in the one, but not in the other. This means that God's undertaking is not *their* undertaking, and that is why they having nothing to do with it. But Christianity in fact consists only in this, that God's undertaking become at the same time fully the undertaking of humanity. This Divine-human solidarity is, in fact, the Kingdom of God, and it *arrives* only in the measure in which it is realized. Evidently, these pseudo-quietists preach a counterfeit Christianity to us. The more passively they subject themselves to the words of a Master whose holiness and greatness serve only as a plausible pretext for them not to think about Him, the more actively they give themselves over in fact to another one, to Mammon.

The indicated counterfeit is usually tied to the denial of any development and progress in the matter of Christian religion. They rashly reach a manifestly absurd conclusion: from the fact that many evolutionists adhere to a unilaterally mechanistic concept about evolution that excludes the action of a Higher power and all teleology, and from the fact that many preachers of historical progress understand by this the limitless self-perfection of man without God and against God, they conclude that the ideas of development and progress themselves have some kind of atheistic and anti-Christian character. Meanwhile it is not only not this way, but the other way around—these ideas are specifically Christian (or more precisely Judeo-Christian). They were introduced into people's consciousness only by the prophets of Israel and the preachers of the Gospel. Both eastern and western paganism in its loftiest expressions—in Buddhism and in Neoplatonism—placed absolute perfection unconditionally outside the process of history, which for it appeared to be either an infinite and purposeless supersession of chance, or a gradual passage to the worse.*[3] Only the Christian (or, Messianic) idea of the Kingdom of God, consistently revealing itself in the life of humanity, gives meaning to history and defines a true concept of progress. Christianity gives humanity not only an ideal of absolute perfection, but also the path to the attainment of this ideal, consequently, it is in essence progressive. Therefore any view that denies this, the progressive element, in Christianity, is a counterfeit that conceals a pagan reaction under the Christian name. Its goal, of course, not always clearly acknowledged is to distract people from the Divine undertaking and to consolidate them in the bad worldly reality that Christ, in conquering the world, came to abolish. Meanwhile false Christians try, although in vain, to snatch away from Christ His victory, in every way maintaining those worldly orders and institutions that have nothing in common with the Kingdom of God. Where does such a protective tendency come from in genuine, noncounterfeit Christianity, which is as alien to the principle of conservatism as it is to the principle of radicalism? On the basis of the Christian religion neither the preservation nor the destruction of any worldly orders whatsoever can interest us *in and of themselves.* If we concern ourselves with the *undertaking* of the Kingdom of God, then we must take up that which worthily serves this undertaking and reject what is contrary to it, being guided in this not by the dead criterion of any abstract -*isms*, but (according to the Apostle Paul) by the living criterion of the mind of Christ [1 Cor 2:16], if we have it in ourselves. If we do not have it, then it is better not to call ourselves Christians. By right those carrying this name must not concern themselves with preserving and strengthening *in any way whatsoever that which* given social groups and orders in earthly Christianity *might become,* but, on the contrary, concern themselves with their regeneration and transformation in a Christian spirit (insofar as they are capable) with their true introduction into the realm of the Kingdom of God.

Thus, the idea of the Kingdom of God necessarily leads us (I have in mind all conscious and sincere Christians) to the obligation to act—within the limits of our calling, for the realization of Christian principles in the collective life of humanity, for the transformation of all our social orders and relations in the spirit of higher truth—that

---

*The view of the world process that we find in the Persian book "Bundegesh" presents a seeming exception. Yet this artifact, though containing in itself a religious element of the ancient Zend[-Avesta], in its full content relates to later times (twelfth century AD), and obviously presumes the powerful impact of Christian ideas.

is, it leads us to *a Christian politics.* Here we come across a new counterfeit of Christianity or, better said, a new variation of the very same disguised anti-Christian reaction. "Christian politics," they say, "is a *contradictio in adjecto,* there can be nothing in common between Christianity and politics: *My kingdom is not of this world* [Jn 18:36], . . ."[4] In no way does it follow, from the fact that the kingdom of Christ is not of this world, that it can not act in the world, rule and govern the world. Otherwise it would be necessary to maintain that since autocratic power is not by the people (but by Divine grace), then it can not govern the people either. According to sound logic, it is the other way around, precisely out of the fact that the kingdom of Christ is not of the world but *from above,* it follows that it has the *right* to rule and govern the world. One of two things: either societies that call themselves Christian must reject this name, or they must acknowledge their obligation to conform all their political and social relations with Christian principles, that is, bring them into the realm of the Kingdom of God; it is in this that a real Christian politics consists.

If, as advocates of pseudo-Christian individualism maintain, all political and social orders are alien or even contrary to Christianity, then from here it directly follows that true Christians must live outside of all political and social orders. But this is a patent absurdity, unmasking these advocates by their own life and activity. But if, on the one hand, it is not possible to abolish social and political forms of life (which would be tantamount to the abolition of man himself as a social and political creature) and, on the other hand, it is doubtless that these forms in their given activity are far from corresponding to Christian principles, far from having been introduced yet into the Kingdom of God, then it directly follows from this that the task of Christian politics is to perfect, to elevate these forms, to transubstantiate them into the Kingdom of God. True, Christian politics has been and is very abused. The Kingdom of God on earth was and is represented as the sum total of people who have verbally acknowledged certain dogmas. Not long ago an adherent of such (again, patently counterfeit) Christianity announced in the press that it is not possible to have intercourse with "liberals" on the basis that they purportedly "do not confess that Jesus Christ cometh in the flesh," as the Apostle St. John the Divine requires [2 Jn 7]. It is not certain what this assertion is based on. I know fierce conservatives who are quite alien to any confession of Christ, and I know liberals about whom such a reproach can in no way be made. But this is not the point. Evidently, our zealot of the faith was luckless in resorting to the authority of St. John the Divine. The text cited, as anyone who occupies himself with the subject knows, is directed against the error of the *docetae* that arose at that time; they acknowledged the supernatural nature of Christ, but denied His actual *incarnation*, having seen only a *phantom* in his corporeal appearance and in his historical being. Afterwards this false opinion took root deeply and was disseminated in various Gnostic sects. But I most resolutely maintain that I am not familiar with a single liberal who is at all guilty of this docetic error. Of course, the text from John the Divine, just as with any word of Holy Scripture, has a general significance too beyond the direct historical meaning. But here as well it is directed not against liberals, but precisely against adherents of that counterfeit Christianity, which is reduced to dead faith on the one hand and to hypocritical doctrines about personal holiness and personal salvation of the soul on the other. Indeed it is they, *in separating* all human tasks from the Spirit of Christ, who deny all the power of His Incarnation, which was in fact accomplished not for Him, but for humanity. In reducing Christianity to an *abstract dogma*, in denying its realization in social and political life, they manifestly demonstrate that they do not confess in fact Christ *who came in the flesh*, and that is why they are subject to the apostolic anathema that one of them so imprudently recalled. In any event the Apostle of love could not reduce all Christianity to dead faith; he, of course, knew the truth that his co-disciple James expressed so well: "the demons also believe, and tremble" [Jas 2:19]. Indeed, an alliance with liberals is not as dangerous as an alliance with demons.

That very same writer on social and political affairs inquired triumphantly: "What does Vladimir Soloviev teach?" I can answer this simply and definitively: I do not have *my own* teaching, but in view of the dissemination of harmful counterfeits of Christianity, I consider it my duty to elucidate the basic idea of Christianity from various aspects, in various forms and on various grounds—the idea of the Kingdom of God as the fullness of human life not only individual, but also social and political, reunited through Christ with the fullness of Divinity; and regarding alliances, I only absolutely avoid them with demons, who believe and tremble.

8

On the Decline of the Medieval Worldview

I call, for the sake of brevity, the historical compromise between Christianity and paganism "the medieval worldview"—a dualistic semi-pagan and semi-Christian order of concepts and life that was arranged and that reigned in the Middle Ages both in the Romano-Germanic West and in the Byzantine East.

Both adversaries and defenders of the medieval worldview usually take it for Christianity itself, or, in any case, acknowledge the connection between them to be as unbreakable as that between content and its corresponding form. I find it useful and important to elucidate the fact that Christianity and the medieval worldview are not only not one and the same, but also that they are in direct opposition. The fact that the causes of the decline of the medieval worldview are not in Christianity, but in its perversion, and that this decline is not at all appalling for Christianity, will also be elucidated by this.

I

The essence of true Christianity is the regeneration of humanity and of the world in the Spirit of Christ, the transformation of the kingdom of this world into the Kingdom of God (which is not of this world). This regeneration is a complex and lengthy process; it is not for nothing that it is compared in the Gospel itself with the growth of a tree, the ripening of a harvest, the rising of dough, and so forth. But, of course, the Christian regeneration of humanity can not just be a natural process, it can not be accomplished on its own, by a path of unconscious turns and changes. This regeneration is a spiritual process ("verily, verily I say to you: whosoever is not born of water

159

and spirit, cannot enter the Kingdom of God" [John 3:5]); humanity itself must certainly take part in it with its own consciousness and its own powers. The essential and root distinction of our religion from other eastern ones, in particular from the Muslim, consists in the fact that while Christianity as a Divine-human religion presupposes Divine action, it requires at the same time human action. In this respect the existence of the Kingdom of God itself depends not only on God, but on us as well, for it is clear that the spiritual regeneration of humanity can not occur apart from humanity itself, can not be just an outward fact; it is an *undertaking* that has been laid upon us, a *problem* that we must solve. It is also no less clear that this problem is not only impossible to solve, but even to recognize in all its significance *at once, in a single act.*

The conversion and the regeneration of even a single person does not take place suddenly. Take Christ's own disciples. If anyone had all the facilities for a complete and speedy spiritual rebirth, they did. However, we do not note any such rebirth during the entire earthly life of the Savior and afterwards up to Pentecost itself. They remained the same as they had been. The appearance of Christ affected them. His spiritual power attracted them and bound them to Him, but it did not regenerate them. They believed in Him as in a fact of a higher order, and awaited from Him the establishment of the Kingdom of God *as an outward fact too.* And it is precisely with them, with these chosen ones, with this salt of the Earth that we can see better than anything how little such a faith in the Divine, as in an outward supernatural fact, means. It is no accident, of course, that the highest praise of Peter for his fervent confession of true faith [Mt 16:17–19] and the following address are famously placed side by side: "Get behind me Satan; You are a temptation to me; for you do not set your mind on divine things, but on human things" (in Matthew 16 [verse 23]). This means that it is possible to have the most zealous, the most fervent and orthodox faith, and yet not have the Spirit of God but resemble Satan—as it is said in another place of the New Testament: "the demons also believe, and tremble" [Jas 2:19]. And the more that such a faith is thus manifested outwardly, forthrightly and with great zeal, the more it is not only contrary to the Spirit of Christ, but the less inward power and durability there is in it. It is not for nothing that it is related in the Gospels how the same zealous disciple of Christ cut off the ear of the High Priest's servant in defense of his Teacher, and then denied Him thrice on that same night [Mt 26; 70–75]. To ascribe this unsound Petrine faith to his particular character is the same as heaping on the Western Catholic church alone (for which the

Apostle Peter is acknowledged as the special prototype) the guilt of pseudo-Christian fanaticism and violence, as this is accepted among us. But something similar is also related in the Gospel about the favorite disciple of Christ—about John (this prototype, as others think, of our Eastern Orthodoxy).

"John answered him, saying, 'Master, we saw one casting out demons in Your name and we forbade him, because he was not following us.' And Jesus said to him, 'Forbid him not; for whoever is not against us is for us' " [Mark 9:38–40].

"And it came to pass that as the days drew near for Him to be taken up (from the Earth), He set his face to go to Jerusalem. And He sent messengers ahead of him. On their way they entered a village of the Samaritans to make ready for Him, but they did not receive Him (there) because His face was set toward Jerusalem. Seeing (this), His disciples James and John said: 'Lord, if you want, we will bring down fire from heaven and consume them as Elijah did?' But he turned and rebuked them and said: 'You do not know of what kind of spirit you are; for the Son of Man came not to destroy men's lives, but to save them.' And they went to another village" (Luke 9: 49–56).[1]

If the main point is faith, then it would seem this is something stronger than faith, when they are immediately, without the slightest doubt, ready to bring down fire from heaven; and yet in the presence of such seemingly great faith James and John did not know the Spirit of Christ, and they did not know it precisely because they believed more than anything in His outward miracle-working power. This power existed, but it was not the point.

II

The Spirit of Christ took possession of the Apostles inwardly and regenerated them only after an outward separation. It took possession of that first community of believers in Jerusalem as well, among whom, according to the words of the Acts of the Apostles, there was one heart and one soul [Ac 4:32]. But the church in a broad sense, Christian humanity in all its scope, has to this day not lived up to its Pentecost; it relates to Christ in the same outward manner as the Apostles related at the time of His earthly life—neither has it yet learned to think in divine terms, neither does it know of what spirit it is. The more widely the preaching about the new spiritual Adam was promulgated across the pagan world, the more the old Adam of the flesh showed resilience and exerted resistance. An accusatory character already predominates decisively in the Apostolic epistles to various churches, special disgraces already appear side by side with special spiritual gifts in these first Christian communities (See the epistles of the Apostle Paul to the Corinthians).

An old and very widely promulgated notion about the era before Constantine the Great as a time of ideal purity, as a golden age of Christianity, can be permitted only with great constraints. There was, of course, a difference, but there was not a complete opposition between those first centuries and the ones that followed. In general at that time as well the majority of Christians related to the Kingdom of God outwardly, expecting its arrival as an external miracle-working catastrophe that must erupt, if not today then tomorrow. But, notwithstanding the vulgarity of such a view, this assumed proximity of the end of the world, on the one hand, and the still more proximate possibility of torture, on the other, sustained Christians of that time at a certain spiritual height and did not allow pragmatic materialism to gain the upper hand. Of course, persecutions were not a common phenomenon everyday and everywhere. Absolutely universal persecutions—throughout the entire Roman Empire—did not exist at all; widespread persecutions continued a very short time; the majority of persecutions had a local and chance character. But since there were Roman laws, by virtue of which it was possible to prosecute Christianity as a criminal and state crime, then the *possibility* of torture hung over Christians always and everywhere, and attached a purgative, tragic character to their life. An important advantage of those centuries over the ones that followed consisted in the fact that Christians could be and were persecuted, but in no way could they in any event be persecutors. In general, belonging to the new religion was much more dangerous than advantageous, and therefore the best people usually turned to it with sincere conviction and inspiration. If the life of the church of that time was not fully permeated by the Spirit of Christ, then in any event higher religious-moral motives predominated in it. Amidst the pagan world *there was* a truly Christian society, far from perfect, but in any event governed by another, better principle of life.

In this respect the curtailment of persecutions and the official recognition of the new religion, at first as fully legal and then also as the reigning one, actually created an important change for the worse. Under Constantine the Great and Constans, the pagan masses flocked to Christianity not out of conviction, but out of slavish imitation or self-interested calculation. A type of feigned, hypocritical, previously nonexistent Christian appeared—one that multiplied even more when under Theodosius, and ultimately under Justinian, paganism was forbidden by law and, apart from a scattered handful of semi-tolerated Jews, every subject of the Greco-Roman Empire was compulsorily obligated to be a Christian, under threat of severe criminal punishments. Of course, there arose a multitude of different shades of superficial and indifferent Christians between the type that thus pledged to be Christian against his will and under constraint, and those who remained real Christians by deep conviction. But all this was concealed without any distinction by the overall organization of the external church, in which all categories of internal merit were erased and became confused. The earlier truly Christian society became blurred and dissolved into a Christianity-in-name, but which in fact was a pagan multitude. The predominant majority of superficial, indifferent and feigned Christians not only preserved in fact the pagan principles of life under the Christian name, but also in every way strove—in part instinctively, and in part also consciously—to establish the old pagan order side by side with Christianity, to legalize and to immortalize it, in principle excluding the task of its inward renewal in the Spirit of Christ. Here then was laid the first foundation of the Christian-pagan compromise that itself determined the medieval worldview and life.

III

I am not talking about an *actual* compromise between absolute truth and our reality. All our life—past, present, and future—until the end of history, is in each of its modes an actual compromise between the higher ideal principle that is realized in the world, and the material milieu in which it is realized but does not correspond to it. When this is fully realized, there will be an end to every compromise, but at that time there will also be an end to history and the entire world process. As long as there is some kind of imperfection in the world, then there is also a compromise of counteracting principles, for what is imperfection but a *concession* in fact of a higher principle to a lower one? True perfection requires only that the ideal principle more profoundly penetrate the milieu counteracting it and more fully take control of it.

If there is struggle and victory, effort and improvement, if the absolute ideal is not denied and is not forgotten, if it remains an inwardly inspirational principle and the ultimate goal of reality, then actual compromise with the environment of reality is only an extrinsic necessity and not an intrinsic falsehood. There is no vacillating faith here. Taking bad reality into account as a fact does not mean believing in it; conceding to it temporarily in trivial things, in order to ultimately eliminate it in great things, does not mean worshiping it. Treatment of illness is also, if you will, a compromise, rectilinear moralists also deny it; yet Christ sanctified it by his example.

But when the pagan world accepted Christianity, the issue was not a compromise in fact, which there had been even without it, but a compromise in principle. The majority of the newly converted wanted for everything to remain as it was. They acknowledged the truth of Christianity as an outward fact, and entered into certain superficial formal relations with it, but only in order that their life remain pagan as before, that the worldly kingdom remain of this world, and the Kingdom of God, being not of this world, would remain outside the world as well, without any vital influence upon it, that is, would remain as a useless ornament, as a simple subordinate accessory to the worldly kingdom. But Christ came into the world, of course, not in order to enrich worldly life with a few new ceremonies, but in order to save the world. He saved the world in principle, at root, at its center, by his death and resurrection, but He alone cannot now promulgate this salvation to the entire sphere of humdrum and worldly life, cannot realize the principle of salvation in all our reality. He can do this only together with humanity itself, for nobody can really be saved forcibly and without one's own knowledge and consent. But true salvation is regeneration, or a new birth, and a new birth assumes the death of a previous false life, and nobody wants to die. Before it was resolved to accept real salvation, as one's own task, as its own exploit, the pagan world wanted to attempt an easy, cheap salvation, a salvation by dead faith and acts [*delami*] of piety, *by acts* [*delami*] but not as a *vocation* [*delom*]. And, moreover, by outward acts; but actual Christianity is prior to everything else an occupation, an occupation of life for humanity and then, after that, acts. But while acts are easy, an occupation is difficult; and abstract faith in unintelligible subjects, that is, a particular verbal confession of such faith, is easier than anything. Christianity was in fact accepted chiefly from this aspect.

Of course, as a morally historical task, as an occupation of humanity in common, Christianity was not confessed clearly and definitively in the first three centuries either, but it nevertheless was then an occupation of life for everyone; it is not an easy task to prepare for torture, for a proximate end of the world. But now torture completely ceased, and the end of the world started gradually to recede into the background more and more. There was no expectation either to die for Christ or to prepare to meet Him at the Second Coming. Both

His first and second appearance, the center and the end of the world process, lost vital significance, became a subject of abstract faith. And actual human life, which should have been an active continuation of the one and an active preparation for the other, remained in its material meaninglessness and in its material indolence between these drawn back boundaries of a divine past and a divine future. In essence pseudo-Christians, who did not have to spill their blood, but who now began to spill the blood of others, wanted to preserve this pagan life as it was, and only to anoint it externally with Christianity.

The essence of religion is in the fact that its truth is not abstractly theoretical, but is confirmed as a *norm of reality*, as a *law of life*. If, for example, I believe not just in words, but in actual fact, in the trinity of Divinity as in a religious truth, then I must understand and accept its moral and vital meaning. For all our dogmas have such meaning, and even if it was not clearly understood at first, it was felt vividly in the Christian world.

IV

I will not begin to set forth now my view on the vital significance of the fundamental Christian truths, in particular truths about the triune Divinity and the God-manhood of Christ. My view is too unusual and, if set forth in a couple of words, would be incomprehensible. But it is possible to elucidate in what the essence of the matter is by comparing it with another simpler religion. The teaching of Islam is rather meager in content, but this particular religion is fully realized in the life of the Muslim world. The notion of God as a single exclusive force is completely one-sided, but for that it defines the entire Muslim system: a single despotism on earth corresponds to a single despot in heaven. Fatalism and quietism, as the predominant vital disposition of all Muslims, correspond fully to a theoretical denial of a freedom of will and in general the independence of the human principle.

Christian teaching, in contrast to Islam, includes in itself *complete truth*. But this truth is not only completely unrealized (which is not possible until the end of the world), but the very task of its realization is also denied by false Christians, which means that the very sense of Christianity is denied. The meaning of Christianity is that the life of humanity be transformed according to the truths of faith. This also means justifying faith through acts. But if this life was left under its old pagan law, if the very thought of its root transformation and regeneration was eliminated, then by the same token the truths

of Christian faith lost their meaning and significance as norms of
reality and a law of life, and remained in abstract theoretical content
alone. And since this content is hardly understandable to anyone,
then the truths of faith were transformed into obligatory dogmas,
that is, into conditional symbols of church unity and obedience of
the people to spiritual authorities. Meanwhile it was not possible
to reject the idea that Christianity is a *religion of salvation*. And here
out of the illicit union of this idea of salvation with ecclesiastical
dogmatism was born the monstrous teaching that the single path to
salvation is faith in dogmas, that without this it is impossible to be
saved. Fortunately, aside from the dogmas, a certain augmentation of
them was preserved—*the sacraments*. Even though their true meaning
was in part forgotten and in part did not succeed in developing, this
most essential element of Christianity had in any case the advantage
of popular accessibility. The most ardent zealot of true belief could
not require that a baby at the breast either anathematize Nestorius
and Eustace or correctly confess a dogma about inseparable and un-
mingled natures. From infancy baptism was sufficient. And if he died
before baptism? Then one could do nothing—and for him it was the
end—there was no salvation. Sensitive souls invented for such infants
various limbos on the portico of hell. And with respect to heretics
and the consciously unbelieving, they were, as is known, habituated
to eternal hellish tortures in advance by means of temporal tortures.
And in what awful measure did the successors of the Apostles realize
here the prophetic saying of Christ: "You do not know what spirit
you are of" [Lk 9:55].

V

There were, however, people amidst this perverted Christianity who
did not exchange a vital and life-creating truth with a dead and
homicidal dogmatism, people for whom Christianity remained life's
occupation. Without such true Christians, the medieval order would
not have held out so long and would not have displayed the spiritual
life that we actually find in it. Why did they not save it and regenerate it? They did not save and could not save Christian society, the
Christian world, because in all their righteousness and holiness, they
mistakenly thought that it was only possible and only necessary to
save individual souls. They achieved what they wanted: they saved
their own and many other souls, but the society and the world, from

which they separated themselves, from which they ran, remained outside their action and went their own ways.

From the time that the truly Christian society of the first centuries dissolved into the pagan midst and assumed its character, the very idea of public community disappeared from the mind of even the best Christians. They left all public life to the ecclesiastical and secular authorities, and placed only *individual salvation* as their task. They had here, of course, the excuse that the authorities indeed carried the Christian title as well and, consequently, could and had to be concerned about a Christian direction of public life. But the point is that every authority is first of all conservative and, apart from exceptional phenomena, such as, for example, Peter the Great, do not undertake radical transformations on their own initiative. The government is in any case the offspring of its society, organically connected to it, and if the society of the Greco-Roman Empire and Romano-German Europe had a predominantly pagan character, then the state had no incentive to concern itself with a Christian direction of public life. Of course, this task was closer to the ecclesiastical authority, but in the West this authority, absorbed by the struggle with the state for its rights, gradually forgot about its obligations more and more, and in the East it did not have independent standing. Here in the East the contrast between a *paganism of the city* and a *Christianity of the desert* was manifested especially acutely. With the sole exception of St. John the Golden Mouth [Chrysostom], the preaching of Eastern ascetics did not have in view any Christian transformations of the social order. It is not possible to indicate in this sense a single definite requirement in all of Byzantine history. Is it any wonder that the state and its laws remained the same pagan ones as the social morals were? Is it any wonder that the codex of Justinian is in essence only the legislation of the pagan Roman Empire touched up with Christian words? In the West it was a little better. There were vivid examples of striving toward social and moral Christianity, beginning with the principal protest of St. Martin of Tours and St. Ambrose of Milan—against the death penalty*—and ending with the activity of Gregory VII.[2] But in general even here the action of church authority in this direction was not sufficiently forceful and successful and could not outweigh the actions of the examples that were given by that same authority in an antithetical sense.

---

*Concerning the leaders of the *Priscillian* sect, executed by the (usurper) Emperor Maximilian in Trier.

VI

Restricting the matter of salvation to personal life alone, pseudo-Christian individualism had to renounce not only the world in a narrow sense—society, public life—but also the world in a broad sense—all material nature. In this, its one-sided spiritualism, the medieval worldview appeared in direct contradiction to the very foundation of Christianity. Christianity is a *religion of Divine incarnation and resurrection of the flesh*; but they distorted it in a kind of eastern dualism, denying material nature as an evil principle. But material nature cannot be an evil principle in and of itself: it is passive and inert—this is a feminine element, which receives one or another spiritual principle. Christ cast out seven demons from Mary Magdalene and inspired her with His Spirit [Lk 8:2]. When feigned Christians removed material nature from the Spirit of Christ, evil spirits naturally installed themselves in this universal Magdalene. I understand here the unusual development of black magic and all kinds of devilry toward the end of the Middle Ages and at the start of modernity. Spirits were called forth, but incantations did not work. Representatives of pseudo-Christianity, themselves resembling believing demons partly in their dogmatism and partly in their false spiritualism, having lost the real power of spirit, could not imitate Christ and the Apostles and resorted to the reverse method. The latter expelled demons for the purpose of healing the possessed, but the former began to kill the possessed for the purpose of expelling demons.

VII

As feigned Christians have renounced and renounce the Spirit of Christ in their exclusive dogmatism, one-sided individualism and false spiritualism, as they have lost and lose it in their life and activity, where has that Spirit concealed itself? I am not speaking about His mystical presence in the sacraments of the church, or about his individual acts on selected souls. Is humanity as a *whole* and its history forsaken by the Spirit of Christ? Where then does the entire sociomoral and intellectual progress of the last centuries come from?

The majority of people who have created and create this progress do not acknowledge themselves as Christians. But if Christians in name have betrayed the purpose of Christ—and would have ruined it, if only they could have—then why can't those who are *not Christians* in name, and who renounced Christ in word, serve the purpose of

Christ? In the Gospel, we read of two sons; one said, "I will go" and he did not go; the other said, "I will not go" and he went. Which of the two, asks Christ, did the will of his Father? [Mt 21:28–32]. It is not possible to deny the fact that the social progress of the last centuries has been accomplished in the spirit of philanthropy and justice, that is, in the Spirit of Christ. The downfall of torture and cruel punishments, the cessation, at least in the West, of all persecutions of different faiths and heretics, the downfall of feudal serfdom and slavery—if all these Christian transformations were done by unbelievers, then all the worse for believers.

Those who are horrified at this thought, that the Spirit of Christ acts through those who do not believe in Him, are incorrect even from their dogmatic point of view. When an unbelieving priest correctly performs Mass, then Christ is present in the sacrament thanks to the people who have need of him, notwithstanding the unbelief and unworthiness of the one who performs it. If the Spirit of Christ can act through a serving priest, who does not believe in the mystery of the church, why can't he act in history through an unbelieving actor, especially when believers banish him? The spirit blows where it will. Let even enemies serve it. Christ Himself, who commanded us to love enemies, of course, not only can love them, but also knows how to make use of them for His purpose. And it would behoove nominal Christians who take pride in their demonic faith to remember yet another thing from the Gospel—the story of Judas Iscariot and Thomas. Judas welcomed Christ with a word and a kiss. Thomas announced his unbelief to his face. But Judas betrayed Christ and "went and hanged himself" [Mt 27:5], and Thomas remained an Apostle and died for Christ.

The unbelieving engines of modern progress acted in favor of true Christianity, undermining the false medieval worldview with its anti-Christian dogmatism, individualism, and spiritualism. While they could not offend Christ by their unbelief, they offended the very material nature in the name of which many of them acted. They put forth against false-Christian spiritualism, which saw in this nature an evil principle, another view that was just as false, one that saw in nature only a dead substance, a soul-less machine. And now the natural earth refuses to feed humanity, as if it is offended by this double falsehood. Here is the common danger that must unite both believers and unbelievers. It is time for both the one and the other to acknowledge and realize their solidarity with earth-matter, save it from necrosis, in order to save itself from death as well. But what kind of solidarity can we have with the Earth, what kind of moral attitude to her, when we do not have this solidarity, this moral attitude, even amongst ourselves. Unbelieving progressives strive—whether for good or for ill—to create such solidarity and they have already accomplished something. Those who call themselves Christians do not believe in the success of their purpose, maliciously censure their efforts, resist them. To censure and interfere with others is easy. Try to do better yourselves, to create a socially vital, universal Christianity. If we are Christians not just in name but in fact, then it depends on us that Christ be resurrected in his humanity. Then the historical Thomas as well will touch his hand to this Christianity, actually resurrected in the flesh, and exclaim with joy: My Lord and my God! [Jn 20:27–28].

9

When Did the Hebrew Prophets Live?

(Ernest Havet, "La modernité des prophêtes" Paris, 1891)

Ernest Havet, who died in 1889, had a certain renown in France thanks to his work, *Le Christianisme et ses Origines*. The booklet in question was published separately after his death. I say *booklet*, and not book, because what appears to be a work of significant size turns out to be a deception created by typographical changes alone. In point of fact this is only a reproduction (without changes and addenda) of a journal article, published originally in two issues of *"Revue des deux Mondes,"* (60 pages in all). It is within such dimensions that the following proposition is argued in Havet's treatise: all the authors of the prophetic books in the Hebrew Bible, that is, the so-called *n'bijim acheronim* (prophetae posteriores) from Isaiah to Malachi, lived after the Maccabean wars of liberation; to wit, that some of them (so-called first Isaiah, Jeremiah, Ezekial, Hosea, Joel, Amos, Obadiah, Jonah, Micah, Nahum, Habbakuk and Zephaniah) lived at the time of the Hasmoneans, Simon and John Hyrcanus (i.e., between 142 and 107 BC), others (namely, so-called second Isaiah, Haggai and Zechariah) saw activity a century later at the time of the Idumaean [Edomite] Herod the Great, and the last in this series of prophets, Malachi, relates to an even later time: he wrote under the sway of John the Baptist's preaching, in the third decade AD. The author of the Book of Daniel (separated in the Hebrew Bible from the other prophets) also wrote at about that time.

Several special qualities and conditions, combined by Havet in a brilliant manner, are necessary for the defense of such a view. He himself directly indicates the first of them—to wit, his unfamiliarity with the Hebrew language, as a result of which he could read the Old Testament only in translations (p. 6). Moreover he announces that he studied the question of the dating of the prophets for an *entire year*, during which he gave a public course on it (Je viens de donner à l'étude de cette question une année entière pendant laquelle j'en ai fait le sujet d'un course public [p. 8]). If a public course entered into the scope of this single year as well, that is, a report of the *results* of study, then for the study itself there now remains not an entire year, but indeed only a few months. Thus, and apart from a lack of knowledge of the Hebrew language, the attitude of this biblical "critic" toward his subject is noted by uncommon carelessness, and the naïveté with which he himself underscores the extremely super-ficial and hasty character of his study is striking. We will familiarize ourselves with other of its properties, which he himself does not own up to, by following his argumentation.

I

Havet begins with an historical outline of the period to which he dates the greater portion of the prophets, namely, the time of the Maccabean revolt and the reign of the national dynasty of the Has-moneans that followed thereafter. He points out that even before—in the third century BC—the Jews, under the jurisdiction of, in turn, the Greco-Egyptian Ptolemies and the Greco-Syrian Seleucids, little by little become Hellenized (pláces dans ce milieu héllénique il s'héllénisent insensiblement [17]). The religious-political movement of the second century did not arrest the cultural Hellenization of the Jewish people, and even the title adopted by Simon Maccabeus as national leader is well-known only in Greek—εϑναρχος [ethnarchos]. On the basis of such documentation it is not possible, of course, to conclude (as, evidently, Havet does), that the Greek language was adopted by all Jews. In actual fact it came into general usage fully only among Jews "of the dispersion" (διασπορα)—in Egypt, Asia Minor, and Europe; in Palestine and Syria only the higher classes made use of it, while the people spoke in Aramaic or the so-called Syro-Chaldean dialect after the Babylonian captivity. In any case it is without doubt that in the era about which Havet speaks, the Hebrew language proper had already fallen out of usage, had died out. How then can we explain the fact that all the social and political commentators of that time—for from the point of view of our author the prophets were precisely social and political commentators who wrote about contemporaneous current events, but concealed them with ancient names—wrote in the most faultless ancient Hebrew language, and their works constitute the classical specimens of this language? If we add to this the fact that Havet also relates all other biblical writing to the Maccabean and post-Maccabean era, then we get the completely fantastic notion that an entire national literature of the highest merit (which our author does not deny) was created in a language that was already dead and that in its life did not possess an actual literature. This would be improbable even if it concerned just two or three writers, for it would have to assume that there was among these writers, apart from creative genius, unprecedented philological knowledge and skill for those times. But when the proposition concerns an entire literature, then it becomes completely inconceivable. This is just as probable as if we imagined that all the Russian writers in the nineteenth century, particularly the political commentators and journalists, suddenly began without any motive or reason to write in the most faultless Church Slavonic of the Gospel of Ostromirovo [eleventh century] and, what's more, in speaking about the last Turkish War, they replaced it with the campaign of Sviatoslav against the Greeks, but they ascribed the Russo-Chinese debt to the times of Jaroslav.

When good Latin began to be written in the period of the Renaissance in Europe, such a rebirth of dead language did not, in the first place, create classically perfect models and, in the second place, already had in front of itself a detailed ancient Latin literature that these new writers strove to imitate as closely as possible (I am not speaking now about the special literary character of these times, which the era of the Hasmoneans in Palestine did not at all have). But the instance of Havet and his discovery is just as if someone would come forward with the announcement that ancient Latin literature did not exist at all, and all the specimens of it known to us—the odes of Horace and Virgil's poem, Cicero's orations and the annals of Tacitus—were all written by unknown monks partly in the era of Charlemagne's successors and partly at the time of the Crusades—at which point the author of such a discovery would conscientiously explain that he himself knows no Latin at all, but came to his view "having studied" French translations of Latin books with some commentaries over the course of a few months.

If the intrinsic impossibility of the proposition that the Hebrew authors, contemporaries of the latter Hasmoneans and even Herod, wrote in the language of Amos and Isaiah, still had need of some kind of extrinsic confirmation, then we would find it in actual, original Hebrew literature, which doubtlessly belongs to this latter period. We have books of the Maccabees, the Wisdom of Solomon, the Wisdom of Jeshua, son of Sirach, the preaching of the Judean Sybil, a multitude of all kinds of pseudo-epigraphy, but all of this, both according to language and according to literary character, does not have anything in common with the canonical writings of the prophets, so that no competent critic would even think of ascribing these two groups of works to one era.

The basic consideration of the prophetic books' language, apparent and inarguable for anyone at all concerned with these subjects, constitutes *une fin de non recevoir* [a preclusion of other complaints] in advance against Havet's view, which was in fact met in the scholarly world either by laughter or contemptuous silence. But in what way does he himself relate to this, by what means does he attempt to remove the chief incongruity of his hypothesis? In no way and by no means. He does not indicate this difficulty with even a word, as if he did not even think that a question about the language of certain literary artifacts and their relation to other artifacts of that same national literature could have any importance in the determination of the period of these artifacts' provenance.

II

Avoiding through silence the general impossibility of his proposition, Havet directly turns to the partial evidence of its likelihood, or even—as he affirms resolutely—its reliability. He finds the cornerstone of the grounds for his theory in Isaiah, chapter 19. In this chapter, that is, properly speaking only in several lines of it, he examines the connection with a certain event from the Hasmonean era. Around 150 BC, Onias, a clansman of the chief priest [usurper] Onias Menelaus, a protégé of the Syrian kings, resettled in Egypt and, winning the favor of the Ptolemy Philometer, received from him permission to build a temple to the God of Israel in the region of Heliopolis.[1] And here we read in Isaiah (19:19): "In that day there shall be an altar to the Lord in the midst of the land of Egypt, and a stone pillar near the border to the Lord" (Bajom hahu jihjeh mizbeah la IHVH b'tok eres misrajim umassebah esel-g'bulah la IHVH). If one takes this verse separately, forgetting about the context, then it is possible, of course, to see here along with Havet an indication of the temple of the Oniases, as even Josephus Flavius noted, and that Isaiah foretold the construction of this temple. But the second half of this verse—about a frontier pillar unknown to history dedicated to the Lord—forces one to see here not so much an indication of a definite fact, as much as a poetical turn of phrase, quite common in the [Hebrew] Bible's parallelismus membrorum: an altar amidst Egypt and a holy pillar at the border.[2] And the general reason why these holy subjects and Egypt are spoken of here will be completely clear if one is not confined to a single verse, but reads the entire chapter, and also glances at the preceding one. We have in these chapters a general Messianic prophecy—relating to an indeterminate distant future—about the onset of a Divine kingdom, when the chief representatives of paganism, Mithraim and Assur (Egypt and Assyria), and also Cush (Ethiopia) will repent in their impiety after terrible catastrophes, will turn to the true God, will render to him deference and will reconcile with Israel and among themselves. We read about Egypt in particular that God will visit this country with his wrath, that it will be subject to great disasters (in part recalling the "punishments" in the Book of Exodus), and that later Egyptians will acknowledge the Lord and will serve Him, and the Lord will heal Egypt, will accept it as his people and will bless it. None of this has any relation to the Hasmoneans and to the Oniases. Once the return of all Egypt is foretold, then the altar to the Lord *amidst* the land of Egypt becomes an image appearing of its own accord; in any case here an altar erected by Egyptians for their proper service to the true God, and not for the Hebrews, is spoken of. Here a pillar in the name of the Lord on the frontier or the neighborhood proper of the Egyptian land becomes comprehensible: it must show that all Egypt, all the region (*g'bulah*) was embraced in these frontiers, began to belong to the true God, or was dedicated to Him.

Meanwhile, if one stands on the point of view of Havet and sees in Isaiah's verse 19 a contemporary's indication of an accomplished event, then where do we put all similar verses in which events not accomplished are spoken of? We are assured that all biblical predictions are prophecies post factum. But when was there an instance such that the entire Nile dried up and completely disappeared (vv. 5–10)? It has not yet been to this day, just as it also has not been that five Egyptian cities (*hamesh arim b'eres misrajim*), that is, the Pentapolis, suddenly began to speak the Canaanite, that is, Hebrew, language (v. 18). Not only was this not the case in the era of the Hasmoneans, but it could not have been, for then in Palestine itself as well the Hebrew language had already fallen out of usage, and Egyptian Jews had undoubtedly adopted the Greek language.

With respect to the general content of all Isaiah 19—the conversion of Egypt and Assyria to the God of Israel—then this prophecy was fulfilled in later times, since both Egypt and the Near East accepted at first Christianity, and then partly crossed over to Islam, and both these religions came out of Judaism and acknowledged the God of

Israel as their true God. The conversion foretold in the eighteenth chapter of Ethiopia (Cush) to the true God was also fulfilled, for in the sixth century Abyssinia became Christian with an admixture of Judaic elements, properly speaking. In this regard it was completely unnecessary to transpose Isaiah to the Hasmonean era, since here as well he would have turned out to be an actual prophet, and not a social and political commentator foretelling events after their realization.

The last three verses of Isaiah 19 are very striking.

> In that day there shall be an open road out of Egypt into Assyria, and the Egyptians shall together with the Assyrians serve (God). In that day Israel shall be the third with Egypt and with Assyria, in a blessing of all the land, whom the Lord of hosts shall bless, saying: Blessed be Egypt, My people, and Assyria, the work of My hands, and Israel, my inheritance.

Havet is not shy in relating this place to the struggle of the Seleucids with the Ptolemies, when Jerusalem crossed over several times from the hand of one to the other. But what do these military-political relations have in common with what is said by the prophet —with the spiritual union of Egypt, Assyria, and Israel in service to the one God who blesses all three?

Havet finds great support for his theory in the fact that, in mentioning the five cities that will speak in the Canaanite language, the prophet notes: one of them will be called *ir ha Heres*. It is possible to translate this title as *city of the Sun*, in Greek Ἡλιοπολις, in Egyptian *On*. And since the temple of Onias was build in the region of Heliopolis (nom), then our author also announces triumphantly that Isaiah points directly to the temples of the Oniases. A little more knowledge and acumen would make such an argument impossible. *On*, or Heliopolis, was from antiquity the birthplace of Ephraim and Manasseh in the memory of the Hebrews, since their mother, Asenath, the wife of Joseph, was the daughter of a priest of Heliopolis (Gen 41:45). Moreover, here as well, according to ancient tradition, Moses too was raised by the priests of the Sun god and learned "all Egyptian wisdom," and in the Chronicles of Manetho he himself is called a priest of Heliopolis.[3] With these recollections it is possible, of course, to explain why Isaiah refers to the city of the Sun in his Messianic prophecies; the recollections, strengthened by the word of Isaiah, could have prompted Onias to select the Heliopolis region for the construction of his temple. Thus, between this temple and the prophecy of

Isaiah there is, perhaps, a connection, but only one directly opposite to the one that Havet proposes.

III

Following the nineteenth chapter of Isaiah, our author finds the second cornerstone for his theory in chapters 24–27, where the fall and destruction of a secure city are incidentally spoken about. He relates this to the capture by the Jews, at the time of Simon Maccabeus, of the Jerusalem fort of Acra, which constituted the last stronghold of the Greco-Syrian power over Judea. The greater part of these four chapters speaks of things not having any relation to the capture of any city or fort; so, for example:

> And he will take away on this mountain the coverings which are cast over all people, and the veil that spreads over all the nations. For he has swallowed up death forever. And the Lord God will wipe away tears from all faces and he shall take away the shame from His people in all the countries. For the Lord has spoken. (25:7, 8)

Or further: "Your dead shall live, they shall arise with bodies. Awake and cry out, you that dwell in dust; for the dew is like the dew of herbs, Your dew, and You shall cast out the evil dead from the earth" (26:19).[4] Amidst similar grandiose predictions are several verses, in which a certain city is spoken of, that Havet picks out and joins together for his purpose. In this form, they do not really represent anything that directly contradicts his opinion, but nothing that would prove it either, nothing that would force us to relate these places precisely to this and *only* this event—the capture of the Jerusalem Acra. If Havet's theory were proved or provable, then reliance on these chapters could serve as support, but as a piece of evidence independently, indeed one of two main pieces, it only underscores the feebleness of the theory. Added to that, the following device of our author is curious.

At the end of the twenty-seventh chapter, it is said that at this time those abandoned in the land of Assur and outcasts in the land of Egypt, the sons of Israel, will gather from Ephrata to the Nile—one by one they will gather and will come to pray to the Lord on the Holy Mount in Jerusalem (vv. 12, 13). There was no such mass return of exiles and returning settlers with regard to the capture of Acra or in general at the time of the Hasmoneans; no historical information of anything similar exists, and the very fact would be improbable to the highest degree. But our author, introducing this prophecy of Isaiah about the gathering of all Jews on the Holy Mount and ascribing it contrary to all verisimilitude to the capture of the Jerusalem Fort, adds on his own with full conviction and relying on nothing: "This means that after the time that the independence of Israel was, finally, ensured, all those who were exiled in Egypt and in Syria, who had exiled themselves, not able to endure the Macedonian rule, return from all corners to the homeland" (p. 63). But where does he learn about this return, which history knows nothing of? Instead of supporting his view with actual facts, attested from other sources, he accepts the self-same still uncorroborated view, or interpretations of prophetic texts according to this view, as an independent basis for the support of *new* facts, not having any other evidence.

Disasters to which Ephraim, that is, the Kingdom of Israel, will be subjected are spoken of at the beginning of the twenty-eighth chapter in Isaiah:

> Alas, the crown of pomp of the drunkards of Ephraim, and
> the flower whose shapely beauty fades, which are on the
> head of the far valleys, there, where they are in a stupor
> from wine! Behold, from the Lord a mighty and strong one,
> like a tempest with hail and destructive foul weather, like
> a flood of mighty waters overflowing, are loosed upon the
> earth with force.

Havet relates this to the capture of Sechem, and then Samaria by John Hyrcanus in the year 129, which is why the Samaritan Temple of Mount Gerizim was destroyed. But the fall of a magnificent city, the inhabitants of which would luxuriate and get drunk, is spoken about in Isaiah. This fully resembles Samaria as the capital of the Israelite kingdom in the eighth century, and not at all the poor Samaritan community of the second century, which could take pride only in its temple, but it is precisely this temple that there is no indication of in Isaiah. To relate the expression "crown of pomp" (*atereth geuth*) to the Gerizim Temple and not to regal Samaria with its palaces, would not only be arbitrary, but also directly incompatible with the text, which connects this "crown of pomp and flower whose shapely beauty fades" not with something religious (according to the concepts of the Maccabean epoch), but only with drunkenness and the drunken stupor of the Ephraimites. Neither is there any basis to see John Hyrcanus, and not the Assyrian king, as the indubitable accomplisher of Divine retribution in the phrase "from the Lord a mighty and strong one" (*hazak v'ammis l'adonai*), a characteristic representation of the Bible, or of one of the Judean kings, who had inflicted heavy blows upon his Israelite rivals. It is already impossible in the words of Isaiah to see contemporary information of an event concerning the destruction of Samaria in the Maccabean era because no true believing Jew of this era would identify the hated Samaritans of that time with Ephraimites. The "drunkards" of Ephraim were in any event their brothers, sons of Israel, whereas the Samaritans of the Gerizim Temple were, for a Jerusalem patriot, worse than pagans.

In the thirty-fourth chapter of Isaiah, the approaching certain ruin of all paganism is described in vivid detail

> Come near, nations, hearken and hear you people! Hear, earth and all that is therein; the world, and all that comes forth from it. For the wrath of the Lord is upon all nations, and his fury upon all their armies; he will give them over to be cursed and to perish. (Isa. 34:1–2)

Further the Idumites (Edom), the Jewish nation's most proximate pagans, are referred to in particular; their complete destruction is foretold, so that their country will revert into a vast desert. This was fulfilled in later times, but Havet boldly relates all this to the war of John Hyrcanus with the Idumites, although this war did not at all end with the destruction of Edom and the reversion of the country into a desert, and although in the text of Isaiah there is not the slightest allusion to the campaign of Hyrcanus, or to any kind of characteristic trait of those times and circumstances. But it is, of course, possible—with a very great desire but with very little sense—to relate the description of the Messianic kingdom (Is 35) to the times of the later Hasmoneans, when the eyes of the blind will open and the ears of the deaf will hear, when the lame will leap like a hart, and the tongue of the dumb will sing praise, when ravenous beasts will no longer be on earth, and all those ransomed by the Lord will return to Zion with the radiance of Eternity upon their heads. If one is to believe Havet, then all this was accomplished at the time of the same Ethnarch John Hyrcanus, about 120 years BC (vv. 5, 6).

Our author announces boldly, but unsupported by evidence, that the four following chapters (36–39) are a later addition, taken from the Book of Kings (ce sont des pages du Livre des Rois, ou figure le vieux prophete, et qu'on (?) [sic] a cru devoir reproduire a la suite du livre qu'on lui attribue [68]). Critics have up to now generally assumed the opposite, that the historical evidence of Isaiah was of the quality of a primary source inserted in the much later Book of Kings at its final redaction. Apparently Havet thought that remaining silent about this generally accepted opinion meant refuting it. However, if he had extended his personal opinion about the relative antiquity of the Book of Kings to the Hebrew annals (*Dibre hajamim*—Chronicles), then he would have found the following inconvenient evidence there: "the rest of the acts of Hezekiah, and his meekness, behold, are written in the visions of Isaiah the prophet, the son of Amos, and in the book of the Kings of Judah and Israel" (2 Chr 32:32).

IV

Proceeding to the prophet Jeremiah, Havet himself admits to the difficulty of subsuming him under his theory, but once he resolves to do so, then no difficulties can stop the game critic. Nevertheless Jeremiah is so unpleasant to our author that he apparently could not force himself to read this prophet in his entirety, but only glanced at him in places. For Havet, this would at least be the most beneficent explanation for his incredible assertion that the destruction of Jerusalem by the Chaldeans is not spoken of at all in Jeremiah's *prophecies* (p. 80). So Havet asserts, but in Jeremiah we read the following:

> And Zedekiah the king sent Jehucal "son of Shelemiah" and Zephaniah, the son of Maaselah, the priest to Jeremiah the prophet, saying—Pray now unto the Lord, our God, for us.—And Jeremiah came in and went out among the people; for they had not put him into prison. And Pharaoh's army came forth out of Egypt; and when the Chaldeans that besieged Jerusalem heard rumors of them, they departed from Jerusalem. And came the word of the Lord unto the prophet Jeremiah, saying: Thus says the Lord, the God of Israel: thus shall you say to the king [of Judah], who sent you unto me to inquire of me: behold, Pharaoh's army, which has come forth to help you, shall return to their own land, to Egypt; and the Chaldeans shall return and fight against this city, *and take it and burn it with fire*. Thus saith the Lord: do not deceive your souls, saying, the Chaldeans shall surely depart from us,—for they shall not depart. And even if you had defeated the whole army of the Chaldeans

that fight against you, and there remained among them only wounded men, every man in his tent will rise up, *and they will burn this city with fire*." (Jer. 37:3–10)

This place does not stand alone in Jeremiah: prophecies about the destruction of Jerusalem proceed through his entire book. I will introduce only a few: "For I have turned My face against this city to evil and not to good—says the Lord;—*it shall be given* into the hand of the king of Babylon, and *he shall burn it with fire*" (21:10).

> And Zedekiah, king of Judah, and his princes will I give into the hands of those who seek their lives, and into the hand of the king of Babylon's army, who have departed from you. Behold, I will command, says the Lord, and they will return to this city, and they shall fight against it, *and take it, and burn it with fire*; and together with it I will make the cities of Judah a desolation so that there will not be an inhabitant." (34:21–22)

In chapter 38 Jeremiah tells King Zedekiah: "And all your wives and your sons shall be led out to the Chaldeans, and you shall not escape out of their hands, for you shall be taken by the hands of the king of Babylon, *and this city shall be burned with fire*" (v. 23).

Apart from these prophetic places and those similar to them that have been missed or avoided by the critic, there is a historical tale in Jeremiah about the destruction of Jerusalem, in chapters 39 and 52, that Havet announces, unsupported by evidence, is taken from the Book of Kings. This assumption (besides its arbitrariness) is completely useless to him, once, apart from these chapters, the destruction of Jerusalem by the Chaldeans is spoken of in Jeremiah in the many other texts that have been cited above, which the undaunted critic did not dare even approach.

The critic separates himself from the breathing, living truth of the exposited events in which Jeremiah himself took part directly (chs. 36–52) with an amazing remark about the improbability of this tale. It seems improbable to him because the Judean king and his confidants were not frightened by the threats of the prophet and did not repent (ni le roi ni ses serviteurs ne s'effrayet des menaces prophetiques, et ne pensent a demander grace. Il est clair que nous lisons la une fiction, non une histoire [93]). But if it had been related in Jeremiah oppositely, that the Judean king and his servants obeyed the prophetic

admonitions and repented of their sins, it is without any doubt that the
very same Havet would have exclaimed triumphantly (and this time
quite rightly): how unlike history this is, what an obvious fable!

V

Rejecting apparent truth as invention, the critic naturally considers
himself in the right to create unprecedented and unheard of facts. A
future gathering of all segments of the Hebrew people, and of the
reconciliation of the house of Judah and the house of Israel, is spoken
about in the thirty-first chapter of Jeremiah. Our author resolutely asserts that such a union and reconciliation were accomplished at the
time of John Hyrcanus. Havet introduces the Messianic prophecies of
Jeremiah about healing and the joy of the people at the restoration
of the kingdom of David after having announced—as always unsupported by evidence and against all probability—that these places relate
to the times of the Hasmoneans and can not relate to any other; he
continues thus (p. 84): "But here is another picture, which also can
be placed at this time. This picture of the return of Ephraim or Israel
(in a strict sense of the word in contrast to Judah), that is, the return
of separate generations: first Ephraim is *reconciled, or sooner resigned*.
And it is enough to open the Book of Ezra to be assured how far it
was from this at the time of Zerubabel. But this occurred at the time
of Hyrcanus, the son of Simon, and here is what is read in Jeremiah."[5]
What follows are the words of Jeremiah about the fact that the Lord
will be God for all tribes of Israel† and the well-known address of
the Lord to Rachel, who is inconsolable:

> Thus says the Lord: a voice was heard in Ramah, lamentation
> and bitter weeping; Rachel weeps for her children and can-
> not be comforted about her children, for they are not. Thus
> says the Lord: restrain your voice from weeping and your
> eyes from tears; for there will be a reward for your work,

---

*Mais voici un autre tableau qui ne peut non plus se placer qu'à cette date. C'est celui
du retour d'Ephraim ou d'Israel en sens resreint où le mon d'Israel s'oppose à celui de
Juda, c'est à dire le retour des tribus séparée: pour la première fois alors Ephraim est
reconcilié *ou plutôt soumis*. Et il suffit d'ouvrir le livre d'Esdras pour s'assurer combien
il s'en fallait qu'il en fût ansi au temp de Zorababel. Mais cela s'est vue sou Hyrcan,
fils de Simon, et voici ce qui se lit dans Jérémie.

†According to the Hebrew Bible [Jer] 30:24, in translations 31:1.

says the Lord, and they shall return from the land of the enemy." (Jer. 31:14–15, according to the Hebrew Bible)

If one is somehow at a loss as to what exactly Havet has in view, what exactly occurred at the time of John Hyrcanus that is of such consolation for Rachel, then let the reader recall that this Judean leader ravaged Samaria and Sechem and destroyed the Gerizim temple! It is a good thing too that Rachel in actual fact had only a very flimsy and distant connection to this new Samaria, ravaged by Hyrcanus, else the consolation would have been quite strange. Here the critic resorts to a conscious and very crude *deception* of inattentive readers: in order to convert the *ravaging* of Samaria into the *reconciliation* of Judah with Israel, or Benjamin with Ephraim, a turn of phrase such as the following is used: then (at the time of John Hyrcanus) Ephraim was first *reconciled or sooner resigned (réconcilié ou plutôt soumis)*. The flagrant absurdity of the very thought is easily concealed by this smooth phrase and at a quick reading can slip by unnoticed. But are resignation and reconciliation in actual fact one and the same thing? And what resignation indeed: with carnage, heaps of ruins, the destruction of a sanctuary! After this the destruction of Jerusalem by the Romans could be considered a reconciliation of Jacob and Esau.*

And here is another specimen of the critical method to which our author is obliged by virtue of his important discoveries: "*the prophecy* (of Jeremiah) about Edom," says he, "must be related, just as Isaiah's, to the conquest of the Idumites by Hyrcanus. And concerning the prophecy about the fall of Babylon, then I relate it again to the invasion of the Parthians in the middle of the second century" (la prophétie sur Edom (49:7) doit se rapporter, ainsi que celle d'Isaïe, à la conquéte de l'Idumée par Hyrcan. Et quant à celle de la ruine de Babylone (chap. 51 et 52) je la rappport encore à l'invasion des Parthes au milieu du II siècle, p. 87). All the arguments of the critic on these two points are spent with these lines: *must be related, I relate*—this is enough and no further grounds are required.

However, when our author engages in reasoning, it comes out even worse. There is powerful denunciation of the "abomination" of human sacrifices in Jeremiah—clear evidence, it would seem, that this prophet wrote before the Babylonian captivity, when such sacrifices could still have been customary in the semi-pagan multitude of Jews. But Havet contrives to date this trait as well to the era of the

---

*In rabbinical literature Rome acquires the title Esau or Edom.

Hasmoneans with the help of the following reasoning (p. 103): human sacrifices are an expression of extreme fanaticism, but fanaticism among the Hebrews must have become acute after the Maccabean wars (ce fanatisme avait eu sans doute un recrudescense pendant les crises douloureuses du milieu du II siècle)—this means that at this time, the Hebrews must have been intensely burning their infants in the Jerusalem temple, evoking by this the denunciation of well-intentioned social commentators like the author of the Book of Jeremiah, apparently written at this time. It is hardly possible, however, to agree that every kind of fanaticism is unfailingly expressed in sacrifices such as the burning of one's children: so, for example, even the extreme fanaticism of negative criticism is content with the sacrifice of sound meaning and historical knowledge.

There is only one remark relative to Jeremiah that resembles anything like a serious argument in Havet, namely, a suggestion that there is no mention of this prophet in the Book of Kings, but this too is intended only for readers unfamiliar with the Bible. And those who are familiar with it know in the first place that subsequent events in Jerusalem before the Babylonian captivity, that is, precisely those events in which Jeremiah took part, are not related in the Book of Kings at all, but the fact of the ultimate catastrophe is communicated only in a couple of words. Here it was identically natural both to mention and not to mention the activity of the prophet, in conformity with the disposition and the intentions of the historian; in any case such a mention was not necessary, for people reading the Bible more attentively than Havet know in the second place that the prophet Jeremiah is mentioned in two holy books that have no less historical significance than the Book of Kings (2 Chronicles 35:25, 36:12, 21, 22, and Ezra 1:1). In light of this, if our author concludes against the authenticity of Jeremiah from a lack of Jeremiah's mention in the Book of Kings, then why does he not draw a conclusion in favor of the authenticity of Isaiah from the opposite fact of Isaiah's mention in the very same Book of Kings? Isn't it clear that bias, and not logic, governs these pseudo-critical exercises?

VI

Justice requires acknowledging moments of illumination in our author, when he himself feels awkward in the historical realm, and it is as if he recognizes to what extent his views are not serious and his arguments impermissible in a scholarly respect. "But I make haste," he says concerning the activity of Jeremiah, "to exit and to lead my readers out of this historical thicket" (de ces broussailles historiques [91]); and further: "But it is time to leave detail, the interpretation of which is sometimes difficult" (p. 93). In another place he notes to himself on sound grounds that: "It is better to be restrained with respect to texts that you [sic] can read only in translation (Il vaut mieux être sobre sur des texts que je ne puis lire que traduits [133]).

But after momentary sobriety the pseudo-critical fever returns with its previous strength. Just as Isaiah and Jeremiah, Ezekiel too speaks about the disasters that the city of Tyre endured at the hands of the Babylonians. But *since* these prophets wrote in the second century, *then this means* Antiochus Epithanus must be put in place of the Babylonians. True, it is known from history that Antiochus Epithanus did not go to war with Tyre and caused no disasters, but this does not matter: he probably wished to ravage Tyre, and Judah rejoiced in advance (p. 121). But Isaiah, having described the fall of Tyre, says later that it will be restored, and that then the riches of its traders will be dedicated to the God of Israel and will go for the maintenance of his priests. And so? *"It is possible to suppose* that this occurred at the time of Hyrcanus" (On peut supposer du'on vit cela au temps d'Hyrcan [122]).

We read in the prophet Hosea that the Jews will be saved by the Lord their God, and not by weapons and battles (1:7). Our author assures us that this cannot relate to any other times but the Maccabean, as if the Maccabees freed their people without the help of weapons and without battles! The same prophet denounces Israelites in Samaria for the worship of an idol in the form of a "calf" (8:4-6)—clear evidence, it would seem, about the antiquity of this prophet. But Havet relates to this otherwise. As always, taking his unproved and unprovable chronological thesis for the undoubted truth, he concludes: since Hosea must have lived in the second century, then this means that the cult of calves was still maintained among the Hebrews in the second century!

And with regard to the prophet *Joel*, we obtain the soothing assurance that a terrible judgment in the valley of Jehoshophat foretold by this prophet [Joel 3:12] was already accomplished by Simon and Hyrcanus ("c'est Simon et Hyrcan qui ont exécuté ce jugement de leur Dieu" [140]).

Amos also gives occasion for our author to make an interesting discovery. "I am not a prophet and not a son of a prophet," says Amos, and Havet sees in this a clear indication that he lived after the ultimate liberation of the Jews from Greco-Syrian rule. The point is the prophets—with which apparently all Palestine was teeming at the time—were highly valued as inciters of popular enthusiasm in the war against the Greeks; when it ended, they began to be, oppositely, feared and persecuted, and that is why they had to disavow their title. There is nothing at all incongruous with the history of the Jewish nation in such an explanation, for those not having read Amos and unfamiliar with him.

Seeing the name *Jonah* on the pages of our critics, I expected evidence that the whale who swallowed the prophet was also a contemporary of Simon Maccabeus and John Hyrcanus, but unfortunately, Havet did not concern himself with this circumstance.

Then we find two curious bits of news with respect to the prophet *Micah*: (1) that the Messiah about which Micah prophesies was, namely, none other than the Hasmonean Simon, *ethnarch* of Judea (p. 150); and (2) in supplement of an earlier intimation—that at this time, that is, in the second century, the official religion of the Jews required the burning of infants, and that they brought them as sacrifice to the God of Israel himself ("c'était bien à Jéhova lui même qu'on faisait ces immolations d'enfants" [152]).

With respect to *Nahum, Habbakuk,* and *Zephaniah,* our author says nothing striking, repeating only that they lived in the second century. Concerning *Haggai* and *Zechariah,* the reader will recall that they lived around the time of the birth of Christ; the Messiah that they proclaimed was Herod (159ff). The title *branch of David* is especially befitting of this Idumite! To him must be ascribed what is said about Zerubabel in these two prophets, and about Cyrus—in so-called second Isaiah. But in order to be unbiased, Havet ascribes to the same Herod what is said about the anti-Christ, the enemy of the sanctuary and God and the people of God—in the Book of *Daniel.*

This book, just as the book of the prophet Malachi as well, was written after Herod, consequently, after the first half of the first century AD. There is one small difficulty here, which is, however, easily eliminated. Both Daniel and Malachi are cited as ancient and holy authorities in the canonical Gospels. When were the Gospels written? If a person of like mind to Havet wanted to surpass his critical boldness while not diverging from his rules and method, then it would follow for him to assert that the Gospels were written at the beginning of the sixteenth century, namely, by Doctor Martin Luther, with the undoubted and poorly concealed intent of basing the evangelical [Protestant] creed on them.

It is impossible not to note still another curious circumstance. There is indication that the Greek translation of the Hebrew holy books, among that number Daniel and Malachi, already existed about 130 years BC; but if these two prophets wrote only in the first century AD, then here is the lone example to date of literary works translated into a foreign language a hundred fifty years before they were originally written.

VII

The abuse of negative criticism achieved an amusing caricature to the point of absurdity in the person of Havet. There was more than a little absurd and laughable, of course, on the opposite side as well. . . . Today we can consider both extremes dead and buried. Germany, the current fatherland of negative criticism, gradually repudiates "hypercritical" arbitrariness more and more, but on the other hand England—to date the immovable stronghold of traditional exegesis—adjoins the general scholarly movement in this sphere, not avoiding even certain temptations, which are nevertheless better than the stagnation previously.

Fossilized rarities of blind literalism are met now only in countries and circles wittingly alienated from knowledge, and at the same time enfants terribles of the opposite tendency, such as Havet, are compelled to bitterly complain about the complete contempt for their theory on the part of scholars, of which "only those who have said nothing about it have shown mercy to it" (ceux-la seulement l'on ménagée qui n'eu ont rien dit [7]).

Truth be told, here as well, as usually is the case, the opposite extremes of traditional and negative tendencies are created on one and the same soil—scholarly abstraction. They are born of one and the same spirit, or, better to say, by one and the same absence of spirit, by the same *indifference* to the essence, to the intrinsic meaning of the Bible and the prophetic writings in particular.

But in the face of indifference and inattention to this essential content—to that which inspired the biblical writers and for the sake of which they acted and wrote—the very problem of the circumstances and time of their activity loses vital interest and at the same time is deprived of the main basis for its correct resolution. For only an understanding of the *meaning* of Hebrew history that was expressed in the Bible gives us a stable point of support for a true assessment of the time and the historical frames of reference in which the bearers of this meaning lived and acted. The necessity of and an interest in special philological and historical research are not eliminated by this, of course, but an understanding of the matter at its essence is also necessary for them, as the point of departure and the guiding thread of intellectual labor.

I do not have in mind at all any kind of metaphysical construction and a priori conclusion of history: I take the matter simply and elementarily. The indisputable fact exists that in ancient times a small and moreover fragmented Hebrew nation endured, and they endured historical catastrophes, the like of which incomparably more powerful, united, and cultured national bodies perished from in the end, and they endured to their advantage, with intrinsic growth and eminence, which means that the Hebrew people endured this not through material power, but through spiritual power. Since the Hebrews did not have other *significant* expressions of the national spirit besides the national religion, this spiritual power was undoubtedly connected with it. But the issue is still not explained by this. There were national religions in all other nations as well, and at first glance it is difficult to find an essential difference between the primary religion of the sons of Israel and the religion of the sons of Moab, Ammon, or Edom. But they perished and Israel remained indestructible, which means that in the religion of the Hebrews there was something greater than its visible national form, there was some kind of intrinsic superiority, thanks to which the spirit of the people was strengthened and became capable of enduring the destruction of its political body. This greater thing that distinguished the national religion of the Hebrews from all others and that was expressed in particular in the prophets was not the abstract idea of monotheism, but was the living consciousness and sentiment that a personal God is the national Providence of Israel and the personal Providence of each Israelite; that He is, *in the first place*, a universal God, Who holds *everything* in His *power*, and *in the second place*, that He is not a God of power alone, but also a God of *truth* [*pravda*], not abstractly conceived, but acting in reality and being realized. From this kind of unity of power and truth it follows that all that happens must end to the glory of this God, that for those who are faithful to Him, physical disasters are only trials, methods, and means to spiritual perfection and happiness. And from this comes the *third* distinctive element of this higher religious consciousness, a belief in a golden age *ahead*, in historical progress, or in a meaning of history, in an ultimate kingdom of truth.

This higher consciousness is in truth *prophetic*, for it anticipates the future and by this very anticipation gives a moral power to people to bring closer this ideal future and realize it. Only such a prophetic consciousness could save the Hebrew nation in extreme disasters, beyond the power of other nations. All extrinsic buttresses of existence were removed from it. What in actual fact preserved the Jewish nation as a single national-spiritual community at the time of the Babylonian captivity? Neither country nor state, nor a single cult, nor even their own language. Everything was lost—everything that other nations had and through which these nations did not save themselves. Israel was saved by the fact that it had one thing—spiritual unity with the living God of Truth. Now one may ask: when did this intrinsic power appear in the Hebrew nation, when did the first bearers and expositors of this higher consciousness live? Isn't it clear that this higher consciousness was *before* the extrinsic catastrophes, for the endurance of which this spiritual power was necessary? According to the natural course of history, the ideal principles that seize onto collective goals first appear in the person of individual chosen people. If at the time of the Babylonian captivity and after the entire Hebrew community, at least in its leading circles, had to adopt a higher religious consciousness for its salvation, then it is clear that individual chosen people had to achieve this consciousness and elevate it *earlier* than the national disaster. They declared themselves prophets in three senses: (1) they *anticipated* the kingdom of truth, ideally defining their religious consciousness through it; (2) they denounced and judged the actual condition of their nation as contradictory to this ideal and *foretold* national disasters as a necessary consequence of such contradiction; (3) they *indicated ahead of time* through their very appearance and activity a way out of this contradiction in the most proximate future of the nation, namely, through the acknowledgment by them of this higher consciousness and their subjection to it.

Thus, on intrinsic grounds we must accept that the major Hebrew prophets lived partly *earlier* than the Babylonian captivity and partly at its start, which is in complete agreement both with ancient tradition and with the opinion of all serious scholars in modernity.

The Bible in general and the writings of the prophets in particular are the most ancient—but now just as before not obsolete—*prophetic* expression of the most exalted and purest spiritual power acting in humanity. Relating to this greatest of universal history's artifacts by being distracted from its special content or intrinsic meaning, and seeing in it only a reflection of extrinsic historical circumstances—means taking the subject not for what it is—means acting unjustly, falsely, *in an unscholarly manner.* On the other hand, looking at the evidence of the living God's historical acts as a fossilized and inviolable relic means demonstrating a dead faith and sinning against the Holy Spirit, who has spoken through the prophets.[6] True scholarship requires understanding that which is really essential in the Bible, namely, the prophetic spirit, and true religiosity requires *acknowledging* this spirit as an eternally living force, which not only determined the fortunes of the Hebrew nation in the past, but also on which the creation of our own future must depend as well.

10

Byzantinism and Russia

I

Pagan Rome fell because its idea of an absolute and deified state was incompatible with the truth revealed in Christianity, by virtue of which supreme state power is only a *delegation* of the authentically Divine-human power of Christ. The second Rome—Byzantium—fell because, while having accepted in words the idea of a Christian kingdom, it rejected it in fact, and persisted in its governmental and legislative contradiction of the higher moral authority's requirements. Ancient Rome deified itself and perished. Byzantium deliberately submitted itself to a higher authority, but considered itself saved by a superficial shroud of Christian dogma and priestly acts that concealed a pagan life, however, it perished as well. This ruination gave a powerful jolt to the historical consciousness of the nation that acquired from the Greeks the conception of a Christian kingdom as well as its baptism. A firm conviction appeared in the Russian national consciousness, insofar as it was expressed in the thoughts and writings of our scholastics, that the signification of a Christian kingdom was being transferred from now on to Russia, that it was the third and final Rome.*

It was permissible for our ancestors to dwell on this idea in its initial cast of instinctive sentiment or presentiment. We are required to verify it through logical deliberation and experience, and then either raise it to the level of the rational consciousness or repudiate it as a childish daydream and arbitrary claim.

II

Two Romes fell, the third—the Muscovite kingdom—stands, and there will be no fourth! . . . If the common characteristic of the old and new

---

*Our scholastics, under the influence of the theological polemic of the Greeks against the Latins, considered papal Rome, and not pagan Rome, to be the first Rome, which, in their opinion, fell away from Orthodoxy.

191

Romes consists in the fact that both of them *fell*, then it is all the more important for us to know *why* they fell, and consequently, *what* the third, the latest Rome, should avoid, in order not to become subject to the very same fate.

If the point were just about the first Rome, then the question about the reason for its fall would not present any difficulty. Rome fell because the principle of its life was erroneous and it could not withstand a clash with higher truth, but what is to be said about Orthodox Byzantium? Its life principle was truth, and its clash with the Turkish Muslims was not a clash with higher truth. Or was it crushed by physical force alone? Yet such a proposition, apart from its impossibility from a Christian point of view, is contrary to both reason and historical experience, which is full of vivid evidence of the fact that physical force alone is powerless. It was not by preponderance of physical force that the classical ancestors of the Byzantine Greeks crushed eastern kingdoms, and not by the numerical superiority of armies that the Aragonese and Castillians finally ousted the Muslim world from the West at the very same time that the Muslim world did away with the eastern empire.

There was an intrinsic, spiritual reason for the fall of Byzantium, and since it does not consist in the subject of faith being false, for that in which the Byzantines believed was true, then the false character of their faith, that is, their false attitude toward Christianity, must be acknowledged as the reason for their ruination: *they comprehended the true idea and applied it unfaithfully.* It was only a subject of their intellectual avowal and ritualistic reverence, but not the motivating principle of life. Taking pride in their orthodoxy [*pravoverie*] and piety, they did not want to understand the simple and self-evident truth that true orthodoxy and piety actually require that we to some extent conform our life to that in which we believe and that which we revere; they did not want to understand that an actual advantage belongs to a Christian kingdom sooner than to others only to the extent that it is founded and managed in the Spirit of Christ.

Of course, it is still quite a long distance from a most sincere and conscientious acknowledgment that vital requirements are connected correspondingly with a confession of higher truth to the realization of these requirements; but in any event such an acknowledgment now arouses one toward efforts in the proper direction, makes one do something toward an approximation of the higher goal, and, not bestowing perfection immediately, serves as an internal engine of *perfectibility.* But in Byzantium it is precisely the vital requirements of Christianity that were themselves denied, no higher task was set for the life of society and for state activity. Imperfection is our common lot, and Byzantium perished, certainly, not because it was imperfect, but because it did not want to perfect itself. These people sometimes repented of their personal sins, but they completely forgot about their *public* sin, and they ascribed the fall of their kingdom only to the sins of individual people. But if the personal sins of a person can ruin him, whereas penitence and reform can save him from ruin, then is it feasible for the fate of kingdoms to be dependent on this? If three righteous men can save a city, then, of course, it is only in the event that they are actually righteous men, that is, not confined to egoistic concerns about themselves alone, but thinking as well about the salvation of the entire city; if they do not do this, then they together with their reprobate fellow citizens are guilty of public sin, through which the city is being ruined.[1]

Kingdoms, as collective wholes, perish only from collective sins—of the whole people, of the state—and are saved only by the improvement of their social system, or its progression toward a moral order. And if personal righteousness is what it is all about, independent of social improvement, then there were no fewer people who were holy in this sense in the Byzantine kingdom than anywhere else. Why then did this kingdom perish? In the Byzantine understanding, if a master did not torture his slaves and he fed them well, then nothing more was required of him with respect to slavery; it was as if a simple idea neither occurred to him, to his confessor, or to the autocrat of the "Greek-Romans" himself: the idea that the good situation of a good master's slaves does not make it easier at all for the unfortunate slaves of his wicked neighbors, whereas the legal abolition of slavery would have immediately eased everyone's lot and would have immediately drawn the earthly kingdom nearer the Kingdom of God, where there is neither master nor slave. Individual events of inhumanity and perversion, no matter how numerous and common, still did not in and of themselves constitute sufficient grounds for the ultimate fall of Byzantium. But we will understand this fall completely if we turn our attention to the following circumstance. Over the entire course of Byzantine history proper (i.e., from the time of the definitive alienation of the Eastern Christian world from the Western—whether one dates this alienation in the eleventh or in the ninth century), it is not possible to indicate a single public action, a single general measure of the government at all that had in view the essential improvement of societal relations in a moral sense—any elevation of a given legal status in conformity with the requirements of absolute truth, any improvement of the collective life within the kingdom or in its external relations; in a word, we will not find here anything of the kind in which it would be possible to note even faint traces of a higher spirit advancing universal history. Even if the villainy and licentiousness of individual people were balanced out by the good deeds of others and the prayers of holy monks, this total and general indifference to the *historical advancement of the good*, to the providential Divine will in the collective life of the people was not balanced and expiated by anything.

The direct successors of the Roman Caesars forgot that they were at the same time delegates of the supreme authority of Christ. Instead of raising the pagan state inherited by them to the height of a Christian kingdom, they, to the contrary, lowered the Christian kingdom to the level of a complacent pagan state. They preferred an arbitrary autocracy of human will, representing the concentrated sum of all individual arbitrary wills in one person, to an autocracy of conscience in accordance with the Divine will. They called themselves autocrats, but in essence they were just like the pagan emperors (if just in this life—and sometimes fleetingly as well)—plenipotentiaries of the multitudes and their armed forces.

Having turned out to be hopelessly inadequate to their higher mission—to be a Christian kingdom—Byzantium lost the intrinsic reason for its existence. This is because the prevailing typical tasks of state administration could even be performed much better by the government of the Turkish Sultan, which, being free of internal contradiction, was more honest and steadfast; and what's more it did not interfere in the religious sphere of Christianity, did not compose dubious dogmas and malignant heresies, and also did not defend Orthodoxy by means of the rash slaughter of heretics and the exultant burning of their leaders at the stake.

After many reprieves and a long struggle with material decay, and just prior to the regeneration of the West, the eastern empire, having long since died in moral terms, was finally swept off the field of history. Even though the intrinsic cause of this lamentable catastrophe was not completely clear to contemporaries, they did, however, note yet another coincidence of events. The Turks brought an end to the kingdom of Constantine at the precise time that a new historical actor found its legs in Eastern Europe, free to take on the work of a Christian kingdom, for the performance of which Byzantium turned out to be pathetically depleted.

III

As a Slavic-Finnish people, enriched by Germans, Russia displayed the superiority of its religious-political consciousness over that of the

Byzantines from the very beginning of its historical life. While he was a pagan, the first Kievan Christian prince devoted himself absolutely to his natural inclinations, but once baptized, he immediately understood the simple truth that neither the Byzantine emperors, beginning with Constantine the Great, nor the Greek bishops ever did (this included, incidentally, those who were sent to Kiev for the instruction of the new Christians). He understood that *true faith obliges*, and it obligates you, namely, to change the rules by which both you and your community live, consonant with the spirit of the new faith. He understood this as even applying in the instance of the death penalty, which was obscure not just for the Byzantines alone; he found it incompatible with the Spirit of Christ to impose the death penalty even upon avowed brigands. The newly baptized Vladimir understood that to take the life of unarmed—and consequently harmless—people in revenge for their earlier evil deeds was contrary to Christian justice. It is striking that in such an attitude to this question he was guided not just by a natural feeling of pity, but directly by his consciousness of true Christian requirements. In answer to the exhortations of Greek bishops, who persuaded him to execute the villains, he did not say that he pitied them, but he said: "I fear sin," that is, I fear acting contrary to higher moral principle. In distinction from his pseudo-Christian mentors, he feared sin more than he did brigands, and it was not his fault if a foreign authority, which he could not scorn, in this instance restricted an autocratic conscience that befitted a Christian state. Finding the death penalty to be unjust, Vladimir also related to war with Christian nations negatively as well, preserving his retainers just for defense of the land against barbaric and rapacious nomads, who were amenable to no other arguments apart from armed force.

Subordinating external politics to a peace-loving spirit, Vladimir manifested the Spirit of Christ in internal affairs, not only from its negative aspect—a justice by virtue of which he considered it a sin to kill even brigands—but also from the positive aspect of mercy, which his constant concerns about the population in Kiev and in other places living in poverty testify to.*

A proper understanding of Christianity also gave notice finally in the radiant, joyous mood that predominated in the life and princely reign of Vladimir and remained in the national memory about him; it was connected with semihistorical and semimythological images and

---

*The fact of these concerns is not as important as their purely moral motive, which become clear from the tale of the chronicler. In Vladimir's reign there was no general national disaster that would have threatened the security of the state, but this prince considered it impermissible to leave anyone at all among his subjects in a helpless situation.

was expressed in the moniker of Little Red Sun.[2] This radiant mood, as we know, neither excluded a consciousness of past sins nor a fear of sin in the present. In true Christianity all this is combined: predicated on the atonement of the past and bestowing a norm upon present reality, it lives in the future, joyously anticipating the advent of full perfection, not of spiritual life alone, but of material life as well. Thus, our first Christian sovereign from all facets faithfully understood and accepted the moral essence of Christianity, which is "righteousness, peace and joy in the Holy Spirit" [Ro 14:17].

IV

A Christian consciousness in Russia did not die with its first spokesman. A hundred years after St. Vladimir, his great-grandson Vladimir Monomakh left an instruction suffused with the same spirit. But the example of this self-same Monomakh sufficiently demonstrates that the realization of a moral order in the world, or at least in a single country, still requires complex historical-political conditions apart from a personal consciousness of truth and personal good will—such conditions are not provided all of a sudden. Vladimir Monomakh, who like his great-grandfather was so suffused with Christian spirit that he considered it impermissible to kill even villains, had to live his entire life on horseback in perpetual campaigns, defending the nation from barbaric predators or pacifying internecine struggles among princes.

In order for a historical nation to fulfill its mission of becoming a Christian kingdom and furthering universal perfection it must first of all *exist*. And the state of affairs that is vividly attested in the instruction of Monomakh, and in "The Lay of Igor's Host" as well, threatened the very existence of the Russian nation. This was not an empty fear, for at hand were examples of nations that had not been successful in developing and that had perished from political disarray.

It was clear to all people of good will and common sense what Russia lacked. An exalted spiritual light was brought into the dark soul of the people and was sustained in it by the reliably heroic virtues of piety and mercy; Christianity brought fruits into the personal life of many, but the whole society was being lost from a fratricidal dissension that made it indefensible against an external enemy who carried with him wanton furor and destruction. It is clear that it was necessary first of all to secure the existence of the national corpus, to unite it through direct and secure organization, that is, to create a strong state. This necessity, which had already been clearly recognized by the immediate successors of Vladimir Monomakh—by Yuri Suzdal'skii and Andrei Bogoliubskii—was only vividly confirmed for everyone by the mongol invasion, against which the weak state of Rus' turned out to be helpless. And if the obvious reason for weakness was the authority of a multitude of princes and internecine strife, then the idea of autocracy appeared for the entire nation as a banner of salvation. Our national worldview gravitated to this as well, and this worldview also strictly defined the character of our monarchy.

As a result of the essential homogeneity of the agricultural population in Russia and the absence of isolated social groups—feudal, urban, ecclesiastical—the Western European concept of the state [gosudarstvo] (Status), as a balance of independent and equivalent elements could not emerge. The word "proprietorship" [gospodarstvo] itself in its initial meaning indicated a head of household [domovladyka] who was not, of course, the representative of equivalent household servants [domochadtsy], but was the sovereign proprietor of a clan community. Even where there was no absolute rule in fact, it remained personified in verbal representation. So, although later historians speak about our "republics" [narodopravstva], these so-called republics expressed themselves otherwise. The Novgorodians called their state "Lord Novgorod the Great," personifying it in the image of a powerful monarch. This monarch lived in enmity against the Muscovite monarchy, but not against the monarchic idea. That the struggle of Riazan or Tver against Moscow was only rivalry for possession of supreme rule, and in no way a principled opposition to absolute rule is clear in and of itself. Local rivalry did not have a basis in the people, who had long since guessed that the Muscovite princes were the real masters of the land; and the decisive support of the spiritual authority, represented by hierarchs such as St. Alexis and monks such as St. Sergius, ultimately sanctioned the supreme signification of Christian rulers, to whom passed as well the historical succession of the Eastern Roman empire later, at the time of Ivan III.[3]

But it turned out quite soon that this historical heritage is not only a gift and an advantage, but also a great *trial*.

Ivan IV must be acknowledged as the first actual bearer of imperial autocracy among us, not only because of the fullness of his power in fact, but also because of a clear consciousness of its character and source. Without question, this is the most significant, distinctive and interesting personality in our history between St. Vladimir and Peter the Great.

V

The most faithful and complete formula of the Christian monarchic idea has, incidentally, come down to us from Ivan the Terrible:

The land is governed by the Divine mercy and grace of the Blessed Mother of God and all the saints, by prayers and our fathers' blessings and seed—it is governed by us, by our sovereigns, and not by magistrates and commanders, and not by governors and military leaders.

This formula is irreproachable; it is not possible to better express the Christian view of an earthly kingdom. But if one compares these perfect words with the historical image of the one who pronounced them, then what a new, staggering, and tragic meaning they acquire. Truly, Russian history does not give ground to any other history in its profound, intrinsic interest.

In Russian literature many have judged Ivan the Terrible from various points of view and expressed different personal opinions about him, both correct and incorrect. As far as I know, they have just not yet subjected him to the final judgment of the supreme instance indicated in Holy Scripture: "a man is acquitted by his words and condemned by them."[4] Meanwhile, this is not only the most correct judgment, but also the most interesting one, because it is only in comparing Ivan the Terrible's abiding words to his personality that his personality acquires a general and instructive significance, whereas apart from this it is only an erstwhile and inimitable incarnation of human evil.

There are negative and positive parts to this formula of Ivan the Terrible: it indicates by whom the land is *not* governed (in the sense of independent authority) and by whom it is governed in accordance with the idea of a Christian kingdom. The land is not governed by magistrates and military commanders; this negative indication is justly placed at the end of the formula, because it has in it only second degree significance. There is nothing characteristic in the fact that the supreme power of Christian rulers is not restricted from below, since this belongs to the power of pagan despots to varying degrees as well: both for Nebuchadnezzar and for Nero, their "governors and military leaders" were not independent participants in governance, but only servants. With all its importance in connection to other definitions, this negative indicator does not in itself differentiate the qualitative essence of governance, being indifferent with respect to both Christianity and paganism.

The essential significance belongs, consequently, to the positive part of the formula. "The land is governed by Divine mercy, and so forth—and the *seed*—by us, by our sovereigns." From the order of address and from the word "seed" it is perfectly clear that the power of the sovereign is confirmed here as a delegation from above with a perfectly defined religious-moral character and mission, to which point the conditions and means, such as the mercy of the Blessed Mother of God, the prayers of all saints, and the blessing of fathers.

Thus, Ivan the Terrible's reign during the period when his character was ultimately determined is not only a collection of all kinds of horrors, but also has a more profound significance in its *deviation* from the monarchic idea formulated by him and its *opposition* to the supreme power proclaimed by him. The Divine mercy and grace of the Blessed Mother of God did not permit Ivan the Terrible to massacre tens of thousands of peaceful Novgorodian people; without the tiniest shadow of doubt, he himself and all Russia knew that in propagating this massacre, he acted directly contrary to that which Divine mercy required; consequently, he was found in open contradiction to the supreme power from which he had a commission as its *seed* to govern the land. It is absolutely clear that the "prayers of all the saints" did not fully empower the pious tsar to kill the Holy Metropolitan Phillip, nor was it less clear that the sources of his power and the most proximate of the sanctions pronounced by him—"the blessing of fathers"—were given to him not to lead the dynasty to its termination by the murder of his heir and to leave his fathers without an ancestral successor.

The reign of Ivan the Terrible was a vivid and distinctive repetition of the contradiction that ruined Byzantium—the contradiction between a verbal confession of truth and its denial in fact. He was sufficiently learned to understand the meaning of Byzantine history, but he did not want to understand it and preferred to share the Byzantine point of view, that *truth does not obligate*. It was all the more unforgivable for the heir of Monomakh to return to that "unbelieving faith" because he already had the example of a better consciousness within proper boundaries, and on the other hand, there was not even a seeming necessity that compelled him to commit the crime. The disorder of the appanage princes that had ruined Kievan Rus, notwithstanding the seeds of healthy life that were planted in it, no longer existed with Ivan IV's accession to the throne; there were no serious opponents to absolute power. Consequently nothing prevented the tsar from using his secure and unrestricted power for Christian principles, pronounced by him himself—the same principles that not only had been understood prior to him, but also to a certain degree had been applied by his Kievan ancestors. Preferring a rotten pagan tradition to the better testaments of St. Vladimir and Monomakh, the unfortunate tsar ruined himself and his dynasty, and led Russia itself to the brink of ruin.

VI

The reign of Ivan the Terrible with all its horrors and its fateful consequences would be an invidious absurdity in a moral sense if deviation from the true idea of a Christian kingdom had just been the personal sin of the tsar. In the interest of what then were rivers of blood spilt for? To whose benefit was the very question of the whole country's existence itself subordinated? But this had not been just a personal sin of Ivan IV. The duplicity of this tsar—who gave himself over to crimes on the order of Nero's, while at the same time citing Divine mercy and the grace of the Holy Mother of God—was supported and in a certain sense excused by the *political vacillation* of the Russian people.

　　The vacillation of the Russian people in their daily routine and their personal-religious spheres in this period, just as that of the majority of other Christian nations, is widely known. "Political vacillation" is precisely what I call this distinctive phenomenon upon which less attention has been cast, and which is quite specific to the Russian national consciousness beginning with the twelfth century. It is the acknowledgment at one and the same time of two irreconcilable kingdom ideals: on the one hand, the Christian ideal of a king as the earthly personification and instrument of Divine truth and mercy—an ideal, supported by the memory of the best and greatest Kievan princes of the Mongol era—and, on the other hand, the purely pagan image of a ruler as the personification of a terrible, all-destructive, power not delimited by anything morally—the ideal of the Roman Caesar, animated and strengthened by the influence of the most immediate impressions of the Tatar hordes.

　　This reversion of Russian consciousness to the ancient pagan deification of a limitless power engulfing everything, a reversion elicited by historical tragedy, was personified in the monarchy, and was rendered in a strange and unusually expressive legend, according to which the authority of Moscow sovereigns received higher sanction from none other than Nebuchadnezzar, that is, precisely from the head of the pagan colossus smashed by Christ and from the most archetypal personification of the idea of limitless despotism, opposed to God and denounced from above.*

Everyone knows the legend about the holy tokens of imperial authority being transferred to the Muscovite rulers from their ancestor, the Grand Prince of Kiev, Vladimir Vesevolodovich, who in his turn received them as a gift from the Eastern Roman Emperor Constantine Monomakh (who transferred to Vladimir that epithet as well). But where did Byzantium itself get these regalia? Our legend answers this question.

After the fall of Nebuchadnezzar's kingdom, the legend relates how Babylon was left neglected, became the habitation of countless snakes, and was ringed by a single huge snake, so that the city became inaccessible. Nevertheless, the Greek Emperor Leo, "baptized as Basil," resolved to acquire the treasure that had once belonged to Nebuchadnezzar. Having gathered an army, Leo left for Babylon and, pausing fifteen fields from the city, sent three men into it, a Greek, an Abkhaz, and a Rusin. The path was very difficult: for a great grass, like the plant *volchets* [*phelipaea ramosa*], grew sixteen versts around the city; there was a multitude of all kinds of vermin, snakes, and toads, which arose from the ground in clusters, as if sown in piles; they whistled and whispered, while others brought a hard frost, like winter. The envoys passed safely on through to the great snake, which slept, and then on to the walls of the city. At the walls there was a staircase with an inscription in three languages—Greek, Georgian, and Russian—announcing that one could safely make one's way into the city upon this staircase. Accomplishing this, the envoys saw a church in the center of Babylon and, entering it, they found on the tomb of three holy boys—Ananius, Azarius, and Misail (who had at one time been consumed in a fiery furnace)—a precious goblet filled with myrrh or wine; they drank from the goblet, became tipsy and fell asleep for a long while; upon awakening they wanted to take the goblet, but a voice from the tomb forbade them to do this and ordered them to go to Nebuchadnezzar's treasure and take "the signs," that is, the imperial insignias.

Among the other valuables in the treasure trove, they found two imperial crowns, and near them a document, where it was stated that the crowns were made by Nebuchadnezzar, the *emperor of Babylon and the entire universe*, for him alone and for his queen,

---

*The origin of Byzantium is ascribed to this legend. However, its Greek text has not been found: in Russia it was very widely disseminated in various versions that are preserved to this day.

but now, they must be worn by Emperor Leo and his queen; besides that, the envoys found in the Babylonian treasury a "semiprecious gem-encrusted chest," in which there was the crown of Monomakh, the royal scepter, and royal purple. Taking the things, the envoys returned to the church, genuflected at the tomb of the three boys, drank once more from the goblet and went the next day along the return path. On the very same staircase one of them stumbled, falling on the great snake and awakening it; when "the great snake heard him, there arose scales on it like waves of the sea, and they began to oscillate"; the two other envoys snatched their comrade away and hastily fled; they arrived at the place where they had left their steeds, and as they finished loading their booty on them, the great snake suddenly whistled; they fell to the ground and lay for a long time like dead men, until finally they came to and set off for the emperor. But the snake's whistle created even more trouble in the emperor's army; more than a few warriors and steeds perished. The rest fled in fear, and only some thirty versts from Babylon did the emperor pause to await his envoys. Upon arrival they related their adventure and gave the emperor Nebuchadnezzar's insignias—the very same ones that, according to other tales—were transferred from one of the Byzantine emperors that followed to the Kievan rulers, and from them to the Muscovites.

A later variant of the very same legend (transcribed in the region of Samara) simply puts Moscow in place of Byzantium, replacing Emperor Leo with the Moscow ruler, namely, Ivan the Terrible. It is *he* who turns out to be the direct successor of Nebuchadnezzar's power!

Tsar Ivan Vasilevich shrieked, crying: who will get the crown, the scepter, the orb of arms and the instructions for using them for me *from the Babylonian kingdom*? For three days and three nights he shrieked, crying; nobody came. Bormà-Iaryzhka arrives and takes upon himself the task of fulfilling the tsar's wish.[5] After thirty years of wandering and every adventure possible, he finally returns to the Muscovite ruler, bringing him the crown, scepter, the orb of arms, and instructions from the Babylonian kingdom, and as a reward he asks of Tsar Ivan only one thing: "allow me to drink in all the taverns tax-free for three years!" The ending is not bereft of significance for this reversion process of the national consciousness in the direction of savage pagan ideals.*

---

*See A. N. Pypin, "A New Epoch," *Vestnik Evropy* (January 1894).

VII

Although Bormà-Iaryzhka, from whom Ivan IV received Nebuchadne-zzar's regalia, represents a factor of no small importance in Russian life and Russian consciousness to this day, he did not have dominant significance in the sixteenth century. A contradiction was felt even then between the acts of Ivan the Terrible and the ideal of a Christian emperor, which, for all that, the Russian people did not reject in favor of the concepts brought from "Babylon" by Bormà-Iaryzhka. Consciousness of a great retreat from the religious foundations of a truly imperial authority existed, and as a result there was an attempt to exultantly uphold these foundations, to raise to a universal level the significance of a spiritual Christian principle desecrated by crude force, and to impart to it new luster in the person of its visible representative. A patriarchy was instituted in Moscow during the time of Ivan IV's direct successor, who prayed for forgiveness of his father's sins; and then under the first two tsars of the new dynasty, clerical authority, in the person of the Patriarch-Sovereigns Philaret Nikitich and Nikon, became almost equal to imperial authority in authority and rights. This clerical reaction against the Babylonian type of monarchy is very striking, but did not lead to good as an ultimate result, and this is for two reasons. Viewed from without, the patriarchate, being properly only a creation of the same state power, could not have secured independence and influence soundly; the elevated significance that ecclesiastical authority achieved among us twice in the seventeenth century, as is known, depended mainly on the fact that Patriarch Philaret was tsar Mikhail Feodorovich's own father, and Patriarch Nikon—the personal friend of Alexei Mikhailovich; and at the first conflict with the source of their power, the hierarchy fatefully displayed its dependency on state authority. Viewed from within, only the undivided predominance of a truly spiritual Christian interest in both authorities could make their union fruitful. But, of course, the patriarchic designation in and of itself does not guarantee the Christian spirit of its bearer, and the example of St. Vladimir and his Greek bishops shows that sometimes worldly sovereigns are more receptive to higher spiritual requirements than are official representatives of the church.

Thanks to the tsar's loyalty to Patriarch Nikon, he was the chief, and happily the only, significant representative of clericalism. He in fact made use of nearly supreme power according to a consciousness of his own rights and advantages. Due to a misunderstanding, he is also extolled for this clericalism by his Catholic biographer (Palmer), who

did not imagine that the conversion of a Moscow patriarch into some
kind of eastern quasi-pope would make any kind of rapprochement
whatsoever of Russia and the East with the present Roman papacy
completely impossible. We recognize the unsuitability of Nikonian
clericalism by its bitter fruit—the church schism—which, however, is
a bad thing that is not without some good, since thanks to it local
clericalism in Russia was ultimately made impossible.

In order to start on the path of a Christian Empire, seventeenth-
century Russia did not need Nikonite clericalism, but a consciousness
of its insolvency and a resolution to actually improve its life. A stable
State was created by Moscow, and national existence was secured.
But for a historical nation, just as for an individual man, it is too
little just to exist—it must become *worthy* of existence. Only he who
has liberated himself from his imperfection is worthy of existence
in an imperfect world. Byzantium perished because it shunned the
very thought of perfection. Every individual or collective being that
rejects this thought inevitably perishes. For a rejection of the task of
perfection can have only two meanings. Either we consider ourselves
already perfect—which is madness and blasphemy, or, knowing our
ugly status, we are content with it, not wishing anything better—which
is a renunciation of the very essence of a moral human being, or of
the image and likeness of Divine infinity within him.

Russia in the seventeenth century avoided the lot of Byzantium:
it acknowledged its insolvency and resolved to perfect itself. The great
moment of this consciousness and of this resolution was embodied in
the person of Peter the Great. If God wanted to save Russia and could
do this only through the free activity of a man, then Peter the Great
was undoubtedly such a man. With all his personal vices and savagery,
he was a historical collaborator with Divinity, a truly providential, or
theocratic, person. The true significance of a man is determined not
by his individual qualities and acts but by the predominant interest
of his life. And there is hardly another example in universal history
of such a man as Peter the Great—an entire, resolute and undeviat-
ing predominance of the single moral interest of the common good.
Having understood from his youth what Russia lacked in order to
start on the path of real perfection, he concerned himself only with
creating the necessary conditions for us to the last day of his life. In
the person of Peter the Great, Russia resolutely denounced and repudiated the Byzantine distortion of the Christian idea—self-satisfied
quietism. At the same time Peter the Great was completely alien to the
Nebuchadnezzarian idea of authority for authority's sake. His authority
was for him an obligation to constantly work for the common benefit,

and for Russia, a necessary condition for its turn to the path of true progress. The transformation of our fatherland and its uniting with European culture could not have occurred without the unrestricted authority of Peter the Great, and he himself viewed his autocracy as an instrument of this providential task. He never even thought about his authority separately from the task that he served, and did not adopt any artificial measures for safeguarding this authority in the form of personal or dynastic interest, to which he, as a result of his own circumstances, even related with hostility. For Peter the Great, everything—even the life of his only son—depended on the interests of his undertaking, and he did not have a single enemy apart from the enemies of his undertaking.

And his undertaking consisted in giving Russia the real possibility of becoming a Christian kingdom—of fulfilling the task that Byzantium disavowed. The well-known spurious testament of Peter the Great obligated Russia to conquer Constantinople and then the entire world. The real testament of Peter the Great, written by his deeds on the best pages of Russian history, obligated Russia, which had learned the lessons of Byzantium, to set about doing what it had to do, but what the empire of Constantine did not want to do, perishing as a consequence. Having adopted the significance of a Third Rome, Russia, in order not to share in the fate of the first two, had to start on the path of the actual improvement of its national life, not in order to conquer the entire world, but in order to be of benefit to the entire world.

VIII

According to the very idea of Christianity as a Divine-*human* religion, a Christian kingdom must consist of free human persons, and just such a person must stand at its head. The concept of the absolute significance of human personality was completely alien to the Byzantine worldview, as is even acknowledged by its supporters. For Christianity, the meaning of Western history is established in the development of this essential principle, which was completely suppressed in the East. Our drawing near to Europe, for which we are obligated to Peter the Great, had its principal importance precisely in this: through European Enlightenment, the Russian mind was opened to concepts such as human merit, the right of the individual, freedom of conscience, and so forth, without which a worthy existence, true improvement, is impossible—and consequently a Christian kingdom as well. Peter the Great did not himself think about this aspect of his undertaking directly, but this does not lessen its significance.*[6]

Within a half century after Peter the Great, people who were joined to the intellectual movement of Europe thanks to his reforms began to clearly understand and loudly announce that enslavement of an individual—the status of serfdom, which pious Moscow, just as pious Byzantium, did not suspect as being anything bad—is a flagrant violation of inalienable human rights, incompatible with and unworthy of an enlightened state. The requirements of such a root change could have seemed materially dangerous, but the moral obligation that flowed from the idea of a Christian kingdom gained sway—following a few individual intellects—even over the thought of Russian sovereigns. A decisive fulfillment of this obligation brilliantly justified Peter the Great's undertaking and the "Petersburg era" of Russian history.

In the liberation of peasants, just as in other reforms of that bent, Russia once again after Peter the Great in the person of its sovereign and on a new and higher stage of its historical development rejected the Byzantine distortion of Christianity, and in fact acknowledged the moral principle that obligates one to act for the good, to actually remedy and improve the life of the people.

It is not possible, however, to say that this was done completely consciously. Flagrant societal sins such as serfdom, death sentences with torture, and justice-for-sale were resolutely condemned and abolished out of conscience; by the same token *some* conditions were fulfilled so that Russia could become a Christian kingdom, or *some* obstacles on the path to this goal were eliminated. But the goal itself was not set clearly or in its total extent, and as a consequence many important conditions for its achievement not only were not fulfilled, but also were not even recognized.

Even strange quirks of our recent history are explained by this shortcoming of cognizance in Russian society. On the one hand, people who had demanded moral regeneration and selfless deeds for the good of the people tied these requirements to teachings by which the very concept of morality is abolished: "nothing exists apart from elements and forces, man is only a variety of the ape, and therefore we should think only about the good of the people and lay down our lives for our lesser brothers." On the other hand, people who

---

*It is not possible, however, to say that he did not think of it at all: among the books that were translated on his order into the Russian language, along with text books of arithmetic and military fortification, were also works by Samuel Puffendorf and Hugo Grotius, exponents of Western legal consciousness of the time.

confessed Christian principles—and with particular sincerity even—at the same time preached the most savage anti-Christian politics of force and extermination. The first contradiction belongs to the past. The second, more profound and ruinous, still hangs over us. It is time, finally, to liberate ourselves from this historical poison, which strikes at the very sources of our life.

IX

The politics of a Christian state, obviously, must be a Christian politics.[7] Here, a question arises first of all about the disposition of such a state to such a society, or to the institution that contains in itself and represents in itself the very foundations of Christianity on Earth, that is, the church.

In Byzantium this question was resolved simply and definitively. The hierarchy of the Greek church rejected very early on its obligation to represent eternal truth to the state—to represent a truth in the name of which it must administer the temporal life of nations and lead them to a higher goal. In Constantinople just about the last representative of the church in this sense was St. John the Golden Mouth [Chrysostom]. He had successors, but they were not superb ones, and several centuries after him the hierarchy lost its authority even to administer church life proper, the organs of which were the ecumenical councils: the last such council in the East was convened, as is known, in 787, and since the end of the century that followed, the ninth, not only no ecumenical, but also in general no independent councils with historical significance convene any longer now in Greek countries; the highest ecclesiastical powers are "ecumenical patriarchs" in the Imperial City, but this is only a fine name, for they find themselves completely in the hands of the secular authority, which, according to its own discretion, elevates them and casts them down, so that in reality the supreme administration of the Byzantine church belongs entirely and undividedly to the emperors, to whom, besides imperial honors, are rendered also bishop's honors.

If this essentially and characteristically Byzantine church-state structure was not the cause, then it was the main condition of the distortion of imperial power in the eastern empire—the main condition of its transformation from a Christian kingdom into a "Nebuchadnezzarian" one, and consequently of Byzantium's fateful ruin as well.

In ancient Rus there were the rudiments of more correct relations between the spiritual and secular authorities, between church and state, but by virtue of historical conditions these rudiments could not develop, and the murder of Holy Metropolitan Phillip appeared on our soil as the most vivid example of Babylonian-Byzantine despotism. The hope of salvation for us was contained in the fact that Muscovite Rus could not be satisfied with this type of autocracy. In modern Russia the first who clearly realized the necessity of an independent religious authority in its true sense—not as a restriction of, but to make up for, autocratic power—was precisely the one among us who is accused (and not without visible foundations) of the enslavement of the church. And, surprisingly, the realization of the true ideal of church-state relations appeared in and was expressed by the great reformer precisely with respect to the affair in which his personality appeared from its most unattractive aspect, and which constitutes the darkest episode of his rule. I mean the affair of Tsarevich Alexei Petrovich. Let us recall the main circumstances and course of this tragic history.

Peter the Great ended his marriage to Tsarevich Alexei's mother during the child's infancy, and out of an affection for the German girl Anna Mons forcibly sent his former empress to a nunnery, locking her away forever; later, when Anna Mons replaced Ekaterina Skavronskaya—and joined the Orthodox Church—Peter compelled his son to be her godfather. All this occurred with the direct participation of the ecclesiastical authorities. At the same time, Peter was concerned with giving his son an education sufficient for the time and strove to train him in military and governmental affairs; under other conditions he could have had a positive influence on him with the example of his own incessant work for the common benefit, but the prince was by nature completely disinclined and incapable of public engagement, and felt good only in private life, where he received less than anything edifying examples from his father; the other, meanwhile, through abuse and beatings required of him that he remake his nature, "change his mores." The natural consequence of all this was that when the prince achieved majority age, he "always wanted to be far away not only from his father's military affairs, but also from other affairs as well, for his father's very person was quite loathsome to him.". . . When he was called by his father for a task or for a special occasion, for example, the launching of a ship, he said: "It would be better if I were at hard labor, or in bed with a fever, than to be there."* Being in such a disposition the son unavoidably was placed on the side of people who, although not directly malevo-

---

*S. Soloviev, "History of Russia" v. 17: ch. II.

lent against his father, related hostilely to his undertaking, dreaming about a turning back.

Peter could not leave Russia in the power of a man who did not understand its historical requirements and was ready to destroy the great "plantation." As an autocratic sovereign, he had the right to remove him from succession to the throne, and as the reformer of Russia, having realized the importance and providential significance of his undertaking, he was morally obligated to act thus, and his words: "better to be a foreigner and good, than one's own and useless" are completely worthy of a great man.*

Taking away his son's legacy, Peter only fulfilled his duty and acted according to pure conscience; but, going further, he was carried away with his own evil passion, and felt this himself, as we will now see; if this good sentiment did not get the upper hand, then it was only because the evil passion appeared with the comely guise of the very societal interest to which he dedicated his life: "If I have not spared and do not spare my life for my fatherland and people, then how can I spare somebody useless like you?"†

When Prince Alexei announced to his father that he wanted a monastic rank, and then under the guidance of a certain Afrosiniia ran off to Vienna and Naples, Peter had direct cause to fulfill *his duty before* Russia, which was to remove such a manifestly unworthy man from succession to the throne in a lawful manner. But evil passion under the guise of higher societal interest suggested to Peter that the rebel-son is dangerous, that it was not possible to leave him abroad, and that there he could be made into an instrument in the hands of Russia's enemies. And here all possible measures are utilized in order to get the prince back, a full pardon is promised him. "If you are afraid of me, then I reassure and promise with God as my Judge that there will be no punishment for you, and that I will show you the best love, if only you hearken to my will and return."‡ This solemn promise was confirmed several months before the actual return of the prince: "I have received your letter, to which I answer: Why ask for the pardon that I have already prior to this promised orally and in writing through Lords Tolstoy and Rumiantsev, and which today I

---

*These words were written before the birth of another son (by Ekaterina) and thus express a serious readiness to completely renounce dynastic interest for the sake of the good of the fatherland.

†Soloviev, "History of Russia."

‡Ibid.

confirm, on which you can rely."* Pardon was promised, without any
other conditions apart from a return to Russia; but when the prince
returned, another two conditions were imposed: his renunciation of
succession and revealing all the people who counseled flight. Alexei
fulfilled both the one and the other: he indicated at first orally and
then in writing his well-wishers and solemnly renounced forever rights
to the throne in Uspensky Cathedral. An imperial manifest published
on that very day confirmed the full pardon:

> And although he, our son, merited death for such offensive
> acts, especially for dishonors inflicted upon us before the
> entire world through his flight and the slanders strewn
> upon us, such as speaking maliciously of his father and
> opposing his sovereign—we, however, being sympathetic
> to him with a father's heart, pardon him and free him from
> any punishment.†

The matter could be considered closed. Adherents of Alexei, so
unworthily stipulated by him, were eradicated; no one any longer laid
any hopes upon him, he evoked only contempt. The circumstances
of his flight and return were well known; when he was on his way
home to Russia, his first well-wisher, Prince Vasily Vladimirovich
Dolgorukii, said to Prince Bogdan Gagarin: "Have you heard—the
fool of a tsar's son is coming here, because his father promised to
marry him to Aphrosinya? Prison for him—not marriage! The devil's
bringing him! Everybody is intentionally leading him on."‡ But to
Peter, who was under the influence of unconquerable rage, serious
dangers from the unfortunate Alexei seemed to loom ahead; of course,
he was now harmless, but what could be expected from him in the
future, after the death of his father? Even though there was no basis
to be certain for sure that the weak and ailing son would outlive his
powerful heroic father, who was only eighteen years older than him,
a passion ignited transforms possibility into inevitability, making it
the cause of actual evil. At the same time that the tsar's unfortunate
son humbly entreated his stepmother to assist in marriage as soon
as possible, the affair concerning him is renewed without any serious
cause on his part. They caught Aphrosinya, who had been hurrying
to be with him, and subjected her to interrogation; they learned some

---

*Soloviev, "History of Russia."
†Ibid.
‡Ibid.

old women's gossip about Alexei's conversations and feelings; it is not possible to bring against him any criminal action apart from the already pardoned flight abroad. Nevertheless they arrested him and subjected him to torture twice. At this point the great tsar felt that the limitlessness of his power did not save him from restrictions imposed by human feebleness, and that his autocratic conscience required supplement and support in the struggle against the malicious passion that had come over him. Distinguished clergy and secular personages were summoned. Peter did not have cause to feel and did not feel any great respect for the Russian hierarchy. But he turned to it in the name of the higher moral authority that his authority represented and on which it was based.

Thus stated the tsar's declaration to the clergy:

> Since you today have already heard enough about my son's crimes, little known to the world, against us, his father and sovereign, and although I have sufficient power according to divine and civil law, and especially according to Russian law (which completely brushes aside suits between father and children and among private persons) in order to execute him for crimes according to my will without the counsel of others—yet, *I fear God and sin,* for it is natural that people see less than others do in their affairs. A doctor, although more skillful than anyone, will not venture to treat his illness himself either, but calls on others. Similarly, we too entrust this our illness to you, asking its treatment, fearing eternal death. If one treated it himself, one would never recognize the force of one's illness—and *all the more in the fact that I promised to pardon my own son with an oath of God's judgment in writing* and then confirmed it in word, if he would tell the truth. Yet although he violated it by concealing most important business, and especially his mutinous plan against us, his parent and sovereign; however, in order not to sin in this, and though his affair is not for spiritual, but civic judgment, which we have given over today for informal discussion, by special pronouncement; yet, wishing all wisdom about this and recalling the word of God, where it admonishes asking in such matters priestly officialdom as well about the law of God, as is written in chapter 17 of Deuteronomy, we desire from you as well, bishops and all clerical officialdom, as teachers of the word of God, that you do not publish this as a decree, but find and show us

true instruction and reasoning from Holy Scripture: What punishment does this profane and Absalom-like *intent* of our son's example merit, according to Divine commandments and other examples in Holy Scripture and according to law? And give it to us in a letter with the signature of your own hands, in order that we, examining it, *would not have a conscience made more heavy by this*. We invoke your priesthood and we hope with God's judgment that you as worthy guardians of the Divine commandments and as true pastors of Christ's flock, benevolent to the fatherland, will act without any dissimulation and predilection in this.*

This declaration to the clergy is a very important document for us in this affair. It is clear what Peter wanted from the clergy. He knew what conscience required of him even without this. But his personal conscience had need of the religious authority's objective support, elucidating and by that strengthening his acknowledged duty. There was one duty here: to fulfill the promise. Peter indicates his right; but this right is abolished by him himself: it is clear that in giving the promise to pardon, he gave up the right to not pardon. He sensed this clearly, and only weakly attempts to restrict the force of the pardon itself, indicating its conditional character: "if he would tell the truth." But this condition was not in the first written promise, according to which the tsar's son returned to Russia. And even if it had been, was it violated by Alexei? The tsar attempts to confirm that it was violated "by concealing most important business and especially his mutinous plan." But the tsar's son could not only not have concealed the most important business, but any business that there happened to be at all, because he had no such business, but only conversations—and drunken ones at that.† The "mutinous plans" and "profane and Absalom-like intent" that were displayed in such conversations expressed only the hostile attitude of a son to a father, which Peter well knew even previously. He himself felt that such accusations were insufficient to annul his sworn pardon; not having the internal fortitude to have done with the suggestions of malevolent

---

*Soloviev, "History of Russia"; our italics.

†Once, the day after such "mutinous" words he asked his house servant: "Was I a nuisance to anyone last evening?" The other said "no."—"And did I not say anything while drunk?"—The servant repeated his drunken words; then the son of the tsar said: "Who doesn't get drunk?—A drunk always says too much. I am truly very much ashamed, that when I get drunk I have many angry and vain words to say, and then later grieve over it" (ibid).

passion and false reason, which told him that he must with one blow save his undertaking from future danger, Peter turned to an outside authority; but this authority did not turn out to be at the height of its calling. In their response to the tsar, the clerical officials did not say directly either yes or no. Introducing examples of retribution and examples of forgiveness from Holy Scripture, they conclude thus: "In brief: the heart of the tsar is in the hand of God. He should elect that portion to which the hand of God inclines."* In this manifest specimen of the Byzantine spirit, or callousness, more striking than anything is the fact that "the clergy did not think fit to say anything concerning the promise, given by the tsar to his son, whereas on the basis of this promise the son of the tsar returned, and Peter indicated his promise precisely, requiring a clear conscience."† Secular officials, after the double interrogation with torture, sentenced the tsar's son to death, "subjecting, however, this our sentence and conviction to autocratic power, will and the merciful consideration by his imperial majesty, the all-merciful monarch." Thus, they too left Peter alone between the voice of his conscience and the sway of malicious passion; he did not find a higher support in his internal struggle; he had to decide himself: remaining to history just a hero, or adding to this the even more elevated merit of moral heroism. On the eve of [the Battle of] Poltava's anniversary Peter suffered a fateful defeat. The reserve book of the St. Petersburg garrison office reads:

> 26th of June (1718) at 8:00 AM they began to gather in the garrison: His Majesty, the Grand Prince (Menshikov), Prince Iakov Fedorovich (Dolgorukii), Gavrilo Ivanovich (Golovin), Fedor Matveevich (Apraksin), Ivan Alekseevich (Musin-Pushkin), Tikhon Nikitich (Strashnev), Peter Andreevich (Tolstoy), Peter Shafirov, General Buturlin; and the torture chamber was made ready, and then, having been at the garrison until 11:00, they dispersed. That same day at the sound of the trumpet at 6:00 AM, being under guard in the garrison, the Tsarevich Alexei Petrovich expired.‡

This affair has no justification, but there is an important mitigating circumstance in it. Recognizing all the force of his autocratic authority, thanks to which he led Russia out upon its present historical

---

*Soloviev, "History of Russia."
†The words of S. M. Soloviev, "History of Russia."
‡Soloviev, Ibid.

path, Peter the Great felt the incompleteness of this authority. He did not want to restrict it outwardly at all ("do not publish this as a decree"), but only to fulfill it inwardly through another, moral principle—through counsel. He understood that in an important private incident, state power, unrestricted in its rights, must rest on good offices of two kinds for the worthy fulfillment of its duties: on the religious authority of an independent priesthood and on the free voice of societal conscience in the guise of the best people, bearers of the national future. Peter searched in good conscience for this assistance and did not find it: in Russia there turned out to be neither priest nor prophet who could have said to the tsar in the name of the Divine will and higher human worth: "you must not; it is not permitted to you, there are eternal limits." In place of this, both the clerical and the secular counselors to which he turned for an elucidation of his *duty*, indicated to him only the *right* of his authority, in which he himself had no doubt at all, but which he considered useless for the resolution of a moral problem.

X

The great autocrat and reformer embodied in himself the best forces of the Russian nation and state—representing national and state progress—but recognized his lack of competence to ultimately resolve a proximate and important matter according to conscience and truth [*pravda*]. When he turned to someone else's authority and someone else's counsel, then didn't truth [*istina*] appear here graphically? The fact that unrestricted *authority* belonging to the monarch by right—as to the bearer of national-state unity—not only does not exclude, but, on the contrary, requires the good offices of two other principles: religious *authority* and moral *conscience*. And isn't there yet another truth [*istina*] displayed here with particular vividness? The fact that these two principles supplementing political power must be independent from national and state restriction, that is, should have universal, supranational significance. It is clear that those to whom the supreme representative of national political unity, the "father of the fatherland," turned for free support—and through whom he wanted to receive that which his moral authority lacked—should represent in themselves something above and more than the fatherland: that they should be the bearers of an all-human or universal consciousness, which relates to the national and state consciousness in the same way as this does to clan consciousness.

A universal consciousness appears in the life of humanity in two forms: as *tradition* of a higher and an all-encompassing truth of rudiments that are already given in life, revealed in positive religion, and as *anticipation* of a future perfect realization of these rudiments in the life of the entire world. People of sacred tradition preserve the ancient pledge of universal unity, or the Kingdom of God; people of an absolute ideal foresee, foretell and bring nearer its actual advance. It is clear from the very distinction between these two designations that the first office has an official character and the second is completely free. The guardians of the given universal-historical sanctum naturally form the institution called the "universal church," with a hierarchical order and a succession. Oppositely, the bearers of ideal perfection can not constitute a definite institution, which, being necessarily imperfect, would contradict their message and would remove all meaning from it; representing human society in its future wholeness, these people can not possess any actual plenipotentiary powers from an isolated part of society in its given transient status. Therefore, if the act of a priest, relying on religious fact as solid stone, has a morally *obligatory authority*, then the voice of a prophet, speaking in the name of an infinity of higher spiritual endeavors, possesses only the power of a morally *desirable* counsel.

Peter the Great was the supreme representative of the genuine interests of his fatherland and acknowledged himself as such. He did not have any doubt in the fact that his son, if he remained alive, would be a great danger for the future of Russia, and that, consequently, the visible benefit of the country required the removal of this man, and positive law gave the tsar the formal right for this. But the autocracy of his conscience did not permit him to be satisfied either with a consciousness of benefit to the state, or a consciousness of his formal right. Moral sentiment revealed to him the truth [*istina*] that has remained obscured to many until now; that earthly interests and rights have genuine significance and worthiness only when they are connected and conform with eternal truth [*pravda*] and the higher good. And as both Byzantine and Russian history clearly show, in order to determine this connection in each circumstance, in order to conform temporal state and national interests with the eternal requirements of the higher order, the conscience of the sovereign must be protected as much as possible from the predominant influence of personal frailties in order to be really autocratic and to fulfill its mission. Left to itself alone, the conscience of an autocrat, just as with any man, can be blinded by passion, deceived by false argument and ignorance, weakened by personal sins. The ultimate resolution of any matter, without doubt, belongs to the autocratic conscience alone, but in order that this resolution be *conscientious*, it should be anticipated and *verified* by the sacred authority of religion and the free conscience of the best people.* Of course, for such a verification to have real significance the representatives of this authority and of this counsel must be completely independent in their office and recognize themselves as such. Their voice must serve the true good of the sovereign and the state, and not the personal will of a man. The great autocrat searched for such independent people to serve authoritatively and to give counsel freely in this matter, but did not find them. Clerical officials responded to him as "wily courtiers," and secular bureaucrats, instead of giving counsel to the tsar, found it necessary to torture the son of the tsar.

The great mind of the reformer clearly saw the essence of autocracy. In order that the supreme power actually be unrestricted, the conscience of the monarch must be free not only from outward restrictions, but also chiefly from inward restrictions inevitably imposed by personal human weakness, and for this, that is, for a true autocracy on his part—in fact, and not just in words—this had to be supplemented and verified by the indisputable authority of religion and the free counsel of the best people, of the true representatives of the societal whole. Was Peter guilty of the fact that he had before him neither an independent ecclesiastical authority nor the freedom of individual consciousness?

XI

Charges continue to this day that Peter the Great somehow reduced the authority of the church and suppressed the nation's vital freedom. But the insolvency of Russia in both respects was vividly demonstrated in the national church schism that took place a half century before the Petrine reforms and, consequently, can not be blamed on the reformer. If one found it necessary and could lay responsibility for the abnormal conditions of Russian life upon one person, to connect it with one name, then this would in no way be the name of Tsar Peter, but indeed only that of Patriarch Nikon.

---

*Even according to Roman Catholic teaching, where the monarchic idea in the person of the pope is elevated to an exceptional height, only the most holy decisions are acknowledged as coming ex cathedra and thus have indisputable and infallible authority, which is preceded by (apart from other, purely religious, conditions) a proper acquaintance of the pope with the opinion of the episcopate by means of an ecumenical council, or through formal or written inquiries and responses.

Since a nation in its collective unity and *particularity* is represented entirely by the authority of the state, ecclesiastical governance can have independent significance and a mission with respect to the nation and the national state only when it represents and bears within itself a supranational universal principle, and while belonging to a given country as the place of its service, has yet a higher point of rest that is outside this nation and this state. Ecclesiastical governance in no way can head the nation, in as much as the nation already has its natural and legal head in the person of the sovereign. Being confined to the national sphere alone, and not connected in fact with any supranational religious center, a spiritual authority can not preserve its independence—otherwise in one country, in one nation there would turn out to be two supreme authorities, two autocracies, two exalted leaders, or two heads on one torso. In fact, ecclesiastical governance of an individual country cannot be genuinely "autocephalic," even if it were to be so called*; if, being confined to the national sphere alone, it has a claim *here* to an independent role, then it will soon get to know the meaninglessness of such claims through experience, willy-nilly completely turning into a subordinate instrument of secular authority.

But Patriarch Nikon made claims precisely to be compared to the tsar in *his* national-state sphere; he wanted to be another sovereign of Russia, until he became convinced that on these grounds he could only be, if not a faithful subject, then a rebellious one. Nikon's voice could not have religious authority in the ears of the tsar, because this was the voice of a political rival. There was no exalted content concealed behind the claims of the Muscovite Patriarch, nothing that would have made him necessary for the common good in the eyes of the tsar; therefore he was justly destroyed out of uselessness, as a simple duplicate of the all-Russian sovereign.

Being incorrect with respect to the sovereign and the state, Nikon was incorrect as well with respect to the nation. He turned all the force of his authority not against the real evils and catastrophes of the nation's life but against the innocent particulars of national Russian tradition (in the sphere of religious ceremony); he fought against these particulars not in the name of any exalted universal principles but only in the name of another, local (Greek) tradition. The clash itself and the division over ceremony could not have taken place if the patriarch

---

*In a special sense the word "autocephaly" designates only a hierarchical independence of national churches among themselves, not touching on the question of relations to secular power.

had stood on grounds of truly ecumenical, universal tradition, which according to its essence gives a place to all particular traditions, not excluding, but embracing them in itself, as various parochial expressions of the same all-inclusive and all-united life.

However the Muscovite Patriarch was not the bearer of ecumenical Christianity, but only of Byzantine "piety"—of the same piety that forgot the true God is "a God of the living," a Sanctuary, obtained by us through religious tradition—the sacred past of Christianity—can be a living foundation of the ecumenical church, inspiring our national and state life only when this past does not distance itself from actual reality and from the tasks of the future. This sanctuary, this sacred tradition must be a perpetual buttress of contemporaneity, a token and a rudiment of what is approaching. In order to govern a Christian kingdom, ecclesiastical authority first of all must not distance itself from striving for the absolute ideal, that is, from the "prophetic" spirit. Herein is its vital force. Only then are the eternal forms of sanctuary handed down to us embodied in a living and infinite content. Then this sanctuary is not only preserved by us as something *finished* and consequently *certain*, as something separate from us, and consequently outside us, but also it is alive within us ourselves, while we are living through it, and we act through it while it does not cease acting within us. The church, as an ecumenical or universal entity, that is, as the unity of everything with God, can only actually be realized through universal history—in the entire life of all humanity, in the entire aggregate of nations and times. Therefore the sanctuary of tradition, that is, the given foundation of the church (in hierarchy, dogma, and sacraments), should not be taken as something accomplished and completed for us *separately* apart from the present and future life of the world. Being separated from its full and eternal meaning, being recognized *only* as completed or finalized, the sanctuary of the church necessarily loses its infinite character, and crosses over into restricted and dead forms: *restricted*, because a completed sanctuary has been completed *at some time* and *somewhere*, within certain extrinsic conditions and borders—dead, because these borders of a phenomenon that has taken place at some time, are separated here from the life of that which is now taking place, abiding everywhere and always. *Having been killed* in Byzantium, sacred tradition began to show signs of life in Russia (for example, the struggle of St. Nil Sorsky and his disciples for the meaning of Christianity), but here as well the historical conditions did not permit it to resurrect, and ultimately smashed it, *before* the Petrine reform, by the fanatics of Muscovite Byzantinism—Nikon and those who were with him.

XII

When the *perfection* of the church is not set ahead of it, but is transferred back into the past, as was the case in Byzantium, and this
past is thus not taken for the *foundation* (as it should be), but rather
for the *apex* of the church edifice—then it unfailingly occurs that the
essential religious requirements and conditions of human life, which
must be fulfilled by everyone and always, are attributed and dated
exclusively to their separate historical expressions and forms—which in
this separateness can only hang over the living conscience in the form
of an outward fact. It would be the same if, say, we just separated,
for example, the spiritual tradition that connects us with some great
writer from the content and inherent form of his works, and attributed
his old publications exclusively to a very dated and imperfect typo-
graphic superficiality, which we would then strive to reproduce with
literal exactitude, assuming the entire debt of our respect for the great
author to be in this. Such was the attitude of Byzantinism to Christ's
undertaking. The essential and the eternal remain in religious form,
of course, here as well, but they no longer occupy the consciousness,
do not interest the will—in the foreground appears that which is
casual and transient, yet painstakingly preserved; and the very flow
of Christian tradition, crammed with dead literalism, now does not
appear in its universal and infinite scope, but is concealed behind the
distinctive particulars of ephemeral and local regulations.

Such a substitution of ecumenical tradition with particular tradition in the Byzantine mind is already manifest at the end of the
seventh century, and appears more strongly in the ninth, then exists
already in the eleventh as if a finalized matter. The causes for the
division of the church, or to be more precise, the rupture in ecclesiastical communion between Rome and Byzantium, serve as indisputable
evidence of this sad fact. We will not speak here about the moral and
cultural-political reasons for this rupture; but the ecclesiastical cause
and pretext in which these reasons were clothed is very characteristic
of Byzantinism.

The celebrated Photius, already at the beginning of his clash
with Rome (which did not want to acknowledge the legitimacy of his
patriarchy during the life of the lawful patriarch, St. Ignatius, who had
not renounced his office), in his second letter to Pope Nicholas (861)
turns attention to certain external particulars of the Latin church, such
as the shaving of beards and the tonsorial on priests, Sabbath fasts,
and so forth. Photius himself was both too educated in general and
too closely connected with the intellectual legacy of the great teachers

of the church to attach essential significance to such trifles and to see an obstacle to church unity in them; however, he clearly hinted in his indications that these ceremonial differences *could* serve as a weapon against Rome. And a few years later he himself made use of this weapon in his encyclicals to the Eastern patriarchal thrones (867), where he condemns (on equal footing with the filioque), as heresy, impiety, and poison, the very ceremonial and disciplinary particulars of the Western church that he had six years previously acknowledged as fully permissible local customs. This fact in any event shows that in the midst of the Eastern hierarchy, to which Photius had turned, there were enough people for whom every superficial divergence from the local Eastern forms of church life appeared as tantamount to a deviation from ecumenical traditions; it seemed to be heresy and impiety. If these people were pious, then there was too much of the old pagan element in their piety, which was connected exclusively to one's own, the clan, the local.

There were already more than a few people of this kind in the Byzantine church at the time of Photius; in two centuries almost all were of this sort. When in the first half of the eleventh century Patriarch Michael Cerularius in his letter to Bishop John of Tranum, and later Niketas Stenthatos (Pectoratus) in his polemical works, both solemnly and relentlessly condemn the Latins as *heretics*, for the fact that they fast on the Sabbath, do not sing alleluias at the great fast, allegedly eat meat of strangled animals, tolerate clean-shaven priests and bishops with rings on their fingers, and use unleavened and not sour bread for the Eucharist—this verdict now does not elicit in Byzantium any protest or doubt, so that it is possible to consider the view that was expressed in such indictments as the decisively prevalent one in the Greek church. Here is how distant the roots of our Russian schism lie.

Standing in the foreground of that part of the eleventh century in which the character of ecclesiastical Byzantinism was fully expressed, as is known, is the question of the use of unleavened bread [*opresnoki*], by virtue of which Western Christianity was then condemned to perdition, as a heresy of the unleavened or of the sour-less (azyme bread).[8] From days of old in the eastern half of the Christian world, sour bread had been used for the Eucharist, but while the ecumenical significance of the church and its sacraments were clearly understood by Eastern Christians, no one thought to elevate their distinctive custom to the level of a requirement obligated for all, and the opposite custom to use unleavened bread for the Eucharist having been established in the Western countries did not seduce anyone in the East and did not at all interfere with full communion with the West. But views changed with the development of Byzantinism, and in the eleventh century the dispute over unleavened bread ends with the division of the church. A supplemental detail of ceremony is taken as the essential condition of the sacrament, and the general obligation of an ecumenical tradition is ascribed to the particulars of a local custom.

The quality of the arguments also corresponded to the question at dispute, which was evidenced in the belittling and the reduction of the significance of religious meaning. The superiority of sour bread was proved by the fact that it is a living bread, inspirited, for it has in it salt and leaven, which impart to it breath and movement, whereas Latin unleavened bread is a dead bread, soul-less, and even unworthy to be called bread, being "like a piece of dirt." One can only regret that the advantage of a living quality and of salt remained in the sour bread, and were not made distinctive properties of the Byzantine mind. However, the real basis in favor of using sour bread was apparently that it was a Greek custom, one's own—whereas the use of unleavened bread was an alien habit, a Latin one. This prevailing motive is involuntarily expressed in the decree of the Constantinople (patriarchal) Synod that pronounced in 1054 an anathema upon the papal legates and upon the entire Western church: "certain impious people"—it says in the decree—"came out of the darkness of the West to the kingdom of piety, and into this city protected by God, out of which flow the waters of pure teaching as from a spring to the ends of the earth." The real impiety of these "certain" people consisted in the fact that they were alien, that they came from the West, whereas the kingdom of piety and the spring of pure teaching could only be here among us, in the East, in our city—although this "pure teaching" was reduced to the fact that in one variety of bread there is a soul, and in the other—there is none. It is a natural and proper thing to love and cherish one's own, that which is native. It is only necessary to recall two things here: first, that it is not possible to impose one's custom on those for whom it is not their own, and second, that there is in the world something more exalted than that which is one's own or someone else's, and that the actual place for this more exalted thing is in the ecumenical church of God.

From a religious and ecclesiastical standpoint Byzantinism thus deviates from the fullness of Christianity not in the fact that it respects the church as a supra-sensory sanctuary, preserving an invariable tradition (for it is so according to its foundation), but in the fact that in separating out the element of tradition from the vital wholeness of universal religion, it restricts and belittles ecclesiastical tradition itself, attributes it to a single part of the church and dates it to a single time in the past, transforming *ecumenical* tradition into a tradition of *local antiquity.*

XIII

The movement toward particularism in the church did not stop with Byzantinism, but consequently went farther. After ecumenical Orthodoxy turned into Byzantine or Greco-Eastern Orthodoxy, new *national* sequestrations began to appear out of it. In this respect, our Russian schism of the Old Believers is only a further result of Byzantinism, or, more precisely, a natural reaction against it, on the very same grounds. Herein is its historical justification.

When Byzantium was the reigning city, the main political center of the Christian East, and the Byzantine Greeks were the people who exercised dominion in the Orthodox world, then on this foundation (there was no other) Constantinople received central significance, and in the church the eastern archbishop of Constantinople called himself the ecumenical patriarch; particular Byzantine tradition was elevated to an ecumenical degree obligatory for all, for Eastern Christians the Orthodox church became a synonym for the Greek church. But then in the fifteenth century, with the simultaneous fall of Constantinople before the Turks and the liberation of Russia from the Tatars, the political center of the Christian East passes over from Byzantium to Moscow; the people of the "pious law" exercising dominion in place of the Greeks become Russians. On the very same historical foundations, upon which Constantinople, as the reigning city, recognized itself as the second Rome—a successor enjoying the full rights of the first ancient Rome—the new reigning city, the capital of Eastern Orthodoxy—Moscow—was declared, as we know, the heir enjoying full rights, with all Byzantium's claims and advantages, not only political, but also ecclesiastical.

Russia received Orthodox Christianity from Byzantium already in the form that it had there in the tenth and eleventh century; along with Orthodoxy, it also received ecclesiastical Byzantinism, that is, a certain traditionalism and literalism, the confirmation of temporal and chance forms of religion side by side with the eternal and essential ones, a local tradition side by side with the ecumenical one. But once such a mixture was accepted and an absolute ecumenical significance was ascribed to a local form of religious tradition, then the question naturally arose among our ancestors: why should this significance belong, namely, to a local *Greek* tradition, and not to the *Russian* one, especially now that the Greeks had lost all their previous actual advantages? This question was resolved definitively by such people as the well-known Arsenii Sukhanov [Hieromonk of Holy Trinity Monastery], who proved to bitter Phanariots [Greek clerics under Ottoman patronage] that the center of the universe was no longer in Hagarite Istanbul, but in pious Moscow; that our great sovereign had no need of the Greeks; that he himself established in himself a still greater ecclesiastical fullness than the one that had been in Byzantium; that it had an all-Russian patriarch in place of a Roman pope, and with him four metropolitans in place of eastern patriarchs. But, apart from power, Moscow had an inherent superiority before Byzantium, which had been defeated by unbelievers. The sincere apprehension appeared that under Muslim leadership it would be difficult for the Greeks to preserve the purity of Orthodoxy, that they could be shaken in faith itself. This meant that true piety must be preserved only in Russia, which finds itself under pious sovereigns; this meant that the local tradition of the Russian, and not the Greek, church should be respected as the true Orthodox tradition.

And here, just as in the ninth to eleventh centuries, when the dark patriotism of the Byzantine Greeks forced them to see the essence of Orthodoxy in the sour breads and the unshaven beards of Greek priests, it was precisely the same in the sixteenth to seventeenth centuries: a similarly dark patriotism of Muscovite people forced them as well to see the essence of piety in the insignificant particulars of local Russian ecclesiastical custom. These particulars, whatever they might have been in and of themselves, became an inviolable relic, and in place of the eternal and universal faith of Christ, an "Old Russian Faith" imperceptibly takes its position in the mind of these pious people.

From the elevated point of view of ecumenical Christianity the position of Russian old-rite followers was incorrect. But whether they were incorrect in a historical sense, with respect to their adversaries then, and partly now as well, that is another question. The point is that their direct opponents—Patriarch Nikon and his like-minded followers did not and do not stand on the point of view of ecumenical Christianity, but on the point of view of a *local literalism*, the same as the old believers—only not the Muscovite, but the previous Byzantine local literalism. The words of Patriarch Nikon are well-known: "By birth I am Russian, but *by faith* and thought—Greek." If it is possible to be *Greek by faith* in place of being simply Christian, then why not be Russian by faith? An *old Russian faith* should not hold sway over a universal Christian faith, but it has in any event equal rights when compared to an *old Greek faith.*

In the acts of the Moscow Council of 1654, it is related how Patriarch Nikon began the correction of ecclesiastical books, out of which our schism came. It is possible to see here with full clarity the essence of the views that the Muscovite patriarch held, and the real character of our ecclesiastical dispute.

> Entering into the book repository (Nikon) found the official document, in it was written in Greek how the patriarchs began to settle themselves in the reigning city of Moscow; this document was written in the summer of 7097 (i.e., 1589). . . . And he found another book, written by the council of ecumenical patriarchs in Greek: the council was in the New Rome, in Constantinople, in the summer of 7101 (i.e., 1593). . . . In this book were assembled these words:
>
> > And since *consequently the Orthodox churches are perfect not only according to divine understanding and piety of dogma, but also according to holy church statute*, it is also correct for us to review all new things for the protection of every church—so that it be taught safely, no addition or deletions are admissible. . . .* And Great Orthodox Russia will be in agreement with the ecumenical patriarchst *in everything."*
>
> Reading this book the sovereign, His Excellency Patriarch Nikon, *fell into great fear lest they had sinned* in some way against the Orthodox Greek law.‡ And he began to examine the necessary places of the Creed of the Orthodox faith: I believe in one God and so forth, and noted that a Russian Metropolitan, the prelate Photius, brought from the Greeks to the reigning city of Moscow 250 years ago the Creed of the Orthodox faith sewn in ornate letters, in agreement with the holy eastern church in everything: then he saw the same Creed in printed Muscovite books, and much was found at variance.

---

*That is: since the Orthodox church is perfect, or has achieved perfection not only from the aspect of dogmatic teaching, but also from the aspect of church discipline and rites, then—and so forth.

†That is, Greek.

‡That is, is there (among us) some kind of deviation from their Orthodox Greek law.

We know what these variances consisted in and what frightened Patriarch Nikon. In the second part of the Creed in place of "begotten, not made" in the Muscovite books was printed: "begotten, and not made"; in the seventh part in place of "Of his kingdom *there will be no end*" in the Muscovite books stood: "Of his kingdom *is no* end"; in the eighth part in place of "and in the Holy Spirit, the Lord, the Giver of life," in the printed Muscovite books read: "and in the Holy Spirit, *true* Lord and giver of life." . . . "Having examined the holy liturgy as well, he found in it things added and things deleted and distorted. In this and in other books he saw many dissimilarities."* All these many dissimilarities in the order of liturgy and in other books were of the same type as in the indicated creed.

Nikon, being by faith a Greek, as he himself declared, fully shared in the fundamental error of Byzantinism that "the Orthodox church achieved perfection" and although it would have been decidedly impossible to determine when precisely it had "achieved perfection," he firmly believed that this had occurred at some time in Byzantium and that this perfection embraced absolutely everyone in the church and did not allow any changes in the minutest details. Thus, in the words of his tablet,

> the commandment of the holy ecumenical councils is fearful, it equally anathematizes additions, deletions, and changes in the smallest letter, even of one character, or iota, the letter i, in the Creed. . . . It is not meet to place, replace, or move anything at all, neither small nor great, neither tone nor syllable, in the Creed of faith, but meet to cherish the whole with full strength and attention, as if it were the apple of your eye, so that we do not place ourselves under the anathema of such great and holy fathers.†

XIV

The undertaking of Patriarch Nikon carried the mark of a triple falsehood. The first falsehood (and here Byzantinism had nothing to do with it) must be acknowledged as his clericalism, by virtue of which he strove to transform religious authority into political power, to become

---

another sovereign in Russia, a threat to the supreme autocratic authority of the tsar; the second of his falsehoods, in which he appeared as
a total and extreme Byzantine, was against ecumenical Christianity,
which he declared with words of the Greeks to be finished, "having
achieved perfection," substituting a living religious truth with the
dead literalism of a local tradition; the third of his falsehoods was
against the Russian people, upon which he arbitrarily imposed this
alien literalism, unjustly condemning and exterminating with terrible
force innocent particulars of our own paternal traditions.

Declaring himself to be a Greek by faith, Nikon turned out not
to be a Greek at all by his intentions and his morality, but rather an
unsuccessful and irrelevant imitator of the medieval papacy. And, as
an example of old historical logic, it is very striking that the Greek
hierarchs, who were called to Moscow for judgment over Nikon,
condemned him for the fault of not being a Byzantine, for a fault
in which they could not really sympathize with him or answer for
him; they condemned him for opposing the tsar and appropriating
political power; and in the two other of his faults, for which the
main responsibility belonged to the Byzantine legacy, not only was
he justified by them, but they also even completed his undertaking,
having committed the Russian followers of the old-rite to a solemn
and pitiless damnation, as criminals subject to both ecclesiastical and
"secular" punishments (Muscovite Grand Council 1666–67).

The entire Russian hierarchy participated in this sorry deed
along with the Greeks, inflicting upon itself a fateful blow. At the
same time that the hierarchy justly rejected Nikon's clerical claims
in its condemnation of him, it had to turn to state assistance for the
forcible suppression of the schism and lost its independence, at once
stepping into an inordinate service role with respect to the state and
into a role of oppression with respect to the people.

What prospect did Peter the Great have to remove from the
"church," that is, from the Russian hierarchy, the independence and
the spiritual authority that it had itself abandoned even before his
birth? To the contrary, he unsuccessfully attempted to reinstate this
spiritual authority. In a matter of great importance to him and to the
state, he turned to the holy order for spiritual direction and support,
as its highest (in a religious-moral sense) representative. Was it his
fault that he received in place of this only the Byzantine stone of dead
literalism and the Byzantine snake of evil flattery?[9]

In three years after the Russian hierarchy was able only to answer the tsar's demand for authoritative leadership with: "the tsar's
heart is in the hand of God," the hand of God placed into the

tsar's heart the wise decision to ultimately replace the patriarchy and to institute an ecclesiastical collegium or synod for management of church affairs under the supervision and leadership "of a good man among officers, one who would know the affairs of the synod and have courage." This college received regulations from the tsar, and its members, just as with the general loyalty oath, had to swear allegiance, in their capacity as church governors, to the sovereign as the supreme or "utmost" judge of this college.

The inclusion of the Russian Church as a department, with a central board at its head, in the general structure of the state administration on the same bases with other departments, fully corresponded to the true situation of the matter, and to condemn Peter the Great for the fact that he did not artificially support the obvious fiction of an independent spiritual authority, would mean—to condemn him for the fact that he did not want to lie to himself and to history. It is imagined that the ecclesiastical hierarchy lost its independence and authority in consequence of the institution of the synod, whereas it is completely clear that the synod could and should have been instituted in consequence of the fact that the hierarchy had already previously lost its independence and authority. The ecclesiastical administration had already in fact been transformed into a branch of the state before it was officially declared in this capacity. This was one of the most natural, forthright, and thus also durable reforms of Peter the Great. Almost all the colleges founded by him disappeared or were subjected to root changes; the "ecclesiastical college" alone, guided by a "knowledgeable and courageous" chief procurator, has now remained in all its inviolability for nearly two centuries—manifest evidence that this institution was not created by individual arbitrary will, but was called forth by actual conditions of our historical life, preserving to this point their strength. But whether these conditions should be acknowledged from a higher point of view as normal, that is another question. It fell to the greatest reformer to feel their abnormality and to suffer from them morally at the most tragic minute of his life, but it was not in his power to change them.

11

The Secret of Progress

Do you know this fairytale?

A hunter got lost in a deserted forest; tired, he sat on a stone by a broad raging stream. He sat and stared into the dark depths and listened as a woodpecker tapped all the while on the bark of a tree. And the hunter's soul became grieved.

"I am alone in life, like I am in the forest," it seemed to him, "it's been a long time since I lost my way on various paths, and there's no exit for me from these wanderings. Loneliness, torment and ruin! Why was I born, why did I come into this forest? What use to me are all these beasts and birds killed by me?" Just then someone touched his shoulder. He looked: there stood an old humpbacked woman—the kind that usually appear on such occasions—worn to the bone, and the color of stale, dried carob [*tsaregradskii struchok*], or boot leather that hasn't been cleaned.[1] Sullen eyes, with two wisps of grey hair sticking out from a cleft chin, and dressed in an expensive but perfectly threadbare frock—nothing but rags.

"Listen, my good young man, on the other side there's a tiny little town—a pure paradise! Once you get there, you'll forget all your woes. One would never find the road on one's own, but I'll take you directly, [for] I'm from those parts myself. Just carry me across to the other bank, otherwise where would poor little me find my balance in this current, hardly able to move my legs? One foot already in the grave, and o-o-o-h-h, I so don't want to die!"

The hunter was a good-hearted fellow. And though he didn't altogether believe the words of the old woman concerning the paradisiacal place, and fording the expanded brook was not appealing, and carrying the old woman was not very becoming ... he took a good look at her, and she started to cough, all a-shiver.

"The venerable one," he thought, "is not yet done for! She's probably a hundred, and what a burden she has borne in her day—it's necessary to take pains for her as well."

229

"Well, granny, climb onto my shoulders, but stiffen your bones, or else you'll crumble to bits, and you won't collect them in the water." The little old woman scrambled up onto his shoulders, and he felt such a terrible weight, just as if he had saddled himself with a corpse in a coffin; he could barely take a step. "Well," he thought, "it'd be shameful to go back on my word!" He stepped into the water, and suddenly it wasn't so difficult, and it got easier and easier with every step. Then some unimaginable enchantment came over him. He was striding forward, looking ahead. But when he came out on the bank, he looked back: in place of the old woman nuzzled up against him was an indescribably beautiful damsel. She led him to her homeland, and he didn't complain about loneliness any longer, didn't harm the beasts and birds, and didn't search for a way through the forest.

Everyone knows this fairytale in one variant or another, and I've known it from childhood as well, but it was just today that I sensed in it a completely un-fairytale like meaning. Modern man, hunting for fleeting, momentary goods and ephemeral fantasies, has lost life's true path. The dark and irrepressible current of life is before him. Time, like a woodpecker, relentlessly marks lost moments. Melancholy and loneliness, and ahead—gloom and ruin. But behind him stands the sacred antiquity of tradition—and in such unattractive forms! But what is to be made of that? Let him just think a bit about how he is obligated to it; let him *respect* its old age by means of an intrinsic sincere impulse, let him *pity* its infirmities, let him *become ashamed* to repudiate it on account of this appearance. Instead of scrutinizing illusive fairies behind clouds in vain, let him strive to convey this sacred burden of the past over the actual currents of history. This is the solitary way out of his misguided wanderings—*the solitary one* because every other one would be insufficient, unkind, profane: the venerable one is not yet done for!

Modern man doesn't believe in the fairy tale, doesn't believe that the haggard old woman will turn into a beautiful damsel. He doesn't believe—all the better! Why have faith in a future reward, when it is required to earn it through real efforts and selfless acts? He who does not believe in the future of an old shrine, should anyway remember its past. Why not carry it out of respect for its antiquity, out of pity for its decadence, out of the shame of being ungrateful. Blessed are they who believe: while standing on this bank, they already see the gleam of imperishable beauty behind the wrinkles of decrepitness.[2] But those who do not believe in a future transformation also benefit—*unexpected joy.* For both one and the other, there is one task: to go forward, having taken upon themselves all the burden of antiquity.

If you want to be a man of the future, modern man, do not forget father Anchises and the clan gods in the smoking ruins.[3] They needed a pious hero to bring them to Italy, yet only they could give him and his clan both Italy and world dominion. But our shrine is mightier than Troy's, and our path with it farther than Italy and all the earthly plane. *He who saves is saved.*[4] Here is the secret of progress—there is, and will be, no other.

Editor's Notes

Introduction: Freedom, Faith, and Dogma

1. V. S. Soloviev, "Opravdanie dobra (predislovie ko vtoromu izdaniiu)," in *Sobranie sochinenii Vladimira Sergeievicha Solovieva* 2nd ed. 10 vols. Edited by Sergei M. Soloviev and Ernst L. Radlov (St. Petersburg: "Prosveshchenie," 1911–14 [Reprint with 2 additional volumes, Brussels: "Zhizn's Bogom," 1966–70]) 8:6. (Hereafter cited as *Sobranie sochinenii*.)

2. "Three Addresses in Memory of Dostoevsky," in *The Heart of Reality: Essays on Beauty, Love, and Ethics*, edited and translated by Vladimir Wozniuk (Notre Dame: University of Notre Dame Press, 2003), 25.

3. This principle of reconciling all diversities in divine unity goes as far back as one could go with Soloviev, to his first published piece, "The Mythological Process in Ancient Paganism" in 1873. See *Enemies from the East? V. S. Soloviev on Paganism, Asian Civilizations, and Islam*, edited and translated by Vladimir Wozniuk (Evanston, IL: Northwestern University Press, 2007), 3–23.

4. See, for example, Judith Kornblatt, "Vladimir Solov'ev on Spiritual Nationhood, Russia and the Jews," *Russian Review* 56/2 (April 1997): 157–78.

5. See Vladimir Wozniuk, "V. S. Soloviev and the Politics of Human Rights," *Journal of Church and State* 41/1 (Winter 1999): 43–45.

6. See "The Jews in Russia," *Times* (London) December 30, 1890, 3, as reprinted in *Politics, Law, and Morality: Essays by V. S. Soloviev*, edited and translated by Vladimir Wozniuk (New Haven and London: Yale University Press, 2000), 291–292.

7. Other, more recent, treatments of similar questions, reflecting an understanding not unlike Soloviev's, can be found in George Florovsky, *Ways of Russian Theology*, 2 volumes, translated by Robert L. Nichols (Belmont, MA: Nordland, 1979–1987); and John Meyendorff, *Imperial Unity and Christian Divisions* (New York: St. Vladimir's Seminary Press, 1989). For valuable comparisons, see also Paul Valliere, *Modern Russian Theology: Bukharev, Soloviev, Bulgakov: Orthodox Theology in a New Key* (Edinburgh: T & T Clark, 2000).

8. V. S. Soloviev, "Kritika otvlechennykh nachal," in *Sobranie sochinenii* 2:116.

9. Ibid., 2:119.

10. See "On So-called Problems," in Wozniuk, *Politics, Law and Morality*, 77.

11. See *Pis'ma Vladimira Sergeievicha Solovieva* 4 Vols. Edited by Ernst Radlov (St. Petersburg: "Obshchestvennaia pol'za," 1908–1923 [Reprint Brussels: "Zhizn' s Bogom," 1970]) 1:24; and *Sobranie sochinenii* 12:360. Also see Konstantin Mochul'skii, *Vladimir Soloviev: zhizn' i uchenie* (Paris: YMCA Press, 1951), 166, 188.

12. See, for example, "On Temptations," "Forgotten Lessons," "The Significance of Dogma," and "The Spiritual Condition of the Russian People," all in Wozniuk, *Politics, Law, and Morality*, 78–84, 108–111, and 126–130.

1. On Spiritual Authority in Russia

Source: "O dukhovnoi vlasti v Rossii," first published in *Rus'* no. 56 (1881), and reprinted in *Sobranie sochinenii* 3: 227–242.

1. *Zemskii sobor*, sometimes translated as "national assembly," a Russian term referring to a more or less representative body of the population, including at times even peasants, that occasionally convened to consult monarchs from roughly the mid-sixteenth to the late-seventeenth centuries.

2. Metropolitan Alexis: Soloviev apparently liked the example of this fourteenth-century Orthodox hierarch and saint, whom he described elsewhere as having gone "to the Golden Horde to mollify the Tatars and suggested to the Russian princes that they submit to the Khan as to a legal sovereign. . . ." See "Retribution," in Wozniuk, *Politics, Law, and Morality*, 113.

3. See the accounts in Mk 14:47, Mt 26:51, Jn 18:10.

4. Archpriest Avvakum Petrov spearheaded the movement in opposition to the Nikonian liturgical reforms and textual "corrections" (see also below, "Byzantinism and Russia").

5. *Streltsy*: literally "shooters," established under Ivan IV in the mid-sixteenth century, soldiers with firearms who gained hereditary rights and privileges, and were utilized in disputes over succession until the end of the seventeenth century, when Peter I disbanded them.

6. "teaching churches": meaning the hierarchy. I am grateful to an anonymous reader of this manuscript for the clarification.

7. "Most powerful bond—religion": one of the anonymous readers of this manuscript suggested that Soloviev was implying with this comment an uncertain "etymology of the Latin 'religio.' "

8. Here Soloviev was adapting the gist of Genesis 3:19.

2. On the Ecclesiastical Question Concerning the Old Catholics

Source: "O tserkovnom voprose po povodu staro-katolikov," first published in *Novoe vremya*, no. 2689 (1883), and reprinted in *Sobranie sochinenii* 4:123–132.

1. Old Catholic: the self-referent title adopted by dissidents who rejected the edicts of the Vatican Council of 1870 that established the dogma of papal infallibility.

2. The eventual decision taken by influential dissentient elements after the Council of 1870 to subordinate their individual views to the authority of the church was known by the phrase *sacrificio dell intelletto*.

3. Professor Dollinger: one of the dissident leaders of the Old Catholics; "unauthorized congregation": *samochinnoe sborishche*.

4. The Russian word for parish (*prikhod*) also has the meaning of "receipts."

5. Dr. Reinkens: another of the dissident leaders of the Old Catholics; Soloviev's use of the phrase *po sluchaiu* (on account of) in his note also carries the sense of "second hand," indirectly extending wordplay on the theme of laying on of hands.

6. Soloviev's indirect reference was to Acts 5:34–39.

3. The Jews and the Christian Question

Source: "Evreistvo i khristianskii vopros," first published in *Pravoslavnoe obozrenie*, nos. 8 & 9 (1884), reprinted in *Sobranie sochinenii* 4:135–185.

1. Soloviev regularly utilized the standard Russian word *evreistvo* to refer collectively to the Jewish people or nation here and elsewhere. Since "Jewry," its technical equivalent in English, might strike some as archaic or grate against the modern ear, I have replaced it throughout this book with one of four terms, depending on context: "the Jews," "Judaism," "the Jewish people," and "the Jewish nation."

2. The reference is to Zechariah 8:23. Soloviev's serious interest in writing about Judaism led him in 1881 to Faivel Bentsilovich Gets, with whom he then shared a good friendship to his last days. After Soloviev's death, Gets wrote that Soloviev began to take lessons from him in ancient Hebrew in the early 1880s, and intensively studied the Bible, Talmud and rabbinic scholarship for three years. These studies led to a number of publications, including *The History and Future of Theocracy* (1884–1886). See F. Gets, "Ob otnoshenii Vl. S. Solovieva k evreiskomu voprosu," *Voprosy filosofii i psikhologii* kn. 56 (1901), cited in Mochul'skii, 148–149.

3. Nicanor, Bishop of Kherson and Odessa (1827-1890): author of *Pozitivnaia filosofiia i sverkhchuvstvennoe bytie* (St. Petersburg: "Obshchestvennaia pol'za," 1875–1888).

4. See St. Paul's Letter to the Romans 11:26.

5. "God-generating" = *bogorozhdaiushchii*

6. Soloviev cited an older Slavonic text.

7. See Genesis 32:24–30.

8. See Exodus 33:11.

9. Soloviev echoed Hebrews 11:1 here.

10. Some lines have been omitted in Soloviev's citation of the Hebrew Bible texts, and some of the verse numbers seem to have been confused. I have made the necessary corrections wherever possible.

11. Matthew 5:5 was cited from an older Slavonic text.

12. "in civitate Dei": an indirect reference to Augustine's conception of the "City of God." This would not be the last time Soloviev would refer to Augustine's work bearing the same title. See, for example, "On So-called Problems," in Wozniuk, *Politics, Law, and Morality,* 77.

13. "God will be all in everything": 1 Corinthians 15:28.

14. Huldreich Zwingli (1484–1531): leader of the Protestant Reformation in Zurich. Soloviev would later analogize the relationship of the founder of Islam, Muhammad, and his chief supporter, Abu Bakr, to that of Melancthon and Luther. See "Muhammad, His Life and Religious Teaching," in Wozniuk, *Enemies from the East?,* 182.

15. A play on words in Russian: *druzhnomu* (amicable), *druzhinnomu* (martial).

16. This argumentation represents a kernel of Soloviev's decade-long unsuccessful and "theocratic" project, which involved reunification of Catholicism, Orthodoxy, and Judaism, and which Pope Leo XIII is said to have referred to after the publication of *Russia and the Universal Church* (Paris: Albert Savine, 1889), as "An excellent idea! But, barring a miracle, an impossibility." Cited in Mochul'skii, 185.

17. See "A Brief Tale about the Antichrist," in Wozniuk, *Politics, Law, and Morality,* 276, 288.

4. New Testament Israel

Source: "Novozavetnyi Izrail,' " first published in *Rus'* nos. 24 & 25 (1885), and reprinted in *Sobranie sochinenii* 4:207–221.

1. A reference to John 1:47, 49.

2. *Evreiskii zhargon*: as one of the first readers of the manuscript suggested, Soloviev's reference in the note most probably meant Yiddish.

3. The scriptural references that Rabinovich cited in Soloviev's recounting vary somewhat from the biblical texts. Compare this to the account of David and Goliath in 1 Samuel 17:32–47.

5. The Teaching of the Twelve Apostles

Source: Introduction to the Russian edition of Διδαχη των δωδεκα αποστολων, first published as "Uchenie XII apostolov," in *Pravoslavnoe obozrenie* July (1886), and reprinted in *Sobranie sochinenii* 4:222–240. The translation of the Didache from Greek into Russian was done by his brother M. S. Soloviev.

1. *Pistis Sophia*: this Gnostic text about the life and teachings of Jesus clearly did not impress Soloviev at all, which should give pause to those who may still consider Soloviev guilty of Gnosticism in some way. See Soloviev's lengthy entry in the *Entsiklopedicheskii slovar'*, F. A. Brokgauz, I. A. Efron (St. Petersburg, 1890-1904), reprinted in *Sobranie sochinenii* 10:323–328.

2. "Philosophoumena": a text discovered in 1851 and presumed to have been written by Hippolytus, who was himself at one time considered heretical (in the Catholic Church he was once known as anti-pope). Soloviev's repeated positive references to Hippolytus in this piece suggest that he did not consider him to be heretical at all.

3. Simon: likely a reference to Acts 8:9–24, the story of Simon the Magician, to whom the first Gnostic heresy is traditionally ascribed—see Soloviev's entry in *Entsiklopedicheskii slovar'*, reprinted in *Sobranie sochinenii* 12: 618–619. Ophites: a Gnostic sect that interpreted the snake's (οφις = serpent) seduction of Adam and Eve through knowledge as a positive phenomenon—see Soloviev's entry in *Entsiklopedciheskii slovar'*, reprinted in *Sobranie sochinenii* 12: 613–614. Basilides: second century Gnostic teacher of Alexandria. See *Entsiklopedicheskii slovar'*, reprinted in *Sobranie sochinenii* 10: 290–292.

4. Adolph von Harnack (1851–1930), prolific Lutheran writer on church history whose works include *History of Dogma* (7 volumes—1889–1922) and *The Apostle's Creed* (1892).

5. Waldensians and Irvingians—the former a twelfth-century movement begun in France and considered a heresy by the Catholic Church; the latter a nineteenth-century movement begun in England and also considered heretical. Both adopted hierarchic elements that Soloviev gently mocks. It is possible as well that Soloviev was punning here on fantastic and Utopian elements of the "New World" that appear in the work of the American writers Henry David Thoreau and Washington Irving, both of whom had an audience in nineteenth-century Russia.

6. The Talmud and Recent Polemical Literature Concerning It in Austria and Germany

Source: "Talmud i noveishaia polemicheskaia literatura o nem v Avstrii i Germanii," first published in *Russkoe obozrenie*, no. 6 (1886), and reprinted in *Sobranie sochinenii* 6:3–32.

1. Karaites: members of a Jewish sect that arose in the Middle Ages who reject the Talmud in favor of the authority residing in the Hebrew Bible.

2. Herrnhuters: a German movement that grew out of a Lutheran group hungering for meaningful faith experience; it subsequently became known as the Moravian Brethren, which later spread to various parts of Europe, including Russia, as well as to America (Herrnhut = Lord's tabernacle); Molokans: an eighteenth-century Russian rationalistic sect that broke from the *dubkhobortsy*.

3. Soloviev frequently resorted to characterizations of a triad in order to point out the synthetic resolution or reconciliation of conflicting elements. See, for example, "Three Forces," in Wozniuk, *Enemies from the East?* 24–33; and "Plato's Life-Drama," in Wozniuk, *Politics, Law, and Morality*, 216–217.

4. This appears to be a reference to the somewhat cryptic comment attributed to Jesus in Matthew 11:12.

5. Soloviev cited an older Slavonic form of John 11:50.

6. Soloviev cited an older Slavonic form of Matthew 23:2–3.

7. The logic of the latter part of this long paragraph draws upon Paul's Letter to the Romans 11:13–29.

8. "semi-German jargon" (*polu-nemetskii zhargon*): of course, Yiddish. Compare with Soloviev's use of the term *evreiskii zhargon* on page 90 and explained in note number 2 under "New Testament Israel" above.

9. Soloviev here played on the Christian theological principle that those who follow Christ as the New Adam carry requisite responsibilities, suggesting that Christians have corrupted the mission and become enemy Edomites.

10. In Polish, *rzeczpospolita*: the 1569 Treaty of Lublin created a united "commonwealth" of the Kingdom of Poland and Lithuania. The Russian in Soloviev's citation: "*zhid, liakh, da sobaka-vera ednaka.*"

11. A play on words: "comprehend . . . take"—*poniat'* . . . *priniat'*.

7. On Counterfeits

Source: "O poddelkakh," first published in *Voprosy filosofii i psikhologii*, no. 8 (1891): 149–163, reprinted in *Sobranie sochinenii* 6:327–339.

1. For a possible source of Soloviev's title to this essay, see 1 John 2:26–27.

2. Soloviev cited an old form of John 1:12.

3. Zend-Avesta: a western (and apparently mistaken) designation for the Zoroastrian Scriptures, under the rubric Avesta.

4. *contradictio in adjecto*: contradiction between noun and adjective.

8. On the Decline of the Medieval Worldview

Source: "Ob upadke srednevekovago mirosozertsaniia," a paper given at a meeting of the Moscow Psychological Society, 19 October 1891, first printed in *Sobranie sochinenii* 6:381–393.

1. Soloviev cites Luke 9:49–56 as his text, but appears to draw on the close parallel of Mark 9:38–40 as well.

2. In Soloviev's note, "Priscillian sect": named for its founder, Priscillian, a fourth- and fifth-century Spanish heresy that was Manichean and Gnostic in nature.

9. When Did the Hebrew Prophets Live?

Source: "Kogda zhili evreiskie proroki?" first published in *Sbornik v pol'zu nachal'nykh evreiskikh shkol* (1896): 255–277, reprinted in *Sobranie sochinenii* 7:180–200.

1. On the Oniases, see Josephus, *Antiquities* 12, 1.
2. A generally accepted definition of parallelismus membrorum is "The fundamental principle of Hebrew poetry . . . generally conceived as the apposition of two clauses or cola corresponding in both meaning and grammatical structure." David Grossberg, "Noun/Verb Parallelism: Syntactic or Asyntactic," *Journal of Biblical Literature* 99/4 (1980): 481.
3. Manetho—Third Century BC Egyptian priest.
4. Soloviev seems to have been citing texts from the Book of Isaiah that have subsequently been refined in later Russian translations as well as in others. I have provided later versions in a few places for the sake of clarification.
5. Soloviev translated Havet's French text into Russian in his footnotes. I have reversed this order and rendered the Russian translation in Soloviev's note into English in the main text.
6. Soloviev echoed part of the Nicene Creed here.

10. Byzantinism and Russia

Source: "Vizantizm i Rossiia," first published in *Vestnik Evropy*, nos. 1 & 4 (1896); reprinted in *Sobranie sochinenii* 7: 285–325.

1. Soloviev's logic suggests the story of Sodom. See Genesis 19.
2. Vladimir the Little Red Sun—the characterization of a lazy sun moving across the heavens is from *byliny*—the narrative songs of early Rus' relating stories of purportedly real events. One of the major figures of *byliny* is Vladimir the Great. Soloviev seemed to favor the image of Vladimir as "the Little Red Sun," as can be seen in his use of it earlier in his career, for example, in the essay "Primitive Paganism, Its Living and Dead Remnants" (1890). See Wozniuk, *Enemies from the East?* 98–99.
3. Saint Alexis and Saint Sergius of Radonezh. On Metropolitan Alexis, see note number 2 under "On Spiritual Authority in Russia" above. In contrast to Alexis' desire "to mollify the Tatars," Soloviev recounted Sergius' blessing of Dmitri of Moscow's "open armed rebellion against the very same Horde" and concluded that both "alike acted in the Spirit of Christ for the good of the people," reasoning that the contradiction was only apparent if one considered the Gospel texts literally. See "Retribution," in Wozniuk, *Politics, Law, and Morality*, 113.
4. This appears to be a slightly altered version of Matthew 12:37.

5. Bormà-Iaryzhka: Several variants of the tale of Bormà-Iaryzhka exist, but the one that Soloviev referred to is likely the one in *Skazki i predaniia Samarskogo kraia*, collected and transcribed by D. N. Sadovnikov and first published around 1884.

6. Both Puffendorf and Grotius were particularly notable for their contributions to an international—or in Soloviev's thinking, universal—legal consciousness and are still considered to be two of the most important forefathers of modern international law.

7. Soloviev addressed the subject of Christian politics from many different aspects and to various depths. See, for example, "Christianity and Revolution" (1881); "Morality and Politics" (1883); and "On the Christian State and Society" (1884), in Wozniuk, *Politics, Law, and Morality*, 1–31.

8. "Opresnoki"—the same word used for the Hebrew Passover bread.

9. See Matthew 7:9–10 and Luke 11:11.

11. The Secret of Progress

Source: "Taina Progressa," was written in 1897, and was first published in *Sobranie sochinenii* 9:84–86, according to its editors (See 9: 434). However, more recently, some Russian internet versions have appended to the article the bibliographical information that it first appeared in *Rus'*, January 5, 1895.

1. *Tsaregradskii struchok*: *ceratonia siliqua*, known as carob, locust bean, Saint-John's bread; in Christian tradition, part of John the Baptist's diet in the wilderness.

2. "blessed are they who believe": a slightly revised version of John 20:29.

3. Anchises: father of Aeneas, the "pious hero" who bore him and the penates out of Troy as it burned. "Man of the future": Although Soloviev uses the words *budushchii chelovek* here, the context suggests Nietzsche's "Mensch der Zukunft" from *Zur Genealogie der Moral*. Later, Soloviev would more succinctly convey the image using a slight variation, *griadushchii chelovek*. See "A Brief Tale About the Antichrist," in Wozniuk, *Politics, Law, and Morality*, 268–269, 318.

4. This phrase carries a resonance of 1 Timothy 4:16.

Supplemental Listing of Soloviev's Relevant Writings

(Chronologically arranged)

The Mythological Process in Ancient Paganism (1873)
The Crisis of Western Philosophy [Against Positivism] (1874)
Metaphysics and Positive Science (1875)
The Experience of Synthetic Philosophy (1877)
Critique of Abstract Principles (1877–80)
Lectures on God-manhood (1877–81)
The Great Schism and Christian Politics (1883)
The Spiritual Foundations of Life (1882–84)
Russia and the Universal Church (1889)
Primitive Paganism, Its Surviving and Dead Remnants (1890)
The Jews in Russia (1890)
The Meaning of Love (1892–94)
Mahomet, His Life and Religious Teaching (1896)
Justification of the Good. Moral Philosophy (1897)
Plato's Life-Drama (1898)
The Idea of a Superman (1899)
Three Conversations on War, Progress, and the End of Universal
    History, with the Conclusion of a Brief Tale about the Anti-Christ,
    and with Addenda (1900)

Most of the works cited above are available in English either separately, in various translations, or in one of the three collections I assembled previously:

Politics, Law, and Morality: Essays by V. S. Soloviev (Yale, 2000)
The Heart of Reality: Essays on Beauty, Love, and Ethics, by V. S. Soloviev
    (Notre Dame, 2003)
*Enemies from the East? V. S. Soloviev on Paganism, Asian Civilizations,
    and Islam* (Northwestern, 2007).

Index of Biblical References

NEW TESTAMENT

General Index

Abraham, 51, 52, 134
Acts of the Apostles, 38, 103, 150, 161, 235, 237. *See also* Index of Biblical References
Aeneas, 15, 240
agriculture and rural life in Russia, 80–83, 86–87, 197
Aksakov, Ivan S., 36
Alexei Petrovich, Prince, 208–213
Alexis, Saint, 20, 23, 197, 234, 239
all-unity (*vseedinstvo*), 51, 152
Ambrose of Milan, Saint, 167
American Christian sects, 40, 73, 139, 237
anti-Semitism, 9–10, 43–45, 92, 121–146, 237, 238
Apocalypse of St. John, 107
Apostle, meaning of the term, 110–113
Apostolic Creed, 98–99, 224–225
Aquinas, Saint Thomas, 6
asceticism, 63–64, 78, 116
Athanasius, Saint, 105
Augustine, Saint, 3, 6, 66–67, 236
Austria and the Austrians, 4, 121, 136, 137
autocephaly, 217
Avvakum, 23, 234

Babylon and the Babylonians, 9, 13, 127, 135, 172, 181, 183, 185, 189, 201

baptism, sacrament of, 114–115, 117, 166, 195
Barnabas, Epistle of, 106, 110
Basilides, 103, 237
Bible. *See* Old Testament, New Testament, Synoptic Gospels, and Index of Biblical References
Bismarck, Otto von, 5, 33–37
bogochelovechestvo. See God-man and God-manhood
Bormà-Iaryzhka, 202–203, 240
Bryennios, Metropolitan Philotheos, 105, 106
Buddhism, 52, 154
"Byzantinism and Russia" (essay by Soloviev), 12–14, 191–227, 239–240
Byzantium and Byzantines, 2, 7, 12–14, 69, 70, 71, 77, 105, 159, 191–227, 234, 239

Catholicism and Catholics, 2, 4, 5, 7, 18, 25, 27, 28, 33–41, 44, 46, 72–73, 74–77, 84–86, 135, 136, 216, 220, 234, 235, 237
Charlemagne, 71–72, 173
church-state relations. *See* religion and the State
City of God. *See* Augustine, Saint
civil society, 18, 80, 82
Clement of Alexandria, 104
Constantine the Great, 10, 11, 12, 70, 74, 162, 194

247